Praise for *GenAI on Google Cloud*

We are moving past the era of "wow" moments in Generative AI into the era of "work." This book provides the essential engineering blueprint for that transition. The authors don't just talk about the potential of agents and LLMs; they show you exactly how to architect, secure, and scale them using the very best of Google Cloud's stack. A mandatory read for any leader serious about turning AI experimentation into enterprise value.

—*Saurabh Tiwary, VP, general manager, Google Cloud AI*

A masterclass in balance, this book seamlessly bridges the gap between foundational theory and hands-on execution. For anyone looking to understand the "why" behind Generative AI while mastering the "how" of building applications, this is essential reading.

—*Burak Gokturk, VP of AI and systems research, Google Cloud*

Won't any book about AI agents be woefully out of date as soon as it's published? Perhaps for some, but not this one. The authors provide hearty treatment to a wide range of topics, focusing on the "why" as much as the "how." Whether you're creating AI strategy, designing architectures, writing code, or operating production systems, this book will stand the test of time as a valid guide towards a successful implementation.

—*Richard Seroter, chief evangelist, Google*

For leaders ready to build the next generation of intelligent applications, this book provides the necessary blueprint. It offers the first comprehensive look at Agent Development Kit (ADK), equipping engineers with the practical frameworks needed to turn agentic concepts into production-grade reality.

—*Julia Wiesinger, group product manager, Google*

While ADK gives developers the framework to build powerful agents, this book provides the essential roadmap from building prototypes to secure, production-grade enterprise systems. It is the missing manual for anyone serious about bridging the gap between writing agentic code and delivering real-world business value on Google Cloud.

—*Bo Yang, lead software engineer, Google (Building ADK!)*

GenAI on Google Cloud

Enterprise Generative AI Systems and Agents

Ayo Adedeji, Lavi Nigam, Sarita A. Joshi,
and Stephanie Gervasi

O'REILLY®

GenAI on Google Cloud

by Ayo Adedeji, Lavi Nigam, Sarita A. Joshi, and Stephanie Gervasi

Published by O'Reilly Media, Inc., 141 Stony Circle, Suite 195, Santa Rosa, CA 95401.

O'Reilly books may be purchased for educational, business, or sales promotional use. Online editions are also available for most titles (*http://oreilly.com*). For more information, contact our corporate/institutional sales department: 800-998-9938 or *corporate@oreilly.com*.

Acquisitions Editor: Nicole Butterfield	**Indexer:** Sue Klefstad
Development Editor: Sara Hunter	**Cover Designer:** Susan Brown
Production Editor: Aleeya Rahman	**Cover Illustrator:** José Marzan Jr.
Copyeditor: Stephanie English	**Interior Designer:** David Futato
Proofreader: Dave Awl	**Interior Illustrator:** Kate Dullea

January 2026:   First Edition

Revision History for the First Edition
2026-01-21:   First Release

See *http://oreilly.com/catalog/errata.csp?isbn=9798341623859* for release details.

979-8-341-62385-9

[LSI]

Table of Contents

Preface

Let's be honest—building a flashy generative AI prototype is the easy part. We've all been there: the excitement of a demo that works perfectly in controlled conditions, stakeholders leaning forward in their chairs, and that moment when someone says, "This is amazing! When can we roll it out?"

And then reality hits.

The four of us—Ayo, Lavi, Sarita, and Steph—have collectively spent thousands of hours helping organizations and developers navigate what comes after that exciting demo moment. We work across different teams at Google Cloud, but we kept encountering the same fundamental challenge regardless of industry or use case: the gap between a working prototype and a production-ready generative AI system is massive, complex, and filled with obstacles that aren't obvious until you're knee-deep in the journey.

During one of our regular knowledge-sharing sessions, we realized that while there are plenty of resources that teach how to build generative AI prototypes, there's surprisingly little practical guidance on the critical path from prototype to production. We started compiling our notes, frameworks, and hard-earned lessons, initially just for ourselves and our teams.

"This could help a lot more people than just us," became our mantra, and that's how this book was born.

We're not here to dazzle you with theoretical abstractions or rehash concepts you can find in a hundred blog posts. Instead, we've created the practical guide we wish we'd had—one that addresses the real challenges of deploying generative AI systems in production environments on Google Cloud, backed by concrete examples and honest insights about what actually works.

This isn't a polished marketing narrative. It's a field guide written by practitioners who've seen both the triumphs and the train wrecks. We've kept our individual voices throughout, sharing our unique perspectives rather than forcing a unified narrative, because that's how real engineering teams work. Sometimes we disagree, and that's valuable too.

Our goal is simple: to help you navigate the journey from prototype to production more efficiently than we did our first time around.

Why This Book Matters

The GenAI and agentic AI landscape is evolving at breakneck speed. New models emerge almost daily, each promising more parameters, better benchmarks, and greater capabilities. Yet across industries, we're witnessing a consistent pattern: organizations struggle not with building impressive prototypes, but with making them production-ready.

This transition from prototype to production represents the true value inflection point. According to industry analysts, more than 80% (*https://oreil.ly/t2006*) of enterprises will have experimented with generative AI by 2026, yet many report no significant bottom-line impact (*https://oreil.ly/pfQ1Z*). At the heart of this paradox is a mismatch in deployment. While "horizontal" tools like chatbots have scaled rapidly across enterprises, their value is often spread thin and difficult to quantify. In contrast, high-value "vertical" applications—those deeply integrated into specific business functions—face far greater hurdles, with analysts estimating that nearly 90% (*https://oreil.ly/_D_qr*) of these transformative initiatives fail to progress beyond the pilot stage. The gap is particularly stark in regulated industries such as healthcare and financial services, where security, compliance, and reliability requirements intensify the challenge.

What separates successful deployments from a pilot experiment? It's rarely about model quality alone. Instead, it's about the surrounding infrastructure—data pipelines, evaluation frameworks, monitoring systems, and governance guardrails—that make the difference between systems that demonstrate potential and those that deliver measurable business value.

Google Cloud's Vertex AI platform has helped hundreds of organizations bridge this gap, providing the foundation for both startups and Fortune 500 companies to move their GenAI applications from concept to production. The patterns and practices we've observed along the way form the backbone of this book's practical approach to building systems that not only work in demos but thrive in the real world.

Writing a book about a field that reinvents itself every few months is a formidable challenge. While specific code snippets, tools, or model recommendations are bound to become dated, the fundamental questions of system design, evaluation, and governance will remain. Our goal is to equip you with a durable framework for answering those questions, regardless of what the next breakthrough looks like.

What You'll Find in This Book

We've structured this book to follow the journey from prototype to production, with each chapter building on the previous one:

Chapter 1, "The Challenge of Generative AI Application Development"
Introduces the unique complexities of building GenAI applications and sets the stage for MLOps for LLMs and agents

Chapter 2, "Data Readiness and Accessibility"
Explores how to handle and prepare data for GenAI applications, covering preparation strategies, annotation techniques, and data augmentation

Chapter 3, "Building a Multimodal Agent with the Agent Development Kit (ADK)"
Guides you through creating a functional agent prototype using Google's ADK framework, demonstrating how to build a customer service agent that handles text, video, and images

Chapter 4, "Orchestrating Intelligent Agent Teams"
Shows how to scale from single agents to multiagent systems, covering agent-to-agent and agent-to-tool communication patterns and enterprise collaboration strategies

Chapter 5, "Evaluation and Optimization Strategies"
Explores frameworks for measuring success in LLMs and agents, from safety and robustness metrics to agent trajectory evaluation and advanced optimization patterns

Chapter 6, "Tuning and Infrastructure"
Covers model fine-tuning techniques and infrastructure optimization strategies to maximize performance and cost-efficiency in production environments

Chapter 7, "MLOps for Production-Ready AI and Agentic Systems"
Establishes a comprehensive approach to operationalizing LLMs and agent systems, from CI/CD pipelines and cost management to monitoring and deployment strategies

Chapter 8, "The AI and Agentic Maturity Framework"
Provides a strategic roadmap for organizational growth, helping you assess readiness across leadership, culture, and operations to move from tactical experiments to transformational AI adoption

Each chapter concludes with a "Looking Ahead" section to prepare you for the topics and themes that will come next. Additionally, we provide a "Learning Labs" section at the end of each chapter, where links to hands-on activities will lead you to further support your understanding of key concepts presented in the chapter.

Our Approach

We believe in learning by doing. Throughout this book, we provide code examples that you can run and adapt to your specific needs. We focus on practical implementations rather than theoretical abstractions, though we provide enough theory to ensure that you understand why certain approaches work better than others.

We've chosen to write this book with our individual voices rather than aiming for a seamless narrative. As you read, you'll hear from each of us directly, sharing our specific expertise and experiences. We believe this approach makes the content more authentic and allows us to connect with you on a more personal level.

Who This Book Is For

This book is designed for several key audiences:

- Machine learning engineers and AI engineers transitioning from traditional machine learning models to complex generative AI pipelines
- Data teams moving from conventional analytics to AI-powered insights
- Software developers with Python skills entering AI-first application development
- Product managers and technical leaders responsible for AI strategy and implementation
- Career transitioners leveraging existing technical foundations to move into AI engineering roles

While we assume familiarity with Python programming and basic machine learning concepts, we've structured the content to be accessible to readers with varying levels of expertise. Some familiarity with Google Cloud and Vertex AI is beneficial but not a prerequisite.

Prerequisites

To get the most out of this book, you should have:

- Experience with Python programming
- Basic understanding of machine learning concepts
- Familiarity with cloud computing principles (though not necessarily Google Cloud specifically)

If you're new to some of these areas, don't worry—we provide references and explanations where needed, and the hands-on approach means you'll learn as you go.

Conventions Used in This Book

The following typographical conventions are used in this book:

Italic
> Indicates new terms, URLs, email addresses, filenames, and file extensions.

`Constant width`
> Used for program listings, as well as within paragraphs to refer to program elements such as variable or function names, databases, data types, environment variables, statements, and keywords.

`Constant width bold`
> Shows commands or other text that should be typed literally by the user.

`Constant width italic`
> Shows text that should be replaced with user-supplied values or by values determined by context.

> This element signifies a general note.

Using Code Examples

Supplemental material (code examples, exercises, etc.) is available for download at *https://github.com/ayoisio/genai-on-google-cloud*.

If you have a technical question or a problem using the code examples, please send email to *support@oreilly.com*.

This book is here to help you get your job done. In general, if example code is offered with this book, you may use it in your programs and documentation. You do not need to contact us for permission unless you're reproducing a significant portion of the code. For example, writing a program that uses several chunks of code from this book does not require permission. Selling or distributing examples from O'Reilly books does require permission. Answering a question by citing this book and quoting example code does not require permission. Incorporating a significant amount of example code from this book into your product's documentation does require permission.

We appreciate, but generally do not require, attribution. An attribution usually includes the title, author, publisher, and ISBN. For example: "*GenAI on Google Cloud: Enterprise Generative AI Systems and Agents* by Ayo Adedeji, Lavi Nigam, Sarita A.

Joshi, and Stephanie Gervasi (O'Reilly). Copyright 2026 Ayo Adedeji, Lavi Nigam, Sarita A. Joshi, and Stephanie Gervasi, 979-8-341-62385-9."

If you feel your use of code examples falls outside fair use or the permission given above, feel free to contact us at *permissions@oreilly.com*.

O'Reilly Online Learning

O'REILLY®   For more than 40 years, *O'Reilly Media* has provided technology and business training, knowledge, and insight to help companies succeed.

Our unique network of experts and innovators share their knowledge and expertise through books, articles, and our online learning platform. O'Reilly's online learning platform gives you on-demand access to live training courses, in-depth learning paths, interactive coding environments, and a vast collection of text and video from O'Reilly and 200+ other publishers. For more information, visit *https://oreilly.com*.

How to Contact Us

Please address comments and questions concerning this book to the publisher:

> O'Reilly Media, Inc.
> 141 Stony Circle, Suite 195
> Santa Rosa, CA 95401
> 800-889-8969 (in the United States or Canada)
> 707-827-7019 (international or local)
> 707-829-0104 (fax)
> *support@oreilly.com*
> *https://oreilly.com/about/contact.html*

We have a web page for this book, where we list errata, examples, and any additional information. You can access this page at *https://oreil.ly/GenAI_on_Google*.

For news and information about our books and courses, visit *https://oreilly.com*.

Find us on LinkedIn: *https://linkedin.com/company/oreilly-media*.

Watch us on YouTube: *https://youtube.com/oreillymedia*.

Acknowledgments

Ayo

I'd like to thank my dad, mom, sister, and friends for their patience and engagement as I've subjected them to countless philosophical inquiries about AI and the future of, well, everything. Through our conversations—sometimes skeptical, always thoughtful—they've taught me how different people see the world and what they value. This understanding has been invaluable in writing a book meant to serve diverse readers with varied perspectives and concerns about AI.

To O'Reilly Media, thank you for the honor and trust of this platform. The opportunity to teach and inspire curiosity about AI—to help others experience that same wonder I felt when I first saw an LLM understand context or an agent solve a complex problem—is truly a gift.

Lavi

This book was written for the builder. My heartfelt thanks to everyone who helped bring it to life.

To my family, my foundation and constant source of strength. To my mom and dad, thank you for the incredible privilege of a life shaped by your unwavering support, a solid education, and the belief that I could achieve anything. Your support has been my greatest advantage. To my sister, brother, and all siblings–your constant encouragement has been a true gift. To my entire family, thank you for always making me believe that I can solve anything and do great things.

My deepest gratitude extends to my friends and all the wonderful colleagues I have had and currently have at Google, who have always bestowed their trust in me and cheered me on through every chapter of my life.

I am also profoundly grateful for the journey that led me here. My school and college education laid the groundwork for the person I am today, and I am indebted to all my previous and current managers and my leadership, who have mentored me, challenged me, and helped build me into the professional I have become.

To my colleagues at Google, thank you for building the tools and infrastructure that are changing our industry and for being an incredible source of inspiration. I am also humbled by the broader AI community; your passion fuels my own. Your relentless innovation is what makes this guide relevant. I am also profoundly grateful to the global developer community. Your curiosity, challenging questions, and passion for building are the driving force behind my work.

To my coauthors, Ayo, Sarita, and Steph: I am incredibly proud of what we built. This book is a testament to our shared commitment to helping others succeed in moving from prototype to production. Thank you for your partnership.

This book is a milestone in a mission I care about deeply: making complex AI accessible to every developer and enterprise. This work is impossible alone.

Sarita

Writing this book has been a profound reminder that no achievement is solitary. My deepest gratitude begins with my family and friends, whose belief in me has been a constant anchor, no matter the physical distance. A special acknowledgement goes to my elder brother, Kishor Joshi, who many years ago used his first paycheck to buy me my first personal laptop. That single gift opened the door to the world of technology for me long before a book like this was even imaginable, and I am forever grateful.

Professionally, I am driven by the people I serve and work with. To my customers and the visionary leaders in healthtech: *thank you for inspiring me daily. Your complex challenges are the motivation behind the practical solutions in this book. Your mission is my mission.*

And to my colleagues at Google—the countless innovators and experts across multiple teams who I am lucky to call friends: *your intellectual curiosity and relentless support made this project possible. This work is a testament to our collaboration.*

Stephanie

This book is the result of the cumulative wisdom, patience, and support drawn from many people. *To every individual who contributed to my journey, directly or indirectly, I offer my heartfelt gratitude.*

I am grateful for the foundational community of my family and friends. Your belief in me, your encouragement, and your understanding made it possible for me to undertake this project. I extend my gratitude to my amazing Google colleagues, professional peers, and all of the students, researchers, and technologists I've had the pleasure of meeting and talking with over these last years. The idea and execution of this book was born out of intellectual curiosity, collaboration, and genuine excitement for the field of AI, with all the potential it holds to improve people's lives. I dedicate a specific and vital thank-you to the customers and stakeholders I have had the privilege of working with. This book exists because of the real-world complexities you bring to the table. Your trust in my counsel, and the honest details of your operational challenges have served as the ultimate proving ground for these ideas. A final dedicated space must be reserved for the incredible collaboration that defined this book: my coauthors. More than just partners in writing, you were the essential sounding boards, technical anchors, and creative force that ensured this vision was realized. Thank you for your tireless effort, intellectual rigor, and shared commitment to seeing this project through every demanding stage. It has been such a joy to work with you on this book!

Ayo, Lavi, Sarita, and Steph would like to specially thank our development editor, Sara Hunter, for her guidance and support throughout this project, as well as the entire team at O'Reilly who helped bring this book to life. We're also grateful to Google Cloud for providing the platform and opportunity to work with so many organizations on their GenAI journeys, which provided the insights and experiences that form the foundation of this book. A big thanks to subject matter experts who reviewed drafts of our book, including Saurabh Tiwary, Burak Gokturk, Ashok Rao, Yasmeen Ahmad, Jason Gelman, Alan Blount, Bo Yang, Julia Wiesinger, Christina Lin, Polong Lin, Dave Elliott, Tanya Singh, Irina Sigler, Blane Clark, and Dr. Pete Clardy.

Most importantly, we want to collectively thank the developers, engineers, and organizations who have shared their challenges and successes with us. Your questions, feedback, and innovative solutions have not only made this book possible but continue to drive the evolution of GenAI on Google Cloud. This book is for you.

## CHAPTER 1

The Challenge of Generative AI Application Development

Dear reader, we are excited to have you on this learning journey with us. The objective for this first chapter is to introduce you to the unique complexities of building and deploying applications powered by *large language models (LLMs)*. We hope this chapter will prepare you for subsequent deeper discussions of LLM operations (LLMOps) and agent operations (AgentOps)—really, extensions of *machine learning operations* (MLOps (*https://oreil.ly/4gv-K*)), which includes the behind-the-scenes work and set of best practices for managing the entire lifecycle of AI and agentic systems, from building and testing to deploying and responsibly maintaining these powerful systems in production.

Overview of LLMs, Generative AI Agents, and Potential Applications to Business Tasks

Let's start by defining some key characteristics of LLMs and their application to generative tasks such as content generation, summarization, recommendation, problem solving, and discovery.

To break it down simply, an LLM is:

Large
 LLMs are trained on enormous datasets, often containing billions or even trillions of words. Many LLMs have "read" a significant portion of the internet and many, many books. The corpus for many of the LLMs you may use as a consumer have been trained on the equivalent of several large libraries. In the case of multimodal model training, this includes libraries of text, images, videos, and audio.

Language

The primary focus of LLMs is on understanding and generating human language.

Model

LLMs use complex statistical techniques to learn patterns and relationships within text data. At its heart, an LLM is a type of neural network (*https://oreil.ly/-Y8BF*), specifically a deep learning model, with multiple layers of interconnected nodes. The most common architecture for these models is the *transformer* (*https://oreil.ly/lFBHd*) *network*. Before the transformer can process any text, the raw input is first converted into a numerical format through vectorization, where every word or token is mapped to a high-dimensional vector. These vectors are the model's native language, representing the semantic meaning of the text; words with similar meanings are mapped to vectors that are numerically close together. Transformer networks excel by utilizing mechanisms like "attention," which allows the model to dynamically weigh and combine these input vectors, thereby understanding the context and relationships between all words in a sequence. This deep, vectorized interpretation allows the model to effectively index and retrieve relevant information based on meaning, rather than just keywords.

In language models, a *token* refers to the basic unit of text that the model processes. Tokens are typically word fragments, complete words, or characters depending on the model. For example, the sentence, "Let's go to the store" might be split into tokens such as ["Let", "s", "go", "to", "the", "store"]. One trillion tokens would be roughly equivalent to several billions of pages of text.

The 2017 paper, Attention Is All You Need (*https://oreil.ly/wVd5C*), published in the *Proceedings of the 31st International Conference on Neural Information Processing Systems* by researchers at Google, is foundational to the development and success of modern LLMs. This paper introduced a novel neural network architecture called the transformer. Importantly, this architecture moved away from the previously dominant recurrent neural networks (RNNs) for sequence-to-sequence tasks such as machine translation. The core innovation of the transformer is its heavy reliance on the attention mechanism (*https://oreil.ly/1RGmG*). Instead of processing sequences step by step like RNNs do, the attention mechanism allows the model to directly access and weigh the importance of all parts of the input sequence when processing each position. The transformer architecture described in the 2017 paper has become the cornerstone of virtually all state-of-the-art LLMs.

So, an LLM is a type of AI model that is trained on a massive amount of text data. This training allows an LLM to understand, summarize, generate, and predict new text. While traditionally focused on text, the most advanced LLMs are often trained on multimodal datasets, enabling them to process and generate content across various formats such as images, videos, and audio, along with text. We can use natural language to communicate with LLMs. Prompting is the act of using natural language instructions (the "prompt") to communicate a specific task, request, or context to an LLM to guide it toward generating the desired output.

The Origins of LLMs

It's difficult to pinpoint the exact moment and person who first used the precise term "large language model;" it emerged as these models grew in size and capability. The underlying concepts and technologies were developed by numerous researchers over decades in the fields of natural language processing (NLP) and machine learning. The abbreviation "LLM" gained traction as the scale of these models became a defining characteristic, but LLMs entered the mainstream conversation relatively recently, around late 2022 and throughout 2023. Several key factors contributed to this:

The rise of ChatGPT
> The release of OpenAI's ChatGPT in November 2022 was a watershed moment. Its user-friendly interface and remarkable ability to generate human-like text, answer questions, write different kinds of creative content, and even code captured the public's imagination like no previous generative AI (GenAI) technology. People could directly interact with a powerful LLM and experience its capabilities firsthand.

Increased accessibility
> ChatGPT made LLM technology accessible to the general public. Previously, interacting with such advanced GenAI models often required technical expertise or was limited to research settings.

Viral media coverage
> Impressive and sometimes surprising outputs from LLMs quickly spread across social media and were widely covered by mainstream news outlets. This generated significant public interest and discussion about the potential and implications of this technology.

Advancements in capabilities
> LLMs had been under development for years, with models such as GPT-3 (released in 2020) demonstrating significant advancements. However, it was the combination of fine-tuning for improved performance and advances in alignment techniques to make models safer that truly brought LLMs into the mainstream.

Debates about impact

The capabilities of LLMs sparked widespread conversations about their potential impact on various aspects of society, including education, work, creativity, and the spread of misinformation. This ongoing debate has kept LLMs in the public eye. Responsible GenAI toolkits (e.g., Google AI (*https://oreil.ly/aKeXZ*)) have emerged to help guide best practices around evaluation of LLMs for bias and include tools for model explainability and safety and security guardrails.

Small Language Models (SLMs)

You may hear the term *small language model* (SLM (*https://oreil.ly/Swr68*)) used to refer to a language model with a significantly smaller number of parameters and a less complex architecture compared to LLMs. SLMs are trained on smaller and often domain-specific datasets and require far fewer computational resources for both training and deployment. SLMs are optimized for speed, cost, and on-device deployment. You might reach for an SLM over an LLM when resource constraints are significant, cost constraints are considerable, or you have a well-defined and narrow task. The most common reason for choosing an SLM over an LLM involves latency-sensitive applications, where user interaction demands near-instantaneous responses. However, it's also important to note that many publicly hosted LLMs now offer streaming modes with very low latency for real-time interaction, making the choice more nuanced and dependent on other factors such as data privacy, offline accessibility, and domain specificity. For example, Google's Gemma family of models (*https://oreil.ly/0UqfU*) is a collection of lightweight open models trained for specific tasks such as coding (CodeGemma), image processing (PaliGemma), and content safety evaluation (ShieldGemma).

Don't automatically assume that bigger models guarantee better performance for all tasks. For many practical applications, a well-trained SLM can provide a cost-effective and efficient solution that meets the specific needs. Conversely, for tasks demanding high levels of reasoning, creativity, or general knowledge, the power of an LLM might be essential, even if it comes with higher costs. Table 1-1 provides a comprehensive comparison of these models across key dimensions including size, computational requirements, and capabilities. The key is to match the model's capabilities and resource requirements to the specific demands of your use case. Later in this chapter, we'll talk more about use cases for LLMs; the importance of a well-articulated use case (with performance metrics and evaluation criteria) cannot be overstated!

Table 1-1. Comparing small and large language models

Feature	Small language model (SLM)	Large language model (LLM)
Size (parameters)	Typically millions to single-digit billions of parameters.	Typically billions to trillions of parameters.
Complexity	Simpler neural network architectures.	More complex architectures (often deeper and wider).
Training data	Trained on smaller datasets.	Trained on massive, diverse datasets.
Computational cost	Lower for training and inference.	Significantly higher for training and inference.
Resource needs	Can run on devices with more limited resources (e.g., mobile, embedded).	Typically requires substantial computational infrastructure such as graphics processing units (GPUs) and more specialized tensor processing units (TPUs).
Latency	Very low latency, often enabling near-instantaneous responses, which is ideal for on-device and real-time interactive applications.	Higher latency for full responses, but can be significantly reduced with streaming APIs for interactive use cases.
General knowledge	More limited and may be domain-specific.	Broader and more comprehensive general knowledge.
Reasoning ability	Generally less sophisticated.	Often exhibits more advanced reasoning and understanding.
Creativity and nuance	May struggle with highly creative or nuanced tasks.	Capable of generating more creative and nuanced content.
Task versatility	Often designed or fine-tuned for specific tasks.	More versatile and can perform a wider range of tasks, including in-context learning.
Data efficiency	May require more task-specific data for fine-tuning to achieve comparable performance on certain tasks.	Can often achieve good performance on new tasks with fewer examples (few-shot or zero-shot learning).

Foundation Models and Multimodality

Another term that you might hear used interchangeably with LLM is *foundation model*. In truth, all LLMs are foundation models because they are large, trained on vast amounts of unlabeled data, and can be adapted for various language-based tasks. But not all foundation models are LLMs. There are specialized foundation models—such as biological models for protein structure prediction or vision models for image generation (like Imagen (*https://oreil.ly/SQiTq*)). While a model like Imagen may leverage a powerful LLM to encode and 'understand' a text prompt, its primary architecture is specialized for generating pixels rather than performing general-purpose, multi-turn linguistic reasoning. The industry is increasingly moving toward architectures that synthesize these disparate capabilities into a single, unified system, resulting in the highly integrated multimodal foundation models illustrated in Figure 1-1.

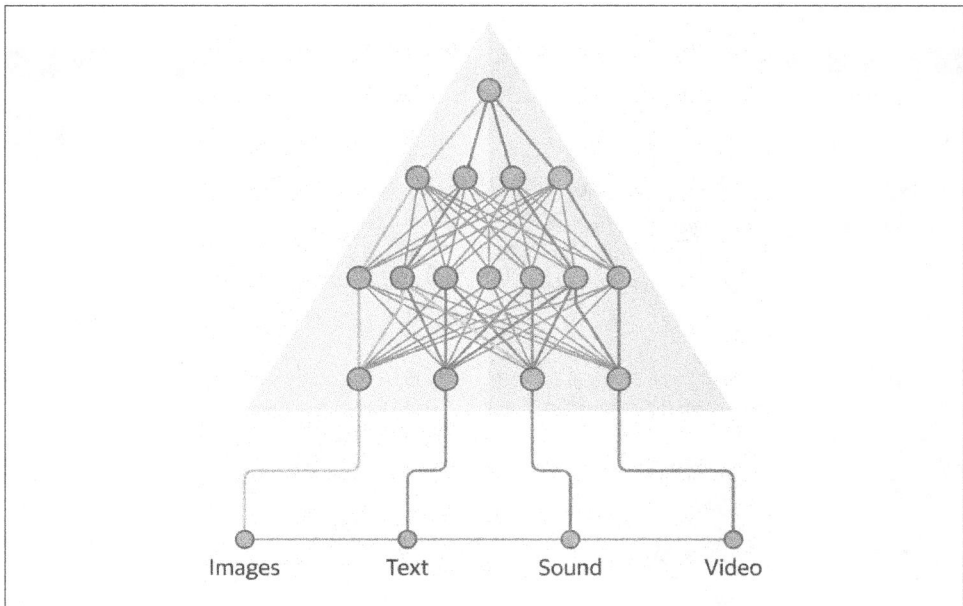

Figure 1-1. Illustration of a multimodal foundation model capable of processing and generating different types of content, including images, text, sound, and video

Google's multimodal Gemini family (*https://oreil.ly/a4oSX*) exemplifies modern foundation models. Gemini 3, for example, functions as an LLM because it is explicitly designed to understand and generate human language with a high degree of sophistication. However, these models are trained on vast datasets of text, images, audio, video, and code. This broad pretraining allows the models to exhibit general-purpose capabilities and be fine-tuned for a wide range of tasks beyond just text, making them multimodal foundation models. These models are often available in distinct versions to match the job at hand; for instance, Gemini 3 Flash is built for high-speed efficiency, while Gemini 3 Pro is designed for deep reasoning and complex problem-solving. Out-of-the-box pretrained foundation models are a key starting point for most consumers of LLMs. Context engineering (covered here and in Chapters 2, 5, and 7) and model fine-tuning (covered in Chapter 6) are common approaches to augment the performance of these models.

What Is Context Engineering?

Context engineering (*https://oreil.ly/CUQHJ*) for LLMs is the strategic design and preparation of all of the input information (e.g, prompt and data) to guide the model's behavior and enable it to perform a specific task more effectively. Prompt engineering, system instructions, Retrieval-Augmented Generation (RAG), and controlled generation are examples of context engineering strategies:

Prompt engineering (https://oreil.ly/tJLIs)
> The practice of crafting effective inputs (prompts) that guide a pretrained LLM to produce a desired, accurate, and reliable output for a specific task. The prompt serves as the functional instructions in a natural language interface that guides the model's reasoning capabilities and dictates its behavior, persona, constraints, and the format of its response. Common techniques in prompt design include:

> *Zero-short prompting*
>> Giving a task without any examples (e.g., translate this text from English to Spanish).

> *Few-shot prompting*
>> Including several examples within the prompt itself, to define and illustrate the desired input-output pattern.

> *Chain-of-thought prompting*
>> Instructing the model to output its reasoning steps before the final answer is output to improve logical coherence and accuracy.

>> You'll read more about prompt optimization, including automated optimization tools available in the Vertex AI Platform, in Chapter 5.

System instructions (https://oreil.ly/uVgjB)
> A fundamental element of prompt design, especially in complex applications like AI agents. A system instruction is a governing, persistent piece of text provided to an LLM that defines its identity, behavioral boundaries, and core constraints for the entire conversation or application session. System instructions establish the primary rules for the model before any user input is processed and are generally fixed and do not change during the course of a single user session, providing a consistent "personality" and set of rules for the LLM. Even in consumer interfaces where a user doesn't explicitly provide one, the platform typically inserts a "hidden" system instruction to establish the model's baseline persona and safety guardrails.

Controlled generation (https://oreil.ly/jY7In)
> A mechanism that can be used to control the structure, format, and guardrails of an LLM's generated output to conform to a predefined schema or format, such as JSON. Guaranteeing a syntactically correct and schema-valid structure for output is critical for the reliability of applications in production environments. Specifically, output engineering/control ensures that LLM responses can be consumed correctly by downstream systems.

Retrieval-Augmented Generation (RAG) (https://oreil.ly/dgksr)
> An architectural pattern for enhancing the factual accuracy, recency, and relevance of LLMs by grounding their responses in external, verified, and up-to-date data sources. RAG also offers users strong interpretability and verifiability by enabling citations. RAG works by fundamentally changing the model's workflow

from relying solely on its pretrained, static internal knowledge to incorporating dynamic, external context. RAG is highly versatile and can be configured to ground LLM responses using virtually any accessible data source, including your own internal proprietary data, external public data, or live third-party data via APIs.

With RAG, when a user submits a query, the RAG system first searches a curated knowledge base (e.g., internal documents, databases, articles) to find the most relevant document segments or "chunks." These retrieved, relevant text chunks are then appended to the original user query, effectively augmenting the model's prompt with fresh, specific context. The LLM receives this augmented prompt and generates its response based on the new, provided context, thereby grounding the answer in verifiable information and minimizing the risk of hallucination.

You'll learn more about RAG in Chapter 2 and will see this important concept come up again in subsequent chapters of this book.

Domain-Specific and Reasoning Models

Some LLMs are referred to as "task (or domain) specific." This is a property of the way these models are tuned for the tasks they are developed to perform. Two examples of task-specific LLMs are SecLM (*https://oreil.ly/YV5Hu*) and Med-Gemini (*https://oreil.ly/JKYbc*), models developed by Google and specializing in the cybersecurity and medical domains, respectively. SecLM is trained on a vast dataset that includes security-related information, threat intelligence, and code analysis data. Its purpose is to specifically assist security professionals with tasks such as threat detection, analysis of malicious scripts, and understanding attack paths.

Med-Gemini is trained on medical literature, research papers, clinical data (likely anonymized and with appropriate safeguards), and other health-related information. Its goal is to specifically assist with tasks such as answering medical questions, summarizing research, and potentially aiding in clinical decision support (under expert supervision). Figure 1-2 shows Med-Gemini in action—it demonstrates its domain expertise by precisely identifying video segments (02:22-02:58) showing how to relieve calf strain with foam roller massage, a capability requiring specialized medical knowledge that general-purpose models might lack. This ability to understand and extract relevant information from medical instructional content showcases how task-specific models are optimized for their domains. Increasingly, general-purpose LLMs, including the Gemini family of multimodal foundation models, have been trained on massive general *and* specialized datasets within their respective domains. This means that users must critically evaluate both general and specialized LLMs for tasks.

MedGemini is an internal Google research product, but try out the MedGemma model, which is part of the Gemma family of open-weight models we mentioned earlier, if you want to get hands-on with a medical domain specific model. SecLM is operationalized in Google Cloud's Security Command Center (*https://oreil.ly/Ley-h*), so go there to experience the insights this model powers.

Figure 1-2. Demonstration of Med-Gemini's task-specific capabilities in analyzing medical instructional content

A new flavor of LLMs has advanced "reasoning" or "thinking" capabilities. This refers to a model's ability to engage in extended internal deliberation before delivering an answer. These models are trained to work step by step through a "thinking stage," where they analyze information, explore multiple hypotheses, and self-correct their logic internally to reduce errors. This incremental reasoning process makes them significantly more reliable for complex math, scientific logic, and advanced coding. A notable example is the Gemini family (starting with version 2.5), which allows users to manage this process through a controllable "thinking budget" (*https://oreil.ly/7GnHb*), balancing the depth of the model's reasoning with the speed of the response.

A Multitude of Models

There are so many LLMs to choose from! It seems like every week there is a new model or new model version released. Choice means that you can thoroughly evaluate and select the best (among many) models to fit your individual use case and that you have the flexibility to move models in and out of your pipelines as needs change. Being able to access a multitude of models and model versions easily, quickly, and within the expectations of enterprise security and privacy is more important than ever. At the time of writing, Vertex AI Model Garden (*https://oreil.ly/ayr1G*), part of

Google's Vertex AI Platform, includes more than 200 first-party, third-party, and open source models—spanning language, vision, audio, and other modalities—for users to choose from for various applications and diverse use cases. This includes pretrained multitask models that can be further tuned or customized for specific tasks, such as generation, classification, detection, recognition, embedding, segmentation, forecasting, translation, and automatic speech recognition. In Chapter 7, you'll hear more about model cards (*https://oreil.ly/MyQLy*), which are simple, structured overviews of how models were designed and evaluated. Model cards can be accessed from within Vertex AI Model Garden and allow you, the user, to make fully informed decisions based on facts about each model.

Generative AI Agents

GenAI agents use the reasoning capabilities of GenAI models (e.g., LLMs) as a cognitive engine to drive autonomous decision-making and actions. Henceforth, an agent can be thought of as an entity that can perceive its environment, make decisions, and take actions to achieve specific goals. Key characteristics of an intelligent agent include the following:

- Perception (i.e., gathering information about the environment)
- Reasoning (i.e., processing information and making decisions)
- Action (i.e., executing choices to interact with the environment)
- Autonomy (i.e., self-directed execution of tasks to achieve a goal)
- Goal-oriented (i.e., working toward specific objectives)

One of the most interesting features of agents is iterative refinement, based on human or internal feedback mechanisms. GenAI agents can refine their generated content based on feedback or changes in the environment, giving them an element of adaptability that is unique and powerful.

As illustrated in Figure 1-3, agents have four key components:

Model(s)
   A model, typically an LLM, serves as the agent "brain" for reasoning, understanding, and responding. The model functions to reason over goals, determine a plan, and generate a response. Multiagent frameworks can leverage different models to complete subtasks as part of an overall process or intent. Models optimized during training for agentic performance (for example, teaching a model not just what to say, but how to behave and reliably choose the correct tools, order of operations, and interpretation of complex content) tend to perform better on sequential decision-making of agentic applications.

Tools

Tools are used to fetch data and perform actions or transactions by calling APIs, functions, or services, including databases or even other agents. In other words, tools bridge the gap between the LLM's capability and the real world by allowing the agent to take actions, access real-time information, and perform calculations or specialized tasks that the LLM cannot do internally.

Orchestration

The orchestration component is the central control plane of an AI agent, managing the cyclical flow and decision-making process across the entire system. This cyclical layer maintains memory and state, including the approach used to plan and sequence actions. It applies advanced reasoning techniques, such as ReAct, Chain of Thought (CoT), and Tree of Thoughts (ToT), to inform decisions, determine which tools to invoke, and decide what new context to retrieve or store. By directing the interaction between the model, the tools, and the environment, orchestration ensures that the agent executes tasks reliably, iteratively refining its plan until the final objective is met.

Runtime

The runtime is the secure environment where the agent's instructions and logic are actually carried out. It is the physical infrastructure that hosts the model and orchestration code and is responsible for making the agent's tools work (like executing code or making API calls). The runtime matters because it governs the agent's real-world reliability: it ensures that the agent is scalable, operates with low latency, and is properly secured and authenticated, which is essential for deploying agents in an enterprise setting. In short, the runtime component of an agent executes the system, when invoked.

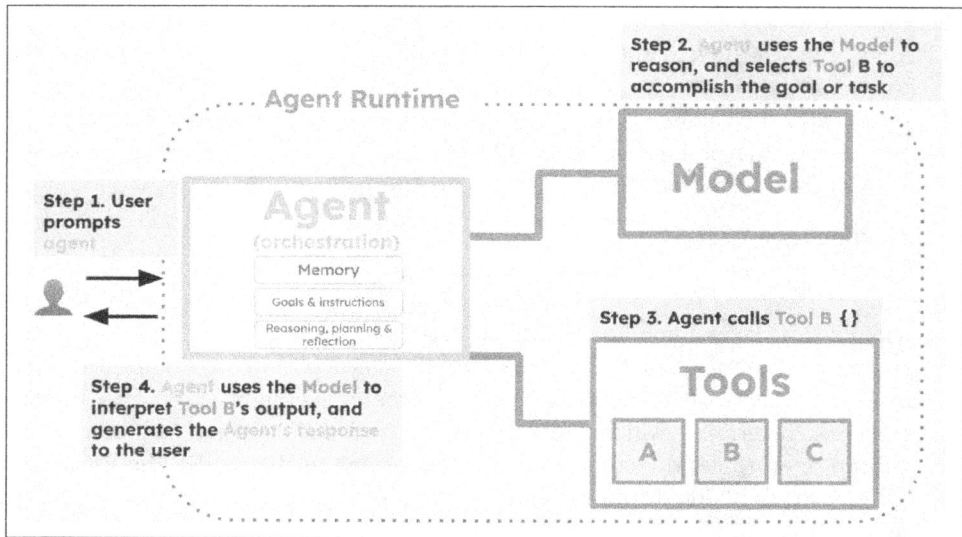

Figure 1-3. Agent overview (reprinted with permission from Megan O'Keefe, developer advocate at Google Cloud) illustrates the complete workflow of an AI agent operating within its runtime environment

As Figure 1-3 shows, the agent runtime serves as the operational environment, encompassing the agent (orchestration), the model (LLM), and the external tools. The process unfolds in four stages, depicted in the figure:

Step 1. Prompt initiation
The user presents a complex goal or query to the agent.

Step 2. Reasoning and tool selection
The agent uses its internal LLM to assess the task. Leveraging its internal memory (which includes crucial context such as chat history and retrieved knowledge) and its goals and instructions, the model engages in reasoning, planning, and reflection to determine that an external action is required. It selects the appropriate tool, B, and formats the required input payload.

Step 3. External execution
The agent's orchestration layer executes the preformatted function call to Tool B within the external tools suite.

Step 4. Interpretation and response
The agent receives the output from Tool B. It again uses the model to interpret this raw data, integrate it with the original context, and generate a final, coherent, and actionable response for the user.

One of the most exciting things about GenAI agents is their potential to automate creative tasks, personalize experiences, and drive new forms of interaction with technology. Agents have widespread application across diverse industries such as sales, marketing, customer service, software development, healthcare, education, consumer goods, and retail. A few illustrative examples of these agents (many of which would likely be multiagent systems that leverage sets of instructions and various LLMs) that we've discussed with user teams include:

AI marketing assistant

An agent that can understand marketing goals, research target audiences, and autonomously generate advertising copy, social media posts, storyboards and visual imagery, and short video content for campaigns and target audiences. Marketing assistants can also dynamically monitor campaign performance and adjust generation strategies for new audience segments or trends in the competitive landscape.

Personalized learning tutor

An agent that can understand a student's learning needs and generate customized practice problems, hints to correct answers, explanations with reasoning, and feedback in natural language. Such agents can adapt and evolve with the user by understanding the changing nature of prompts.

Code developer agent

An agent that can understand software requirements with codebase awareness and generate relevant code snippets, entire functions, or even complete applications. Such an agent could also test and debug the generated code. Developer agents can be particularly useful for enforcing standards and best practices across an organization.

Scientific research assistant

An agent that can understand a researcher's specific domain and hypotheses, utilize RAG against a specialized database of academic papers, and autonomously generate hyper-relevant findings, synthesized summaries, and cross-referenced evidence. Research agents employing scheduled workflows monitor new data sources daily and proactively alert users to new critical information relevant to their area of interest, accelerating hypothesis testing and literature review.

Agent Architectures

Multiagent GenAI applications are increasingly emerging as potential tools for completing complex and multistep tasks, especially in areas of deep scientific research. Applications using multiagent frameworks share a common environment, make individual and collective decisions, and take individual and collective actions to achieve specific goals. Imagine a team of specialized AI robots that need to work together to solve a complex problem, much like a team of human experts collaborating on a project. Multiagent frameworks must provide rules, tools, and infrastructure for these AI robots to communicate, coordinate, and interact effectively.

As illustrated in Figure 1-4, there are several common architectural patterns for structuring LLM-based applications, from simple single-model approaches to more complex multimodel systems.

Google Cloud provides tools and services for building, deploying, and managing no-code, low-code, and high-code agent applications through Gemini Enterprise (for business users), Vertex AI Agent Builder (for developers), and the open source Agent Development Kit (for developers). We will talk more about these products in Chapters 3 and 4.

> Not every GenAI application is an agent application. Nonagentic GenAI applications include zero-shot or few-shot learning, RAG (Retrieval-Augmented Generation), and fixed hard-coded sequences of zero-/few-shot invocations.

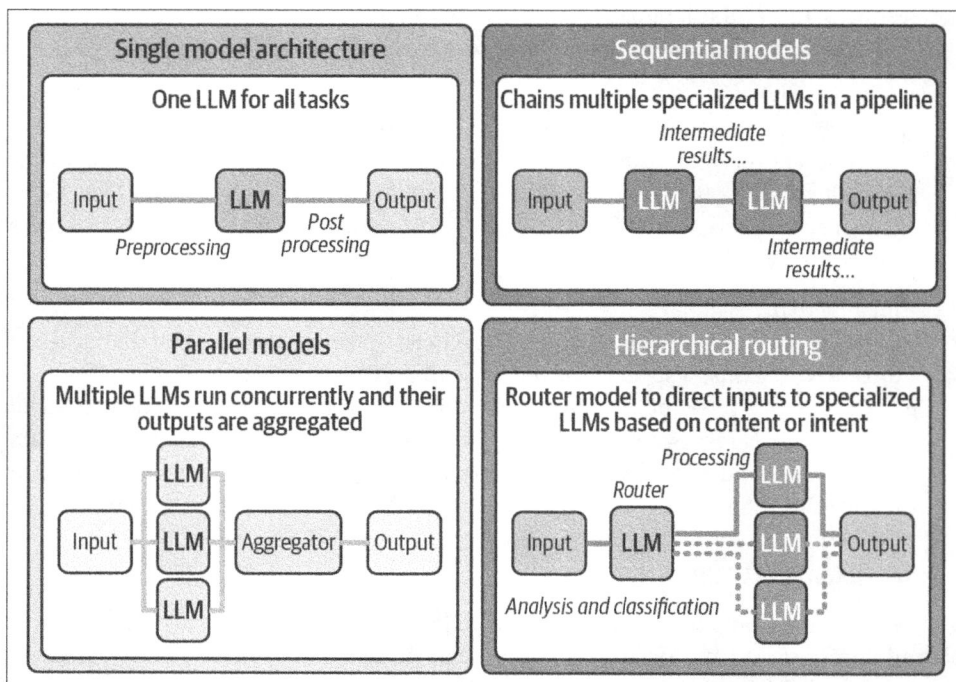

Figure 1-4. Common architectural patterns for LLM applications

You may come across the term "AgentOps" for preparing and managing (i.e., operationalizing) agents in production. In the context of agents, specifically, AgentOps often includes specific provisions for managing tools, orchestration, memory, and reasoning outputs.

We have reached a truly unique moment in time where underlying generative technology has matured significantly, the resources to build and deploy AI systems are more readily available, and the potential for real-world impact is becoming increasingly clear. This confluence of factors makes the current moment a truly transformative and exciting time for the field of GenAI, LLMs, and AI agents.

Challenges in Development, Deployment, and Maintenance

GenAI applications present a unique class of technical and operational challenges unlike traditional software or even conventional machine learning systems. The generative, probabilistic nature of the underlying models introduces complexities that ripple throughout the entire application lifecycle.

In our work assisting organizations deploying LLMs and agents to production environments, we've observed how established MLOps practices often require significant adaptation. Generative models don't behave like classification or regression models—their outputs can't be evaluated with simple accuracy metrics, their performance characteristics change based on prompt construction, and they interact with data in fundamentally different ways.

These differences manifest as specific technical obstacles at each stage of implementation. Let's examine these challenges systematically, from initial development through deployment and into ongoing maintenance, to help you navigate this complex terrain more effectively.

Development Challenges

During the development phase, teams encounter several fundamental obstacles that can significantly impact project success.

Data

LLMs require massive amounts of high-quality data for pretraining to learn general language representations. Acquiring datasets of sufficient scale (often trillions of tokens) and diversity can be a significant hurdle. The sheer volume of data poses logistical challenges for storage, processing, and management. These challenges are a main reason that most business users leverage pretrained foundation models rather than training their own from scratch.

Beyond scale, data quality and representation directly impact model performance. Low-quality or poorly representative data leads to models that generate nonsensical, biased, or factually incorrect outputs, eroding reliability and trustworthiness of applications. Common data quality issues include noise from irrelevant content, factual inaccuracies, repetitive content that skews learning, societal biases that models can amplify, and even malicious data poisoning designed to degrade performance.

Data preparation is another critical challenge, including cleaning, preprocessing, and formatting messy real-world data. For privacy and compliance, organizations must implement anonymization techniques to protect sensitive data such as personally identifiable information (PII) and protected health information (PHI).

> In Chapter 2, we'll explore comprehensive strategies for data readiness and accessibility, including detailed approaches to addressing these data challenges.

Models

Model development presents numerous challenges and choices. Prompt engineering—crafting effective prompts to elicit desired LLM behavior—can be highly subjective, with small changes significantly impacting output quality. LLMs have finite context windows (*https://oreil.ly/iYgDk*), requiring careful prioritization of information in prompts.

Fine-tuning introduces additional challenges despite using smaller datasets than pretraining. The computational requirements remain substantial for models with billions or trillions of parameters, potentially taking days or weeks and incurring significant costs. The technical expertise required can present barriers for many organizations seeking to customize models for specific domains.

Hallucinations represent a significant challenge for LLM applications. Unlike traditional information retrieval systems, LLMs predict the most probable next token based on learned patterns rather than retrieving facts from databases. This fundamental approach can lead to factually incorrect or nonsensical information presented with high confidence as illustrated in Figure 1-5. Grounding techniques that anchor responses to verifiable external knowledge can help mitigate this issue, but comprehensive evaluation remains essential.

The lack of explainability further complicates development. While we can observe inputs and outputs, the complex internal decision-making processes of LLMs remain largely opaque, making it difficult to diagnose issues or implement targeted improvements.

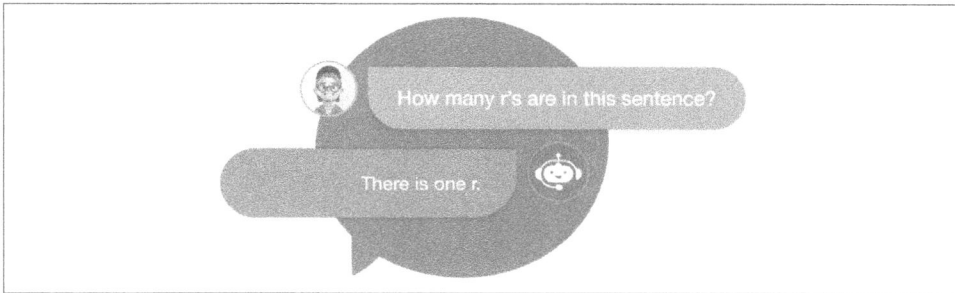

Figure 1-5. Example of a hallucination in an LLM chatbot response

> Chapters 6 and 7 will detail iterative processes for developing production-ready models, including techniques for addressing hallucinations and improving explainability.

Evaluation

Evaluating GenAI applications requires a nuanced approach that goes beyond traditional machine learning metrics. While conventional machine learning models might be assessed with straightforward metrics such as precision and recall, LLM and agent evaluation encompasses multiple dimensions of quality that are often subjective and context dependent.

Qualitative evaluation typically involves assessing how well responses address the original prompt, the logical flow and structure of the generated content, the naturalness and grammatical correctness of the language, factual consistency with real-world knowledge, the overall usefulness and informativeness of responses, and whether content avoids harmful or inappropriate material. These aspects often require human judgment, introducing challenges of consistency and scalability. For agents, evaluation also extends to the trajectory—the sequence of reasoning steps and tool calls—to ensure the system reached the correct answer for the right reasons.

Quantitative evaluation approaches include reference-based metrics that compare generated text against ground truth examples. Methods such as BLEU (*https://oreil.ly/WGTdH*), ROUGE (*https://oreil.ly/zRmI6*), and BERTScore (*https://oreil.ly/m0i0g*) measure various aspects of similarity between generated and reference texts, though they don't always correlate perfectly with human judgments of quality. Other metrics such as perplexity (*https://oreil.ly/zyJ0-*) measure a model's uncertainty in its predictions, while coherence (*https://oreil.ly/3qBd0*) metrics assess readability and logical flow.

A/B testing provides another valuable approach, comparing different models or prompting strategies through structured comparisons. However, designing fair comparisons and interpreting results correctly requires careful consideration of biases and context.

In Chapter 5, we'll explore comprehensive evaluation and optimization strategies, providing frameworks for both qualitative and quantitative assessment of GenAI applications.

Deployment Challenges

Moving from development to production introduces a new set of technical and operational hurdles that organizations must address.

Infrastructure

At the heart of successful GenAI deployment is the challenge of resource optimization. The sheer size and computational intensity of LLMs demand a robust, specialized infrastructure that often surpasses the requirements of conventional applications. Planning and provisioning the right hardware and software stack to serve these models is a key operational undertaking with implications for both performance and cost.

Industry-standard graphical processing units (GPUs) are excellent for parallel processing, while tensor processing units (TPUs) are efficient for large-scale AI workloads. Central processing units (CPUs) are perfectly suitable for smaller, highly optimized models that have less demanding and infrequent inference requests. Compared to GPUs and TPUs, CPUs may also be a more cost-effective and widely available option for compute hardware. The delicate trade-off between high performance and sustainable, cost-effective infrastructure to meet user demands is something that is often revisited by practitioners as demand for GenAI applications grows and must scale across internal and external users.

In addition to compute hardware, developers have choices about deployment environments (cloud-based, on-premises, hybrid cloud, or even edge deployment for smaller models running directly on user devices). Decisions about deployment environments involve trade-offs between cost, security, control, and scalability. Finally, serving and orchestration frameworks are crucial for efficiency, serving GenAI applications to users while managing memory and performance. Software stack choices include tools such as Docker and Kubernetes to package dependencies for consistency in deployment and scaling. LLMOps platforms can be a great choice for managing an entire GenAI product lifecycle, including deployment challenges.

The infrastructure complexity outlined immediately translates into challenges for scaling and maintaining performance. Latency represents a key challenge, particularly for conversational applications where response time directly impacts UX. Balancing performance with resource efficiency requires careful optimization across the entire stack, from model selection and quantization to serving infrastructure. Ultimately, these models require significant computing power, making scalability a critical concern as usage increases. Organizations need infrastructure that can efficiently scale to handle growing demand without performance degradation or excessive costs.

The cost implications of GenAI deployment can be substantial, encompassing compute resources, energy consumption, and potentially API fees for managed services. Organizations must carefully analyze the value delivered by GenAI applications against these ongoing operational costs, considering both direct expenses and opportunity costs of alternative approaches.

Integration

GenAI applications rarely exist in isolation—they must seamlessly interact with existing enterprise systems, databases, and business processes. For instance, a customer support agent might need to access customer relationship management (CRM) data to personalize responses, query knowledge bases for accurate information, and integrate with ticketing systems to track issue resolution, as illustrated in Figure 1-6. Building these integrations requires developing robust connectors that extract information, transform it into formats suitable for LLM consumption, and incorporate it effectively into the application workflow.

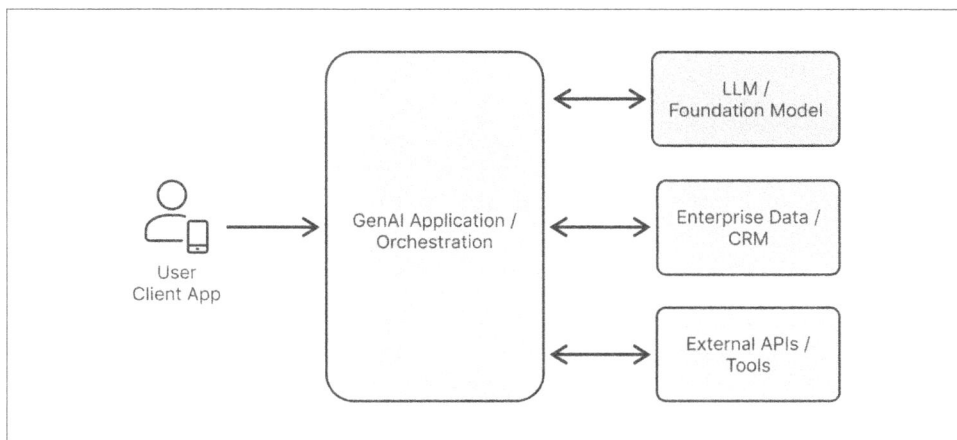

Figure 1-6. High-level architecture of a GenAI application integrated with enterprise data and external APIs

When working with third-party or self-hosted LLM services, API management introduces additional complexity. Organizations must implement strategies for rate limiting, authentication and authorization, versioning, and error handling to ensure reliable operation at scale. This often requires building abstraction layers that shield application logic from the underlying model implementation, enabling flexibility as models evolve.

Security

Security considerations for GenAI applications extend beyond traditional application security to include AI-specific vulnerabilities. Prompt injection attacks can manipulate models into ignoring safety guardrails or generating unauthorized content by crafting deceptive inputs. Adversarial examples might cause misclassification or incorrect outputs through subtle manipulations that exploit model sensitivities. Data breaches could expose not only user data but potentially training data or model weights, creating additional risk vectors that organizations must address.

Privacy concerns are equally important, particularly as LLMs may process sensitive personal information. Without appropriate controls, these models might inadvertently memorize or reveal confidential data from training sets or user interactions. Organizations must implement comprehensive governance frameworks and security measures to protect data, ensure compliance with relevant regulations, and maintain user trust.

Chapters 6 and 7 will provide a practical, prototype-to-production approach addressing the preceding model deployment challenges in detail, with specific guidance on infrastructure, integration, and security considerations.

Maintenance Challenges

Once your GenAI application is developed and deployed, your work to maintain the application in production begins. There are many important considerations for the long-term use of applications to drive business outcomes.

Drift

Model drift poses a significant challenge for GenAI applications over time. As language evolves with new terminology, emerging topics, and shifting usage patterns, models trained on historical data gradually become less effective at understanding and generating appropriate responses. Similarly, changes in data sources, user behavior, or business requirements can impact performance, creating a widening gap between model capabilities and operational needs.

The complex, interconnected nature of language means that even seemingly minor shifts can have cascading effects on model performance. New cultural references or domain terminology may be entirely absent from training data, while once-common expressions might become outdated or change in meaning. This dynamic environment requires continuous monitoring and periodic updates to maintain application effectiveness.

Monitoring

Ongoing monitoring is essential for maintaining high-quality GenAI applications in production. Unlike traditional software that might function identically for years if unchanged, GenAI applications operate in a constantly evolving linguistic and informational landscape. Organizations must implement comprehensive monitoring systems that track not only technical metrics but also semantic drift, hallucination frequency, bias emergence, and other quality indicators specific to GenAI.

This proactive approach enables early detection of performance degradation, allowing teams to implement targeted interventions before issues significantly impact users. Without robust monitoring, organizations risk declining performance, increasing inaccuracies, and potentially harmful outputs that could damage reputation and trust.

Version control

Managing the complex ecosystem of components that compose GenAI applications presents significant challenges. Organizations must track not only model versions but also the associated training data, fine-tuning datasets, prompt templates (*https:// oreil.ly/2I2xk*), integration code, and configuration parameters. This comprehensive version control enables reproducibility, facilitates debugging, and allows rolling back to previous stable states when needed.

Deciding when and how to update production models requires careful consideration of multiple factors. Performance metrics may indicate degradation requiring intervention, while new model architectures might offer substantial improvements in capabilities or efficiency. Organizations must develop clear criteria and processes for evaluating potential updates, balancing the benefits of improved performance against the risks and costs of change.

> In Chapter 8, we'll explore a multistage maturity model for GenAI applications, including detailed approaches to monitoring, maintenance, and continuous improvement.

Addressing Challenges with Modern Platforms

We've painted a pretty daunting picture of the challenges in building production-grade GenAI applications—and we've seen firsthand how these obstacles can derail promising projects. But here's the good news: you don't have to solve all these problems from scratch.

The market has rapidly evolved to provide platforms that tackle many of these pain points out of the box. We're not talking about magical solutions that eliminate all complexity but rather tooling that handles the heavy lifting so you can focus on what makes your application unique.

In our work with organizations across industries, we've seen teams leverage everything from fully managed offerings to more customizable, component-based approaches. AWS Bedrock (*https://oreil.ly/RkzPn*) provides a unified API for multiple foundation models with governance features baked in. Hugging Face's Inference API (*https://oreil.ly/14mWt*) simplifies deployment for thousands of open source models. Specialized providers such as Together AI (*https://oreil.ly/VoSjk*) and fal AI (*https://oreil.ly/igXKW*) offer optimized infrastructure for specific workloads. Even xAI has entered the arena with its Grok (*https://oreil.ly/ea3Kx*) model, which is integrated into the X platform. Each has distinct strengths and limitations that we've watched teams navigate when choosing the right fit for their needs.

Though this book focuses primarily on implementing solutions with Google Cloud's Vertex AI Platform (*https://oreil.ly/2Quf3*), many of the principles and patterns we discuss apply across provider platforms. Vertex AI offers a comprehensive end-to-end environment that addresses the challenges we've discussed in this chapter, and more. What makes Vertex particularly effective for production deployments is the connective tissue of supporting services for data preparation, model training, model evaluation, model serving, and monitoring. Vertex AI combines data engineering, data science, and machine learning engineering workflows, which means that traditionally siloed teams can easily and effectively collaborate using a common toolset.

We (your authors) have also helped many teams who have stitched together functional AI/ML pipeline components across multiple provider platforms—perhaps using one vendor's embeddings service with another's chat completion API—and seen both the flexibility this offers as well as the integration challenges it can create. What matters most isn't which specific platform you choose but rather understanding the patterns that lead to successful production deployments. We'll help you build that understanding throughout this book, showing you how to implement reliable production patterns regardless of your specific technology stack.

> In Chapter 8, we'll revisit AI and agentic platforms and how they can help to accelerate the maturity of your enterprise strategy and cohesive and scalable developer practices.

Industry Use Cases and ROI

"So what's the actual business impact?" It's a question we hear in nearly every executive briefing, and rightfully so. The technical capabilities of LLMs are fascinating, but what ultimately matters is whether they move the needle on business outcomes.

We've had front-row seats watching organizations transform prototypes into production systems that deliver measurable returns. A retail client we worked with started with a simple product description generator that saved their copywriters hours of tedious work. But the real return on investment (ROI) emerged when the company integrated it with its inventory system and customer data, creating personalized product recommendations that boosted conversion rates by 23%. What began as a productivity tool became a revenue driver.

In financial services, we've witnessed the evolution from basic chatbots to sophisticated assistants that handle complex customer inquiries about investment options. One bank we advised initially measured success by call deflection rates (which were impressive at 40%), but later discovered the real value was in increased customer satisfaction and higher retention rates for digitally engaged customers.

Healthcare organizations face some of the most stringent requirements for accuracy and compliance, making production deployment particularly challenging. Yet we've helped teams build systems that accelerate administrative workflows such as prior authorizations—reducing processing time from days to minutes while maintaining compliance with regulatory frameworks. For one healthcare provider, this translated to millions in annual savings and faster patient care.

Manufacturing clients have surprised us with creative applications that blend structured data analysis with unstructured text generation. One team built a system that interprets equipment telemetry, generates maintenance recommendations, and automatically schedules technician visits—reducing unplanned downtime by 25% and extending equipment life.

The telecommunications sector has found particular value in applying LLMs to knowledge management, with one company we worked with dramatically improving field technician efficiency by providing contextual troubleshooting guidance based on service histories, equipment specifications, and previously successful resolutions.

These experiences align with broader industry research. The 2024 "ROI of Gen AI" study (*https://oreil.ly/eJLLT*) by Google Cloud and the National Research Group found that back-office business processes represent the largest area of measurable return, with organizations reporting significant impact in human resources, legal, procurement, and enterprise technology support. The study also indicates that while initial investments often target productivity improvements, organizations are increasingly leveraging these technologies for strategic initiatives such as innovation and customer experience enhancement. Google's 2025 update (*https://oreil.ly/ZoVgN*) on the ROI of AI reported that the most common cross-industry applications for AI agents were customer service and experience (49%), marketing (46%), security operations and cybersecurity (46%), and tech support (45%), as illustrated in Figure 1-7.

What separates organizations that capture significant ROI from those that don't? In our experience, it's rarely about having access to the best model or the most sophisticated technology. It's about rigorously focusing on specific business problems, building robust data and operational foundations, and creating tight feedback loops that allow systems to continuously improve. The returns come from thoughtful and intentional implementation rather than technological wizardry.

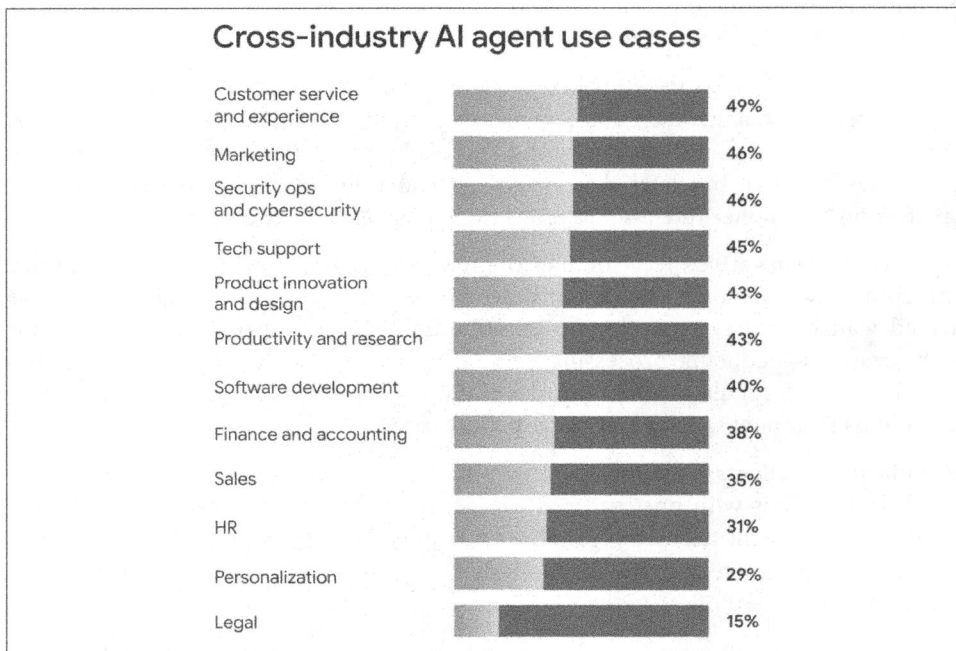

Cross-industry AI agent use cases

Use case	Percentage
Customer service and experience	49%
Marketing	46%
Security ops and cybersecurity	46%
Tech support	45%
Product innovation and design	43%
Productivity and research	43%
Software development	40%
Finance and accounting	38%
Sales	35%
HR	31%
Personalization	29%
Legal	15%

Figure 1-7. Top cross-industry use cases for AI agents by deployment frequency (source: Google Cloud, The ROI of Gen AI, 2025)

Looking Ahead

Throughout this chapter, we've explored the fundamental concepts of LLMs and identified the key challenges that organizations face when developing production-grade systems. While these challenges are significant, they're also well understood and addressable with the right approaches and tools.

In the chapters that follow, we'll address these challenges, providing practical guidance and implementation strategies drawn from our experience helping organizations successfully navigate the journey from prototype to production. Our discussions will scale across the stages of GenAI evolution that we've witnessed over the last two years: from direct (out-of-the-box) foundation model interactions through prompt and system engineering, to grounding and augmenting the behavior of foundation models with external data, to equipping LLMs with tools (like APIs) and reasoning capabilities, to goal-oriented automation with a single dedicated agent or through multiagent orchestration and the development of collaborative AI systems. As we move through Chapters 3 and 4, we'll show you what it looks like to transition from building systems that can respond with external data and actions to a system that can autonomously execute multistep goals; we'll build agents together! Across Chapters 5, 6, and 7, you'll learn how to evaluate, tune, and apply MLOps to safely deploy and maintain your AI products. Finally, in Chapter 8, we'll bring together your learnings across the first seven chapters by applying them to an AI and agentic maturity framework to guide your organization.

In the next chapter, Chapter 2, we'll dive deeper into preparing for GenAI experimentation through "data readiness and accessibility"—a critical foundation for successful GenAI applications.

Learning Labs

To reinforce the concepts covered in this chapter and explore the fundamentals of Generative AI, we recommend exploring the learning resources available in the Chapter 1 folder of the book's GitHub repository (*https://oreil.ly/cWyiA*). Key resources you will find linked there include:

- **Courses**
  - Introduction to Generative AI (*https://oreil.ly/5Zz3x*): A free introductory course that explains GenAI fundamentals, model types, and applications
  - Google AI Essentials (*https://oreil.ly/nGHsO*): A productivity-focused specialization that teaches how to use generative AI tools to speed up daily work tasks and generate ideas
  - Google Prompting Essentials (*https://oreil.ly/CLEoY*): A hands-on specialization teaching the "5 steps of effective prompting" for text, data analysis, and multimodal tasks

- **Video Tutorials**
  - Introduction to Artificial Intelligence (AI) (*https://oreil.ly/8qQj6*): An overview of how AI, Machine Learning, and Generative AI differ and how they automate cognitive tasks
  - Introduction to Responsible AI (*https://oreil.ly/3pQwX*): A breakdown of Google's three core AI principles—bold innovation, responsible development, and collaborative progress
  - Intro to AI Agents (*https://oreil.ly/ms-wU*): A discussion on agentic architecture, defining agents as "AI with a job" and exploring tool usage versus autonomous reasoning
  - Prompt Engineering for Developers (*https://oreil.ly/NGn2N*): A practical guide to improving model outputs using the "Persona, Task, Context" framework and Chain of Thought reasoning
  - How to use Retrieval Augmented Generation (RAG) (*https://oreil.ly/lqiKJ*): A walkthrough of the RAG data flow, explaining how to use embeddings and vector databases to ground LLM responses
  - Intro to multimodal RAG systems (*https://oreil.ly/ciVUw*): A technical tutorial on building RAG systems that can reason across both text and images using multimodal embeddings

## CHAPTER 2

Data Readiness and Accessibility

In Chapter 1, we explored how GenAI applications represent a fundamentally different class of AI systems compared to traditional machine learning models for classification and regression tasks. The generative, probabilistic nature of GenAI systems introduces unique complexities across the entire lifecycle, and as we'll see, this starts with the data.

"Wait, I thought LLMs were all about the models?" a CTO once asked Sarita after their team had spent months fine-tuning parameters but still couldn't match their prototype's performance in production. This is perhaps the most common misconception we encounter when working in the field. While the models get the spotlight, it's really the quality, accessibility, and governance of your data that ultimately determine whether your GenAI application succeeds or fails in the real world.

When our team works with organizations transitioning from prototype to production, we typically find they've underestimated the data challenges by an order of magnitude. Industry analysis suggests that data preparation can consume up to 80% of the total effort in AI projects (*https://oreil.ly/WlIdd*). With GenAI, this becomes even more pronounced, particularly when building systems that need to be reliable, accurate, and trustworthy.

The Amplified Importance of Data for GenAI

"Garbage in, garbage out" (GIGO) takes on an entirely new dimension with GenAI, as illustrated in Figure 2-1. For traditional ML models, the consequence of poor data is typically a quantitative drop in accuracy. For LLMs, however, the failure is qualitative and more insidious: they can confidently generate completely fabricated information, perpetuate subtle biases, or produce plausible-sounding but entirely incorrect outputs.

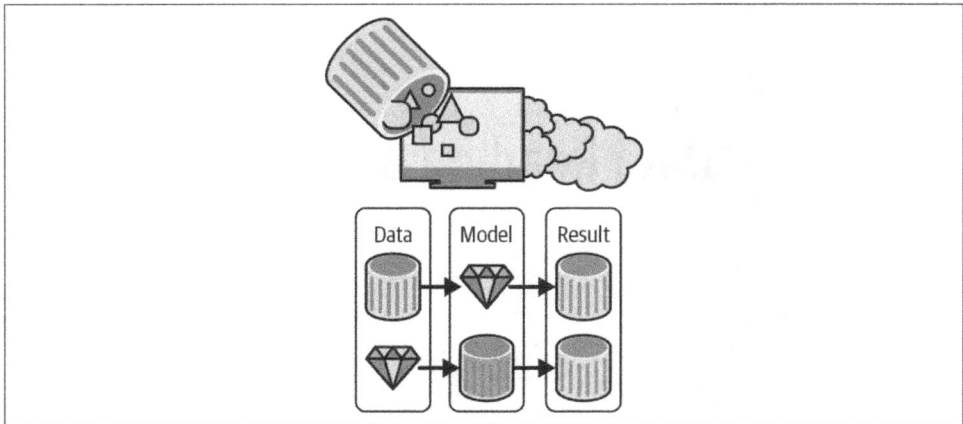

Figure 2-1. Illustration of the garbage in, garbage out effect of bad data

Sarita recalls working with a healthcare provider whose initial RAG system was generating clinical treatment recommendations that sounded medically valid but included completely fabricated medication names and dosages. The issue wasn't with the LLM or the retrieval mechanism, but with inconsistent preprocessing formatting applied to the provider's clinical documents that caused critical information to be missed during document chunking (*https://oreil.ly/4Y-7t*). For example, if one clinical note lists "Medication: Drug X, Dosage: 500 mg" all on one line, but another note lists "Medication: Drug X" and then "Dosage: 500 mg" two paragraphs later, a simple chunking strategy would likely split the medication from its dosage. When the RAG system retrieved only the chunk with "Drug X," the LLM would lack the dosage context, leading it to generate fabricated outputs like Sarita observed.

These risks from poor data quality and preparation become even more acute with agentic systems. When such a system uses an LLM not just to generate text but to reason and autonomously take actions—querying databases, calling APIs, or making decisions—the consequences of data issues cascade rapidly. A seemingly minor data quality problem can trigger a chain reaction of errors, potentially leading to significant real-world impacts.

One financial services client we worked with built an agent to help customers restructure debt. In testing, it performed flawlessly. But in production, it began recommending impossible payment schedules because the client's production database contained subtle inconsistencies in how interest rates were stored across different account types—something their test environment didn't capture. This is a classic example of a *semantic data issue* rooted in a lack of a united enterprise governance strategy. For this client, the "interest_rate" column in their "mortgage" database was stored as a float (e.g., 5.5), while in the "credit_card" database, it was stored as a string with a percentage (e.g., '5.5%'). The agent, lacking the context of this semantic difference, treated both as raw numbers, leading to catastrophic calculation errors. A key architectural solution is a *semantic layer*, which sits between the data sources and the AI to provide a single, authoritative definition for all business terms, preventing this type of error *before* it can impact the agent.

> The semantic layer is a metadata translation layer that sits between complex, technical data storage (like data warehouses or data lakes) and business users' tools (like dashboards, Business Intelligence [BI], or AI agents). It allows users to query data using familiar business terminology instead of technical table names and columns.

What Data Readiness Really Means for GenAI Applications

These experiences taught us something crucial: the definition of "data ready" for GenAI applications is fundamentally different from traditional ML systems. Data readiness is a state achieved when organizational data has undergone meticulous preparation and optimization to ensure that it can be seamlessly, effectively, and reliably utilized by LLMs and agentic systems. It signifies that data is not merely available but appropriately formatted, thoroughly cleaned, contextually enriched, actively governed, and demonstrably trustworthy.

When Ayo was consulting with a retail client struggling with its recommendation engine, he explained it this way: "It's not just about having a lot of data; it's about having the right data, in the right shape, at the right time."

In the following sections, we'll unpack exactly what these dimensions—the right data, the right shape, and the right time—truly mean in practice when moving from a prototype to a production system.

From Data Fault to Learning Failure: Why Agent Improvement Stalls

Think of an agent's ability to learn from its mistakes as a cognitive process. Data errors aren't just bad inputs; they are traps that can sabotage this process. We can use a simplified memory model to understand why:

Short-term memory (STM) is flooded
> An agent's "short-term memory" is its immediate context—the plan it's currently executing and any recent error messages. A production environment with poor data quality can flood this context with repetitive, low-level data faults (e.g., thousands of the same "parser error").

"Cognitive overload" masks the real problem
> In more advanced agentic architectures, a key goal is for the agent to identify high-level planning failures, learn from them, and store that knowledge for the future (a form of "long-term memory"). However, if the agent's immediate

---

context is constantly clogged with noise from data errors, it becomes impossible for the system (or the developers who maintain it) to distinguish a meaningful strategic failure from the countless trivial data faults.

Long-term learning "starves"
The agent gets stuck in a reactive loop, perpetually handling the same data inconsistencies without ever getting the chance to solve higher-order problems. As a result, its ability to genuinely improve stalls. This is how issues like semantic inconsistency, data voids, and poor accessibility don't just cause a single error; they create a cycle of failure that prevents the agent from becoming more capable over time.

Key Dimensions of Data Readiness

Let's break down these dimensions through the lens of what we've learned helping dozens of organizations move from prototype to production.

First, data must be *discoverable*. In one manufacturing organization we worked with, the data scientists had built a promising prototype for an LLM that could answer questions about equipment maintenance procedures. But when they tried to scale it, they hit a wall—nobody knew where all the maintenance documentation lived. Some was in SharePoint, some in an ancient document management system, some in email attachments, and some existed only as printed manuals in maintenance shops.

"I can't ground an LLM on data I can't find," the lead data scientist told us in frustration. We ended up creating a "data map" that identified not just where information lived, but who owned it and how frequently it changed—essential context that the company's data catalog had never captured before.

Similarly, *accessibility* often becomes a roadblock. Steph recalls a financial services client that built a prototype chatbot for customer service. It worked beautifully in the lower development environment where the data science team had unfettered access to customer data. In production, however, privacy requirements meant that the LLM could access only redacted data through specific secure APIs, which completely changed how the data needed to be structured and how the prompts needed to be engineered.

The most deceptive requirement is often *quality*. "Surely our data quality is good enough," a retail executive once told Ayo. "We've been running our business on it for years." But what's "good enough" for operational systems or even traditional analytics can be catastrophic for generative models. Missing values in a database might be acceptable for a dashboard showing aggregate sales trends, but for an LLM generating detailed product descriptions, those gaps become confabulations—plausible but entirely fictional claims that can mislead customers or violate regulations.

Format requirements also differ dramatically for GenAI applications. A major insurance company we consulted with had beautifully organized policy documentation in well-structured PDFs that humans could easily interpret. Yet their LLM consistently misinterpreted coverage details because tables were being processed as jumbled text by the company's ingestion pipeline. Steph helped the company's team develop custom parsers that could extract tabular information and convert it into structured JSON that preserved the semantic relationships between policy elements—relationships that were visually obvious to humans but completely lost in the raw text extraction, as illustrated in Figure 2-2.

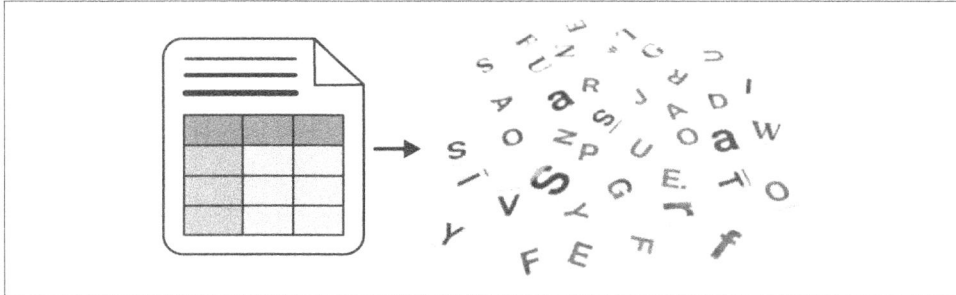

Figure 2-2. Without a proper preprocessing step, such as the automated extraction provided by Document AI or BigQuery's `ML.PROCESS_DOCUMENT` *function, structured data (left) can be misinterpreted by an LLM as jumbled text (right)*

Layout-Aware Parsing with Google Cloud

Newer models such as Gemini 3 Pro with optical character recognition (OCR) capabilities have significantly improved native table parsing and understanding. However, table extraction remains challenging in many production scenarios, especially with complex layouts or poor-quality scans. For mission-critical applications, we often recommend specialized document processing services such as Google Cloud's Document AI (*https://oreil.ly/tKk-H*), Microsoft Azure's Document Intelligence (*https://oreil.ly/N6jZQ*), or Amazon Textract (*https://oreil.ly/XtQ10*). These services offer more reliable structured data extraction, custom parsing rules, and domain-specific processors (e.g., for invoices, receipts, or contracts), as illustrated in Figure 2-3. The extra processing step adds complexity to your pipeline but dramatically improves downstream model performance by providing properly structured data rather than relying on the model's ability to interpret raw text. Developers can also leverage BigQuery's built-in AI functions, such as `ML.PROCESS_DOCUMENT` (*https://oreil.ly/3SBWa*), to automatically extract tabular information and convert it into structured JSON that preserves the semantic relationships between document elements.

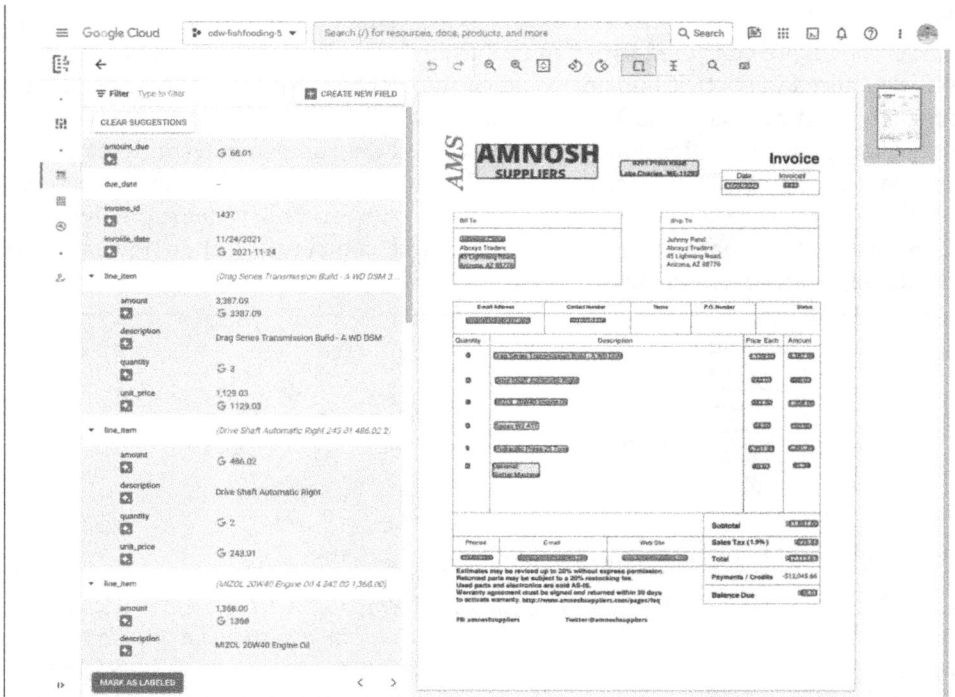

Figure 2-3. Semantic Feature Extraction and Layout-Aware Parsing within Google Cloud Document AI, illustrating how complex documents are transformed into structured data and task-optimized embeddings

Finally, *governance* takes on new significance. Data usage policies that worked for traditional applications often fail to address the unique ways LLMs can combine, interpret, and generate information. One healthcare organization we worked with had to develop entirely new governance frameworks to ensure that its clinical decision support system respected not just patient privacy regulations, but also considered fairness, provenance tracking, and auditability requirements that simply hadn't been relevant for its pre-GenAI systems.

What Does Data Governance Mean?

Data governance is a set of policies, processes, and roles that ensure data is managed as a critical asset throughout its entire lifecycle—from creation to retirement. The primary goal of a data governance strategy is to maximize the value, quality, reliability, security, and compliance of an organization's data. Data governance answers the fundamental questions: who can access the data, how can it be used, and who is accountable for its quality and meaning?

The semantic layer is a critical component for achieving centralized data governance, particularly for ensuring common and central definitions of business terms. In addition to centralizing business definitions (functioning as a "central source of truth"), the semantic layer standardizes logic for AI applications and agents and importantly, makes it easier to enforce, comply with, and audit data policies. For example, access and security rules can be applied at the business term level rather than the technical column level. For instance, "*Only managers can view the 'Gross Revenue' metric*" is simpler to manage and audit than applying permissions to 20 different columns that contribute to the calculation of Gross Revenue.

In Chapter 7, we'll do a deeper dive into data governance and related concepts.

The Interconnected Nature of Data Readiness

What makes data readiness particularly challenging for GenAI systems is how interconnected these requirements are. A healthcare company we worked with learned this the hard way when it tried to address data quality issues in isolation, without tackling the underlying governance gaps.

"We spent months cleaning our customer interaction data," the CIO explained, "only to discover that without clear data ownership and consistent standards across departments, the quality problems just kept reappearing." The company's LLM-powered customer support bot would work well for a few weeks, then gradually start making more errors as fresh, inconsistent data flowed into the system.

The solution ultimately involved creating a unified data readiness framework that recognized how discoverability, accessibility, quality, format, governance, and security reinforce each other, as illustrated in Figure 2-4. When the company implemented role-based access controls as part of its governance initiative, it also improved data quality by ensuring that only authorized personnel could modify certain data elements. When the company improved metadata tagging for security purposes, it simultaneously enhanced discoverability.

This holistic approach mirrors what we've seen work across industries. Data readiness for GenAI systems isn't a series of independent checkboxes, it's a coherent strategy that addresses longstanding "data debt" while preparing for the unique demands of these powerful models.

The components in this framework are grouped by their conceptual role. Quality, format, and governance represent the inherent properties and policies of the data itself. Discoverability and security represent the mechanisms of control and access.

Finally, accessibility represents the core action of delivering the right data to the right people, enabled by all other components.

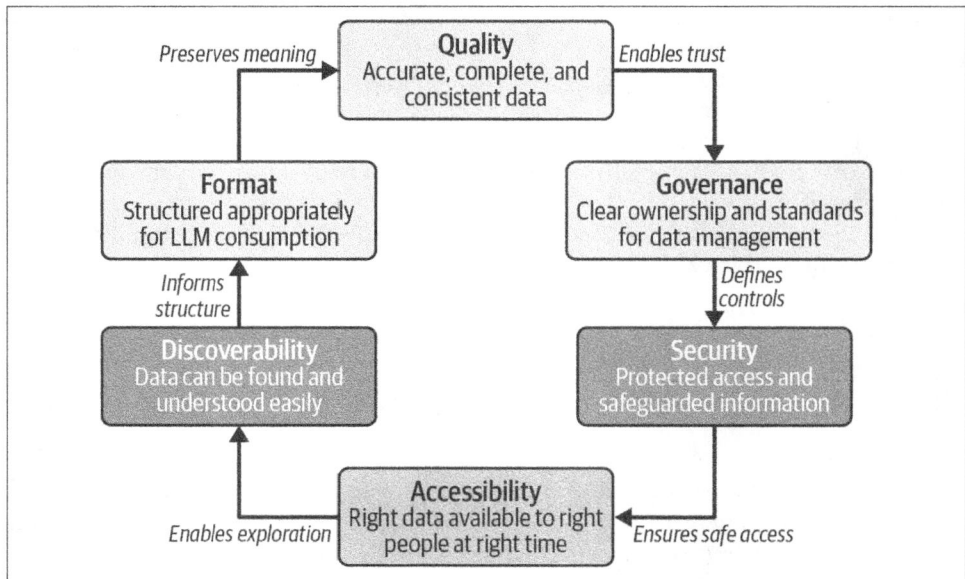

Figure 2-4. *The six components of data readiness for GenAI: an interconnected cycle*

Managing Prompts as Data Assets

In the rush to build, teams often hardcode prompts or treat them as simple configuration files. However, in a production data architecture, prompts are critical data assets that define your application's behavior and must be managed with the same rigor as your training datasets. Keep the following in mind:

Versioning and lineage
> Just as you version your datasets, you must version your prompt templates. A "data-ready" architecture treats prompts as managed artifacts—stored in version control or a dedicated prompt registry—ensuring that you can always map a specific model output back to the exact combination of data version *and* prompt version that generated it.

Context window management
> Data readiness also means managing the scarcity of the context window. This involves strict governance over what data is allowed to enter the window, using summarization chains to compress verbose retrieved content, and enforcing token budgets to ensure that your critical system instructions are never pushed out by noisy retrieval results.

In Chapter 7, "MLOps for Production-Ready AI and Agentic Systems," we'll dive deeper into the operational side of this concept. We'll explore "PromptOps" and the specific CI/CD workflows required to manage prompt versions, test them systematically, and deploy them alongside model iterations in a production environment.

The Human Element: Roles in the Data Readiness Journey

Successful GenAI implementations depend not just on understanding the interconnected nature of data readiness, but on having the right people with the right skills to make it happen. In our work with organizations across industries, we've observed that the most successful teams recognize that data readiness isn't owned by any single role—it's a collaborative effort requiring diverse expertise.

Each role brings a unique perspective and set of skills to different parts of the data readiness cycle. As we walk through these key personas, you'll notice that the boundaries between them often blur in practice. The data scientist exploring a new dataset might identify quality issues that the data engineer needs to address, while governance questions raised by compliance teams influence architectural decisions made by ML engineers.

Let's look at how these roles collaborate to build the foundation for successful GenAI deployment, starting with the explorers at the frontier: data scientists.

In Chapter 8, we'll revisit this critical concept of team synergy through the lens of *AI maturity*. We'll show how an organization's journey from the "Tactical" to the "Strategic" and "Transformational" phases is defined by its ability to break down these silos. The "aha moment" is this: low-maturity organizations keep their *business subject matter experts (SMEs)* and technical teams separate, leading to "pilot purgatory," where projects work in a lab but fail in production. High-maturity organizations, in contrast, use AI and agentic platforms to *embed* these domain leaders directly into the development lifecycle, ensuring that technical execution is, by default, aligned with measurable business value and strategic goals.

Data Scientists: The Explorers

Data scientists are often the first to venture into unexplored data territories when organizations begin GenAI initiatives. Their initial challenge is typically discovery—finding relevant data sources that could inform or ground their models.

In one organization we worked with, the data science team spent three weeks searching for product information that should have taken minutes or hours to locate. The data existed but was scattered across inventory systems, marketing databases, and even spreadsheets maintained by individual category managers.

This discovery process requires both technical skills and detective work. Effective data scientists develop systematic approaches to mapping data landscapes, often beginning with broad questions using tools such as BigQuery (*https://oreil.ly/JKiYM*) to understand available datasets. Tools such as Dataplex Universal Catalog (*https://oreil.ly/k1OTJ*) can accelerate this process by providing a centralized catalog with context about data assets across the organization. Beyond merely locating data, data scientists need to understand provenance, freshness, completeness, and potential biases. This discovery process is also becoming more conversational; data scientists can now use natural language interfaces—such as Dataplex Semantic Search (*https://oreil.ly/uLKJg*) or Looker Conversational Analytics (*https://oreil.ly/REBLR*)—to ask questions about datasets, their quality, and their lineage.

> We'll go deeper into BigQuery and Dataplex later in this chapter. BigQuery enables powerful SQL queries across vast datasets, helping data scientists quickly explore and understand available data. Dataplex complements this by providing metadata management, data governance, and discovery capabilities in a unified platform. Together, these tools streamline the critical early stages of GenAI data preparation by making relevant data more discoverable and accessible across the organization.

Once relevant sources are identified, the next challenge is data wrangling (*https://oreil.ly/yTiIT*) and integration. Building a customer support chatbot, for instance, might require combining knowledge base articles (unstructured text), historical support tickets (semi-structured), and customer profiles (structured data from CRM systems). Data scientists typically perform this exploratory work in a unified notebook environment. Using BigQuery notebooks (*https://oreil.ly/Oc0oP*) powered by Vertex AI Colab Enterprise, they can work interoperably with Python, SQL, and even Spark, combining data-wrangling libraries with BigQuery's powerful analytics all in one place.

For GenAI applications specifically, data scientists face unique preparation challenges. Sarita recalls working with a legal team building a contract analysis system: "Their challenge wasn't lack of data—they had thousands of contracts. The challenge was preparing that text appropriately for the LLM. We had to experiment with different chunking strategies, embedding approaches, and metadata schemas before finding the right balance."

One hard-earned lesson from numerous implementations is that data preparation for generative models is inherently iterative. Initial assumptions about chunk size, embedding approaches, or filtering criteria almost always evolve as testing reveals gaps or performance issues. This requires planning for flexibility from the beginning, with data pipelines that can adapt to changing requirements without complete redesigns.

ML Engineers: Building the Bridge to Production

ML engineers occupy a unique position between data preparation and model deployment, focusing on how data directly impacts model performance and optimization. While data scientists explore data possibilities and data engineers build foundational infrastructure, ML engineers design the systems that transform raw data into model-ready formats and ensure that models perform consistently in production.

"The most painful failures we've seen are when a meticulously tuned model suddenly underperforms in production," Ayo notes. A retail client spent months fine-tuning a model for sentiment analysis in customer reviews, only to watch it deteriorate within weeks of deployment. The investigation revealed that the client's training data hadn't accounted for seasonal shifts in customer language and product references. The fine-tuned dataset was perfectly curated but not representative of real-world variation.

ML engineers develop specialized expertise in understanding how data characteristics affect model behavior. In one healthcare company, the ML engineering team discovered that including or excluding certain data fields in their training process dramatically impacted how well their LLM could recognize policy exclusions. They conducted a systematic feature importance study that evaluated model performance across different data combinations: "We created what we called 'data ablation tests' for the LLM," Sarita said. "By systematically removing different types of data from the context—policy dates, coverage limits, exclusion clauses—we could measure exactly how each element affected response accuracy. This informed both our data preparation strategy and our prompt engineering approach."

Through these systematic evaluations, ML engineers transform abstract data-quality concerns into measurable performance impacts. This evidence-based approach creates a continuous feedback loop between data preparation decisions and model outcomes, turning what might otherwise be a static, one-time process into an ongoing optimization cycle that evolves as new patterns emerge in both data and user interactions.

For fine-tuning and adaptation tasks, ML engineers design specialized data pipelines that enforce rigorous quality standards. When a healthcare organization needed to adapt a general LLM for medical terminology, the ML engineers built a comprehensive fine-tuning data pipeline with multiple safeguards (*https://oreil.ly/bIIyJ*). Their system verified medical term consistency against external terminology databases while carefully balancing case distribution to prevent specialization bias across different medical fields. They didn't stop at basic quality controls—the team also implemented data augmentation techniques to improve model robustness and created targeted synthetic challenge cases that addressed known model weaknesses. This multilayered approach ensured that the LLM could reliably process medical language with the precision that healthcare applications demand.

As models move to production, ML engineers build monitoring systems that track the alignment between training data distributions and real-world inputs. They develop automated retraining triggers that detect when data drift exceeds acceptable thresholds, ensuring that models remain effective as language patterns evolve.

Beyond technical implementation, the fundamental contribution ML engineers bring to data readiness is a performance-centered perspective. They view data not as static content to be processed, but as the dynamic foundation that directly shapes model behavior and UX. This perspective ensures that investments in data quality remain tightly coupled with business outcomes throughout the model lifecycle.

Data Engineers: Architecting the Foundation

While ML engineers focus on model-specific data pipelines, data engineers build the underlying infrastructure that makes everything possible. For GenAI applications, this infrastructure requires thoughtful planning to handle diverse data types and access patterns.

Steph recalls working with a retail client who needed an advanced product recommendation system that could handle millions of products with rich semantic search capabilities. The client's requirements included both powerful filtering and sub-100 ms semantic search latency across its growing catalog.

The data engineering team designed a multilayer architecture that leveraged Google Cloud's complementary services. At the foundation layer, they used Cloud Storage to store the original product documents and images in their raw form. For structured data management and vector search capabilities, they implemented a solution combining BigQuery with Vertex AI Feature Store (*https://oreil.ly/fq2T2*). BigQuery served as the centralized repository for product data, metadata, and embeddings, enabling complex queries and joins across the product catalog. Vertex AI Feature Store provided ultra-low latency vector serving by maintaining synchronized copies of the most relevant embeddings optimized for similarity search.

This integrated approach was transformative. First, it eliminated the need to maintain duplicate data across separate systems. This, in turn, shortened the idea-to-prototype timeline by days or even weeks, as teams could now discover and reuse features built on common business attributes. Second, data from BigQuery seamlessly flowed to the Feature Store's optimized serving layer, simultaneously enabling both powerful analytics *and* the required sub-100 ms semantic search performance. Finally, the architecture scaled automatically as the product catalog grew, maintaining consistent performance without requiring manual intervention.

DevOps and SREs: Operationalizing the Foundation

A perfectly architected data foundation is still just a blueprint. The "prototype-to-production gap" that Steph and Ayo mentioned—like the chatbot that failed under real-world privacy rules—is closed by the operational teams: Developer Operations (DevOps), Security Operations (SecOps), and, as Steph notes, Site Reliability Engineers (SREs).

These personas are the bridge from "it works" to "it works *reliably, securely, and at scale.*"

For them, the data foundation is not a static asset but a dynamic system that must be versioned, deployed, and monitored. Their core focus is the *CI/CD (continuous integration/continuous delivery) pipeline*, which is uniquely complex for GenAI. A RAG application (*https://oreil.ly/Vc5oF*) isn't just code; it's a living system of code, models, and constantly changing data.

This is where a *GitOps*-centric approach, as seen in modern RAG architectures, becomes essential. In this model, the "source of truth" in a Git repository defines the entire state of the application:

CI

> When an ML engineer updates the agent's logic, a CI pipeline is automatically triggered. This process runs tests, scans for vulnerabilities, and—most critically—builds the agent's code into a *container*. This containerization step is special because it packages the agent's complex logic and all its specific dependencies (such as Python libraries, data connectors, and environment variables) into a single, portable unit. This ensures that the agent runs identically in development, testing, and production—a massive challenge for AI systems that this approach elegantly solves. This container is then pushed as a versioned artifact into *Artifact Registry*.

CD

> The GitOps controller detects the new image in Artifact Registry (*https://oreil.ly/Sr-P6*). It then automatically manages a progressive rollout of the new container to the production environment, which is often a scalable, serverless service like Cloud Run (*https://oreil.ly/Qg0Ld*).

This same pipeline also handles *data* changes. When new documents are added to the RAG knowledge base, it's this CI/CD process that triggers the data ingestion, chunking, and embedding jobs that update the vector database.

This is where the SRE mindset, so core to Google's culture (*https://oreil.ly/K6H4K*), is critical. An SRE's job goes beyond just deployment. They are responsible for the *reliability, performance, and cost-efficiency* of the entire system. They are the ones asking the following:

- "What is our service level objective (SLO) for RAG retrieval latency?"
- "What are the SLOs for the data ingestion pipelines that refresh the vector database?"
- "How are we monitoring real-time token consumption and GPU utilization for capacity planning?"
- "What is our error budget—the acceptable amount of failure—for failed tool calls?"
- "Is this agent's cost scaling predictably with its usage, or are we exposed to runaway costs from inefficient tool calls or agent reasoning loops?"

While the data engineer *builds* the road, the DevOps and SRE teams *operate* it—installing the guardrails, managing the flow of traffic, and ensuring that it can handle rush hour without collapsing in production.

Business SMEs and Domain Leaders: The "Why" Behind the "What"

This brings us to the final, and arguably most critical, group of personas we identified: the *business subject matter experts (SMEs)* and *domain leaders*. These are the stakeholders who understand the nuance of what the data *means*.

While the technical teams build the *how*—the pipelines, models, and infrastructure—the domain leader defines the *why*. They are the "guardrails" for business logic, context, and risk:

- In the financial agent failure, an SME is the person who could have explained, "Hold on, 'interest rate' isn't one thing. It has three different semantic meanings depending on the account, and you *cannot* treat them as the same number."
- In a healthcare setting, SMEs are the clinical leaders who define the "persona" of an agent (e.g., "Persona 1: clinical peer" versus "Persona 2: patient-facing assistant") and the critical "conditions" that govern its behavior (e.g., "Discharge" versus "Pre-Visit").
- SMEs can often alert developer teams to data assumptions that, while statistically valid, could be clinically dangerous or biased. For example, in a healthcare setting, an SME understands that historical healthcare utilization (cost) is a proxy for systemic access and institutional bias (*https://oreil.ly/ma5sB*), not a direct measure of patient clinical need for high-touch services such as care management programs. As a result, an SME might suggest that models for clinical risk use

features such as lab values or chronic disease comorbidity counts instead of proxies such as healthcare cost, to avoid reinforcing historical disparities in care access.

In short, these personas are the connective tissue between the AI's technical capabilities and its real-world business value. Without their active and continuous involvement, even the most advanced agent is just an impressive technical demo—a system that can *execute* a task but doesn't understand the *purpose* of the task.

The biggest architectural insight we've gained is understanding the relationship between data storage and serving strategies. Not all data requires the same infrastructure or access patterns. Smart data architects recognize that GenAI applications need thoughtfully designed systems that balance performance, cost, and operational complexity.

The foundation built by data engineers determines what's possible for the entire GenAI application. When done right, it's invisible to end users but enables seamless scaling, consistent performance, and sustainable operations even as data volumes grow exponentially. Their work creates the technical foundation that allows data scientists and ML engineers to focus on extracting insights and building powerful UX.

Strategic Data Patterns: The Foundation for Reliable GenAI Systems

Now that we've explored how different roles approach data readiness, let's examine the key architectural patterns that enable GenAI systems to transition successfully from prototype to production. These patterns have emerged across industries as critical foundations for reliable, scalable AI systems.

The Unified Data and AI Platform

Successful GenAI implementations invariably build on a unified data and AI foundation. In Google Cloud, this typically manifests as a "Data and AI Lakehouse" architecture, illustrated in Figure 2-5, which seamlessly connects data storage, processing, governance, and AI capabilities.

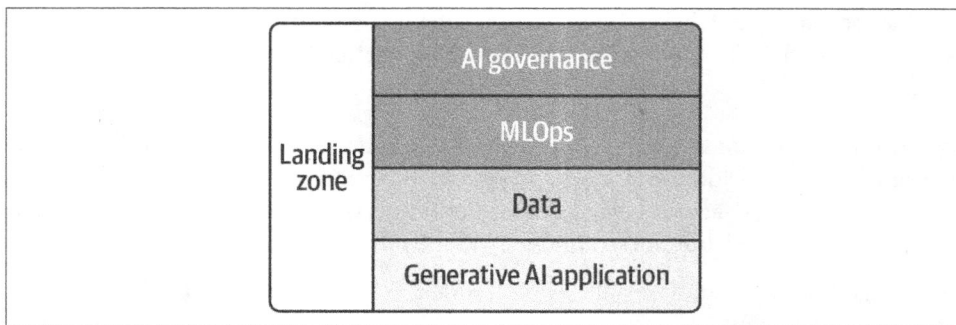

Figure 2-5. The building blocks of a unified platform

At the foundation layer sits Cloud Storage—the versatile landing zone for raw data including documents, images, logs, and media files. This provides the elasticity and flexibility needed for scaling with unpredictable data volumes.

BigQuery forms the core of this unified platform, acting as both a serverless data warehouse and data lakehouse. Its ability to analyze structured data in native storage while directly querying data in Cloud Storage, other clouds (via BigLake (*https://oreil.ly/7jnWf*)), or open table formats (Iceberg, Delta Lake, and Hudi) eliminates data silos and minimizes complex extraction, transformation, and load (ETL). This open foundation is key because it unifies analytical and operational engines, allowing both BigQuery and AlloyDB to interoperate on the same data.

Crucially for GenAI applications, BigQuery now integrates generative AI capabilities directly with functions like `ML.GENERATE_TEXT` (*https://oreil.ly/mCi-z*) and `ML.PROCESS_DOCUMENT` (*https://oreil.ly/TShE5*). This integration enables powerful document processing directly within your data platform, without requiring complex data movement or separate infrastructure.

The ability to query data where it lives is key. Object tables (*https://oreil.ly/dHoeM*) take this integration even further, enabling seamless analysis of unstructured data (such as images, PDFs, and audio) directly from Cloud Storage. In the same way, BigLake extends this capability to structured open table formats such as Apache Iceberg, Delta Lake, and Hudi, allowing you to analyze all your data within a single platform. For example, Example 2-1 shows how you can process a collection of contracts stored in Cloud Storage and extract structured information using Document AI, all within a SQL query. For a deeper dive, refer to the Google Cloud example repository (*https://oreil.ly/k2dYX*) to parse responses from Document AI into chunks and metadata, then generate vector embeddings for the chunks.

Example 2-1. Process contracts with Document AI and join with client data directly in BigQuery

```
-- Create an object table pointing to documents in Cloud Storage
CREATE EXTERNAL TABLE `project.dataset.contracts_object_table`
WITH CONNECTION `us.cloud_storage_connection`
OPTIONS(
  object_metadata = 'SIMPLE',
  uris = ['gs://company-contracts/*'],
  max_staleness = INTERVAL 1 DAY,
  metadata_cache_mode = 'AUTOMATIC'
);

-- Create a Document AI processor model reference in BigQuery
CREATE OR REPLACE MODEL `project.dataset.contract_processor`
REMOTE WITH CONNECTION `us.document_ai_connection`
OPTIONS (
  remote_service_type = 'cloud_ai_document_v1',
  document_processor = 'processors/12345abcde'
);

-- Process documents and extract structured information
SELECT
  uri,
  -- Extract specific entities from the JSON results
  JSON_EXTRACT_SCALAR(
    ml_process_document_result, '$.entities[0].mentionText'
  ) AS contract_value,
  JSON_EXTRACT_SCALAR(
    ml_process_document_result, '$.entities[1].mentionText'
  ) AS effective_date,
  JSON_EXTRACT_SCALAR(
    ml_process_document_result, '$.entities[2].mentionText'
  ) AS expiration_date,
  -- Join with other structured data
  c.client_name,
  c.account_manager
FROM
  ML.PROCESS_DOCUMENT(
    MODEL `project.dataset.contract_processor`,
    TABLE `project.dataset.contracts_object_table`
  ) AS doc
JOIN
  `project.dataset.client_data` AS c
  ON REGEXP_EXTRACT(uri, r'contracts/([^/]+)') = c.client_id;
```

Vertex AI completes this foundation, providing end-to-end ML/GenAI lifecycle management. Its Model Garden gives access to foundation models, while Vertex AI Workbench (*https://oreil.ly/Oyay-*) or Vertex AI Colab Enterprise (*https://oreil.ly/_vwUa*), Pipelines (*https://oreil.ly/Mb4rp*), and the Model Registry (*https://oreil.ly/TcigO*) support development, deployment, and governance workflows. The deep integration between BigQuery, BigQuery Notebooks (*https://oreil.ly/obapT*), and Vertex AI minimizes data movement, reducing both complexity and cost.

This unified platform is not just about connecting data sources (the *multimodal data* (*https://oreil.ly/1s33z*) layer at the bottom) or managing them (the *Dataplex governance layer* (*https://oreil.ly/pUR_C*)). It's about enabling a *multiengine* layer where autonomous systems—such as Gemini Enterprise (*https://oreil.ly/m_vXg*) (formerly Agentspace) and agents—can operate alongside traditional SQL and BI.

This architecture is what allows all the personas we discussed in "The Human Element"—from business users to data scientists and platform engineers—to collaborate on a single, secure foundation, moving from simple data analysis to building and deploying autonomous agents.

The effectiveness of this unified approach, as depicted in Figure 2-6, becomes evident when compared with fragmented alternatives. Organizations that attempt to build GenAI applications across disconnected databases, storage systems, and AI platforms typically struggle with data inconsistencies, governance gaps, and significant operational overhead that ultimately undermine model performance.

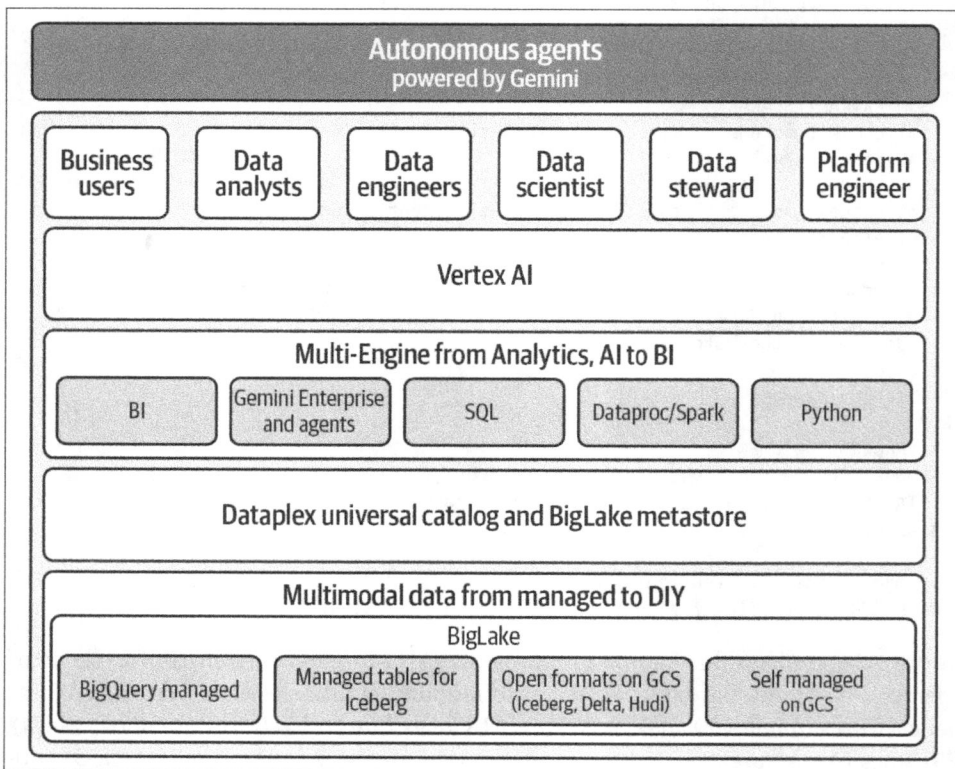

Figure 2-6. Google Cloud autonomous data to AI platform

Please refer to Google Cloud's data-to-ai GitHub repository (*https://oreil.ly/5svpt*) for a complete, end-to-end reference architecture that implements this AI Lakehouse pattern using Terraform and Vertex AI notebooks.

In Chapter 1, we introduced the core concept of RAG. We defined it as the primary architectural pattern for enhancing the factual accuracy and relevance of LLMs by grounding them in external, verifiable data, and we promised to go deeper in this chapter. Now, we'll do just that.

As our conversations with technical teams have evolved, we've seen that RAG isn't one simple thing. It's a spectrum of complexity and design patterns. This is the evolution from "Naive RAG" to "Advanced RAG" and, ultimately, "Agentic RAG," and it represents the true data-readiness challenge. Let's explore this evolution of RAG paradigms (*https://oreil.ly/mnr88*), from its foundational data pipeline to the advanced, agent-driven systems that power production AI.

From RAG to Agentic RAG: The Evolution of a Data Pattern

While often described as an architectural pattern, RAG is fundamentally a data engineering challenge. Naive RAG systems frequently fail in production not because of model limitations, but because they treat data retrieval as a simple semantic search. They fail because they lack metadata filtering and semantic relationship mapping, placing an impossible burden on the embedding model to "guess" context that should have been structured during ingestion. To succeed, we must move from simple retrieval to the advanced, data-centric patterns of GraphRAG and Agentic RAG.

The DIY RAG pipeline: a data engineering challenge

At its core, a Naive RAG system—as illustrated in the leftmost panel of Figure 2-7—is a complex data pipeline that addresses the data readiness challenges we've discussed. Building this from scratch—the do-it-yourself (DIY) approach—is a significant engineering effort. We've found that this DIY RAG implementation challenge can consume 60% to 70% of a project's timeline, time that's spent on data infrastructure rather than the AI's behavior.

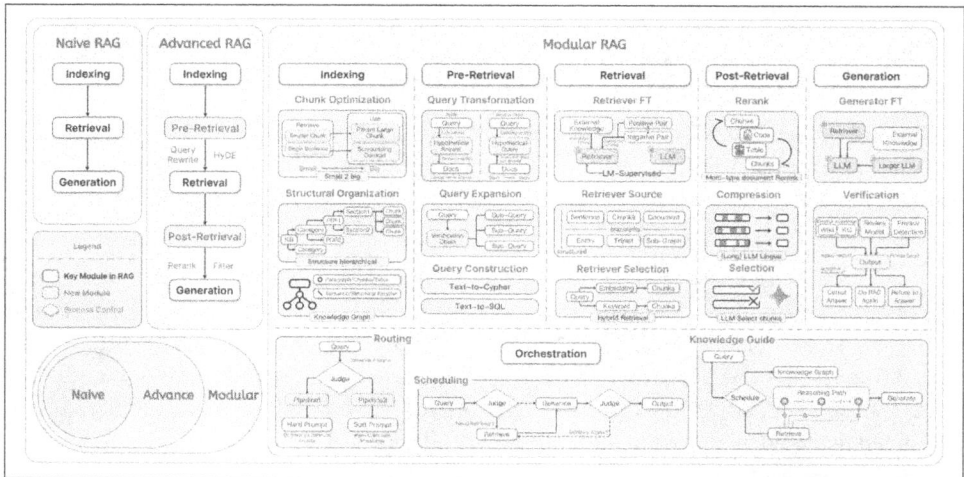

Figure 2-7. Adapted from Yunfan Gao et al. (2024), "Modular RAG: Transforming RAG Systems into LEGO-like Reconfigurable Frameworks" (https://oreil.ly/nlFNd)

The complete data flow involves several critical stages, each with its own data-readiness pitfalls:

Stage 1: Data preparation and chunking

This is where most prototypes fail. Documents (PDFs, structured, unstructured, semi-structured OR in the case of healthcare, additional FHIR (*https://oreil.ly/v49yn*) bundles, DICOM (*https://oreil.ly/0KtyI*) metadata) must be parsed and segmented. As Sarita saw with a healthcare client, "inconsistent formatting... caused critical information to be missed during chunking," leading to "fabricated medication names and dosages." A robust DIY pipeline must handle tables, semantic boundaries, and overlapping chunks to maintain context.

Stage 2: Embedding generation

These text chunks are converted to vector representations. A critical, often-missed failure point is *embedding model consistency*. The *exact same* model version must be used for indexing documents and embedding user queries at retrieval time. A mismatch here leads to a silent failure where the system retrieves irrelevant documents.

Stage 3: Query processing and filtering

The user's query is also embedded. But a "things, not strings" vector search isn't enough. A production system must perform *metadata filtering*. For a query such as "Find imaging for female patients 30-50 with emphysema," the system must *first* filter on structured `PatientSex` and `PatientAge` DICOM tags *before* running a vector search for "emphysema."

Stage 4: Context assembly

The retrieved chunks are assembled into a prompt. This is a key data-shaping step. A well-designed assembler, like the one a healthcare client built, formats the context with metadata (source, date) to help the LLM weigh the authority of different sources, which reduced hallucinations by 35%.

> In vector search (*https://oreil.ly/VLN0P*), *top-k* refers to retrieving the k most similar items to a query, where k is a configurable number (often 3 to 10 for RAG applications). The choice of k represents an important trade-off: too small a value might miss relevant information, while too large a value can introduce noise and increase computational costs. Production systems often use adaptive approaches that adjust k based on query complexity or confidence thresholds rather than using fixed values, as demonstrated in the logic of Example 2-2.

Example 2-2. Assemble retrieved document chunks into a coherent context for the LLM code

```
def assemble_rag_context(query, retrieved_chunks, max_tokens=6000):
    """Assemble chunks into a coherent context for the LLM."""

    # Sort chunks by relevance score in descending order
    chunks = sorted(
        retrieved_chunks,
        key=lambda x: x['score'],
        reverse=True
    )

    context_pieces = []
    current_length = 0

    for i, chunk in enumerate(chunks):
        source_type = chunk.get('source_type', 'Unknown')
        source_date = chunk.get('publication_date', 'Unknown date')
        source_author = chunk.get('author', 'Unknown author')

        header = (
            f"SOURCE {i+1} [{source_type} from "
            f"{source_author}, {source_date}]"
        )
        context_piece = f"{header}:\n{chunk['text']}\n"

        # LOGIC FIX: Check length before adding
        # If adding this chunk exceeds the limit, stop adding.
        chunk_tokens = len(context_piece) / 4
        if current_length + chunk_tokens > max_tokens:
            break
```

```
        context_pieces.append(context_piece)
        current_length += chunk_tokens

    combined_context = "\n".join(context_pieces)

    prompt = (
        f"Please answer the following question based ONLY on the "
        f"provided sources:\n\n"
        f"Question: {query}\n\n"
        f"Sources:\n{combined_context}\n\n"
        f"Answer:"
    )

    return prompt
```

Stage 5: Feedback and continuous improvement
A production RAG system must capture user feedback to refine retrieval quality and identify gaps in the knowledge base.

This DIY complexity is the primary driver for adopting managed services.

The RAG trade-off: choosing your vector store (DIY versus managed)

The DIY pipeline we just described is powerful and flexible, but it's also brittle and operationally expensive. Sarita recalls a healthcare client who spent three months building a custom RAG system (like the pgvector solution in our financial example (*https://oreil.ly/YKA85*)), only to have it crash under production load.

This DIY complexity, as shown in Figure 2-8, is the primary driver for adopting managed services, and it brings you to the most critical decision point in your RAG architecture: *choosing the right vector store.*

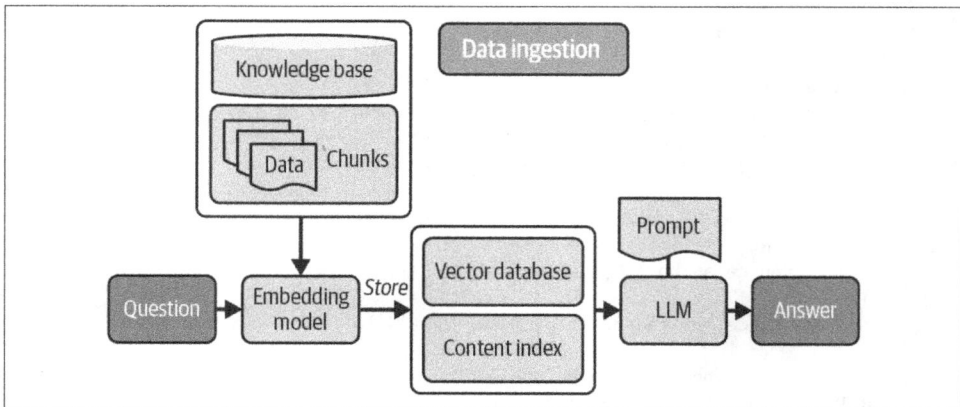

Figure 2-8. The RAG pipeline in a simplified version

Each option offers different trade-offs between performance, integration flexibility, and operational complexity, as shown in Table 2-1. Consider the trade-offs:

DIY/database-integrated (e.g., Cloud SQL (https://oreil.ly/TGKsH), BigQuery (https://oreil.ly/7wT0v))

> This approach, used in our "Enterprise RAG Knowledge Engine," gives you maximum control. By using Cloud SQL (PostgreSQL) with pgvector, you colocate your vector data with your operational or business data. This is ideal for hybrid search (mixing vector search with SQL filters) and low-latency serving. Similarly, BigQuery vector search (*https://oreil.ly/L8Ur7*) is powerful for unifying vector search directly with massive analytical datasets, eliminating data movement.

"Managed"/specialized service (e.g., Vertex AI Search (https://oreil.ly/wrgxo), Vertex AI RAG Engine (https://oreil.ly/oy2qD))

> For many teams, managed solutions such as Vertex AI Search provide a practical middle ground. It handles the *entire* complex pipeline we've described—from ingestion and chunking to retrieval and context assembly—with significantly reduced operational overhead, as depicted in Figure 2-9. It is especially powerful for operationalizing production flows because it can ground responses in data living directly within operational systems such as AlloyDB (*https://oreil.ly/rzBPt*) or BigQuery.

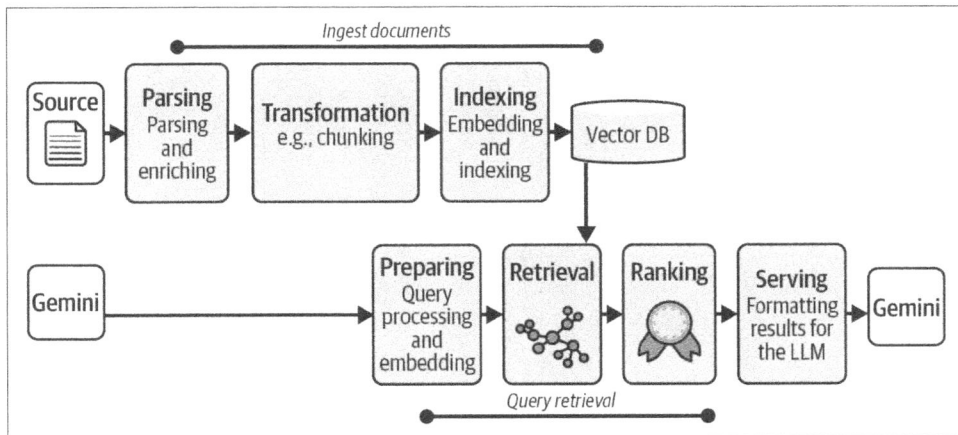

Figure 2-9. Vertex AI RAG Engine (https://oreil.ly/IZhai) is a managed orchestration service, streamlining the complex process of retrieving relevant information and feeding it to an LLM

Vector store: choosing the right approach

The choice of vector storage technology represents a critical decision point in GenAI architecture. Each option offers different trade-offs between performance, integration flexibility, and operational complexity, as shown in Table 2-1.

Table 2-1. A PoV on vector storage on Google Cloud

	Operational							Analytical	Special-purpose
	AlloyDB	BigTable	Cloud SQL (PostgreSQL)	Cloud SQL (MySQL)	Firestore	Memorystore	Spanner	BigQuery	Vertex AI Vector Search
Workload Profile	OLTP/HTAP	OLTP	OLTP	OLTP	OLTP	In-memory	OLTP	Analytics	AI/ML
Data Model	Relational	Wide Column	Relational	Relational	Document	Key-Value	Relational, Key-value, Graph	Relational	Vector
Max Vectors per Search Space	Billions	-	100's of millions	10 million (https://oreil.ly/r8nM1)	~50k per Collection (+ pre-filtering)	100M	10 billion+ (https://oreil.ly/YC744)	10 billion (https://oreil.ly/9Pow_.)	Billions (https://oreil.ly/l7HhU)
Max Dimensions per Vector	64k (https://oreil.ly/Z8sf)	-	64k (https://oreil.ly/A76HK)	16k (https://oreil.ly/pMfu_)	2,048 (https://oreil.ly/Jgoju)	32,768 (https://oreil.ly/fixZ_z)	64k (https://oreil.ly/-az00)	1,600 (https://oreil.ly/-ZHJb)	-
Max Vector Storage Capacity	128 TB (Preview) (https://oreil.ly/8CGqG)	Petabytes (https://oreil.ly/NoLVP)	64 TB (https://oreil.ly/LsnPg)	596 GB (per table) (https://oreil.ly/R779N)	Unlimited	300 GB (https://oreil.ly/kwRKb)	Unlimited	Unlimited (w/ reservation) (https://oreil.ly/w5hXl)	Up to 17.5 TB (https://oreil.ly/mohZd)
Latency	<10 ms	-	10s ms	100s ms	100s ms-sec	<3 ms	10s ms	~1 sec (batch)	<10 ms
Consistency	Strong (https://oreil.ly/Nmkb6)	Topology Dependent (https://oreil.ly/hy5Ks)	Strong (https://oreil.ly/SIzPn)	Strong (https://oreil.ly/kgFi1)	Strong (https://oreil.ly/C5xJ5)	Eventual (https://oreil.ly/_PLj_)	Strong (https://oreil.ly/KEBtA)	Strong (https://oreil.ly/Kc66bl)	Eventual (https://oreil.ly/LN0it)
Data Freshness	Real-time (https://oreil.ly/d3CyS)	Real-time (https://oreil.ly/mgw5n)	Real-time (https://oreil.ly/Wpw46)	Real-time (https://oreil.ly/3gtLj)	Real-time (https://oreil.ly/EDAVO)	Near-real-time (https://oreil.ly/SFnP)	Real-time (https://oreil.ly/i5FHy)	Near-real-time (https://oreil.ly/gkR3U)	Near-real-time (https://oreil.ly/b56q7)
Filtered Hybrid Search	Yes (https://oreil.ly/IVWIZ)	Yes (https://oreil.ly/eXJkh)	Yes (https://oreil.ly/OtSG4)	Yes (https://oreil.ly/MMqA3)	Limited (https://oreil.ly/fhh7Q)	Limited (https://oreil.ly/9iIgr)	Yes (https://oreil.ly/aG3O5)	Yes (https://oreil.ly/TLENr)	Limited (https://oreil.ly/84gj8)
Multiranked Hybrid Search	No	No	No	No	No	No	Yes	No	Yes

Access Control	Fine-grained (https://oreil.ly/svCQE)	Fine-grained (https://oreil.ly/qulKk)	Fine-grained (https://oreil.ly/jy5Hd)	Fine-grained (https://oreil.ly/6dSO_)	Fine-grained (https://oreil.ly/m5z1J)	Limited (https://oreil.ly/wJqi2)	Fine-grained (https://oreil.ly/IxwxU)	Fine-grained (https://oreil.ly/8RAUK)	Course-grained (https://oreil.ly/2OYgX)
Embeddings Management	Built-in (https://oreil.ly/82lI2)	External (https://oreil.ly/F7Xkb)	Built-in (https://oreil.ly/kPOF_)	External (https://oreil.ly/IaRi6)	External (https://oreil.ly/wnP5J)	External (https://oreil.ly/F8oI1)	Built-in (https://oreil.ly/CohSy)	Built-in (https://oreil.ly/829EU)	External (https://oreil.ly/ZC7Ut)
OSS or Proprietary	OSS Compatible	OSS Compatible	OSS	OSS	Proprietary	OSS	Proprietary (w/ PostgreSQL interface (https://oreil.ly/0dTUr))	Proprietary	Proprietary
ANN Index Support	IVF, HNSW, (https://oreil.ly/Brsrf) ScaNN (https://oreil.ly/CW869)	None (https://oreil.ly/OUNyc) KNN ONLY	IVF, HNSW (https://oreil.ly/TbDNF)	TREE_SQ, TREE_AH (https://oreil.ly/9ncWV)	None (https://oreil.ly/cOZfB) KNN Only	HNSW, FLAT (https://oreil.ly/CpR6k)	ScaNN (https://oreil.ly/NSiqm)	IVF, TreeAH ScaNN (https://oreil.ly/CQQ5F)	ScaNN (https://oreil.ly/qmxHj)
Availability SLA	up to 99.99%	up to 99.999%	up to 99.99%	up to 99.99%	up to 99.999%	up to 99.99%	up to 99.999%	up to 99.99%	99.90% (https://oreil.ly/nartA)

Beyond these managed options, open source vector databases and libraries such as Chroma (*https://oreil.ly/9bWJ0*), Milvus (*https://oreil.ly/EToYJ*), and Faiss (*https://oreil.ly/dQGsW*) can be deployed on Google Kubernetes Engine (GKE) or Compute Engine. These solutions offer more customization control but introduce significant new complexities, including data duplication, data movement, and additional operational management. This "DIY versus managed" decision comes with trade-offs. We've seen enterprise customers that require highly custom chunking strategies, specialized medical embedding models, or complex multistep retrieval logic that go beyond a managed framework's options. This need for more advanced, custom logic is what leads to the next step in the RAG evolution.

Navigating Vector Database Selection

A comprehensive comparison guide (*https://oreil.ly/q952w*) provides a detailed breakdown of different vector database options available on Google Cloud Platform (GCP). The selection of an appropriate vector database on GCP can be navigated using a decision tree approach, prioritizing the key use cases and associated business-centric context. There is not a one-size-fits-all vector database that is the right choice for every use case.

When implementing vector search for production GenAI applications, consistency between embedding models used during indexing and retrieval is critical. Using different embedding models or versions for these processes can significantly degrade search relevance. Additionally, vector dimensions and distance metrics (cosine similarity versus Euclidean distance) must remain consistent throughout your pipeline. Organizations often underestimate the operational complexity of maintaining this consistency, especially as models evolve. Much of the powerful search capability in Google's managed services, including BigQuery, AlloyDB, and Vertex AI Vector Search (*https://oreil.ly/K8nym*), is powered by Google's own ScaNN (*https://oreil.ly/4w2Rm*) (Scalable Nearest Neighbors) algorithm. ScaNN is the fundamental Google Research technology that AlloyDB uses for vector indexing. The release of ScaNN for AlloyDB (*https://oreil.ly/YmEVF*) leverages some of the ScaNN library techniques to accelerate vector index creation, accelerate vector search, and deliver low-memory footprint. We'll cover the basics here, but for those interested in additional details, there are many articles on the research powering ScaNN published in prestigious research publications, including PMLR (*https://oreil.ly/O_2SE*) and NeurIPS (*https://oreil.ly/wZ3zW*) papers. ScaNN is also available in the Google Research Github repository (*https://oreil.ly/iKlsA*).

For full control and customization for your RAG applications, you can leverage Document AI (*https://oreil.ly/Xv6VH*) for parsing documents, text embeddings API (*https://oreil.ly/32eKr*) for vectorization, Vertex AI Vector Search for indexing/retrieval, ranking API (*https://oreil.ly/vZidO*) for reranking, and Gemini API for synthesis, grounded by Vertex AI grounding (*https://oreil.ly/TCaQf*).

You can learn about the Vertex RAG Engine with Gemini through GCP sample code (*https://oreil.ly/XzuWx*).

Advanced RAG: from vectors to agents

When a Naive RAG system isn't smart enough, the architecture must evolve. The two most powerful advanced patterns we see are GraphRAG (*https://oreil.ly/li7cn*) and Agentic RAG (*https://oreil.ly/3tGSz*).

GraphRAG: retrieving relationships, not just documents

Standard vector search is excellent at finding semantic *similarity* but terrible at understanding semantic *relationships*. It answers "what" but often fails at "why" or "how."

We call this the "L'Occitane" problem. A standard RAG system, when asked "Where can I freshen up?" might retrieve "Public Showers" (relevant) but also "L'Occitane en Provence" (semantically similar, as it sells toiletries, but functionally wrong) (Figure 2-10).

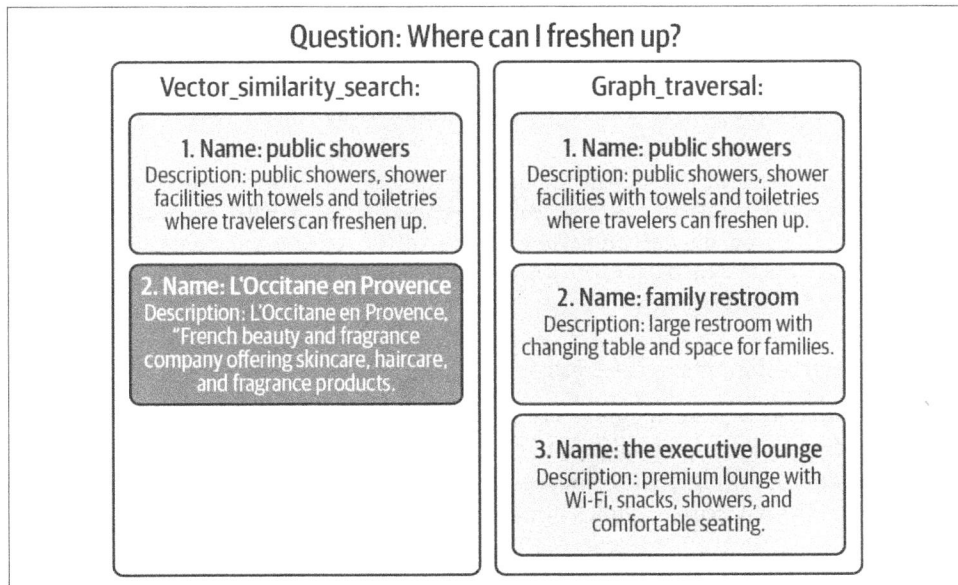

Figure 2-10. A simple example for vector search similarity response versus one with graph traversal

GraphRAG solves this by combining vector search with a *Knowledge Graph (KG)* (*https://oreil.ly/PFwU7*). Instead of just finding similar documents, it finds *related entities*, as illustrated in Figure 2-11, and explained with the following:

Step 1 (vector search)

The query finds the "Public Showers" node in the graph.

Step 2 (graph traversal)

The system then traverses the graph from that node to find related entities, such as `Public Showers -> SIMILAR_TO -> Family Restroom`.

Step 3 (the "aha moment")

The context sent to the LLM now includes "Public Showers" and "Family Restroom." It has eliminated the irrelevant "L'Occitane" result and added a relevant option ("Family Restroom") that vector search alone would have missed. This improved precision is the difference between a toy and a trustworthy system.

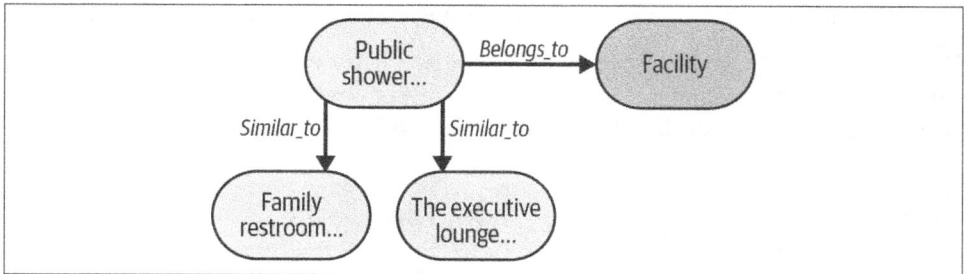

Figure 2-11. Example graph traversal for neighboring nodes

> Refer to the Google Cloud Architecture center for an advanced RAG architecture that combines vector search with Knowledge Graph queries (*https://oreil.ly/9bIWg*) to retrieve interconnected, contextual data, which results in more detailed and relevant GenAI responses.

Agentic RAG: orchestrating specialist retrievers

The most advanced pattern is *Agentic RAG*. This pattern addresses the reality that enterprise data lives in many different, complex systems. A single RAG pipeline can't effectively query multiple data sources at once—for instance with the healthcare example, a FHIR database, a DICOM metadata store, and a PDF knowledge base.

Instead of one monolithic pipeline, an Agentic RAG system uses a *multiagent architecture,* which we'll explore in detail in Chapter 4. It involves the following:

- A primary coordinator or routing agent receives a user's query (e.g., "What is the discharge summary for the patient with emphysema from yesterday?").

- This coordinator *plans* and *delegates* the task to specialized subagents.

- The coordinator might first call the `agent_1` to query structured electronic health record (EHR (*https://oreil.ly/035dw*)) tables and FHIR bundles to identify the patient.
- Then, it passes that patient's ID to an `agent_2` (knowledge base agent) to perform a vector search on unstructured data, such as PDF discharge summaries (*https://oreil.ly/XeI00*) (Figure 2-12).

This "agentic workflow pattern"—which involves planning, memory, and specialized tools—is the true state of the art for production AI. It moves RAG from a simple data pipeline to an intelligent, autonomous system.

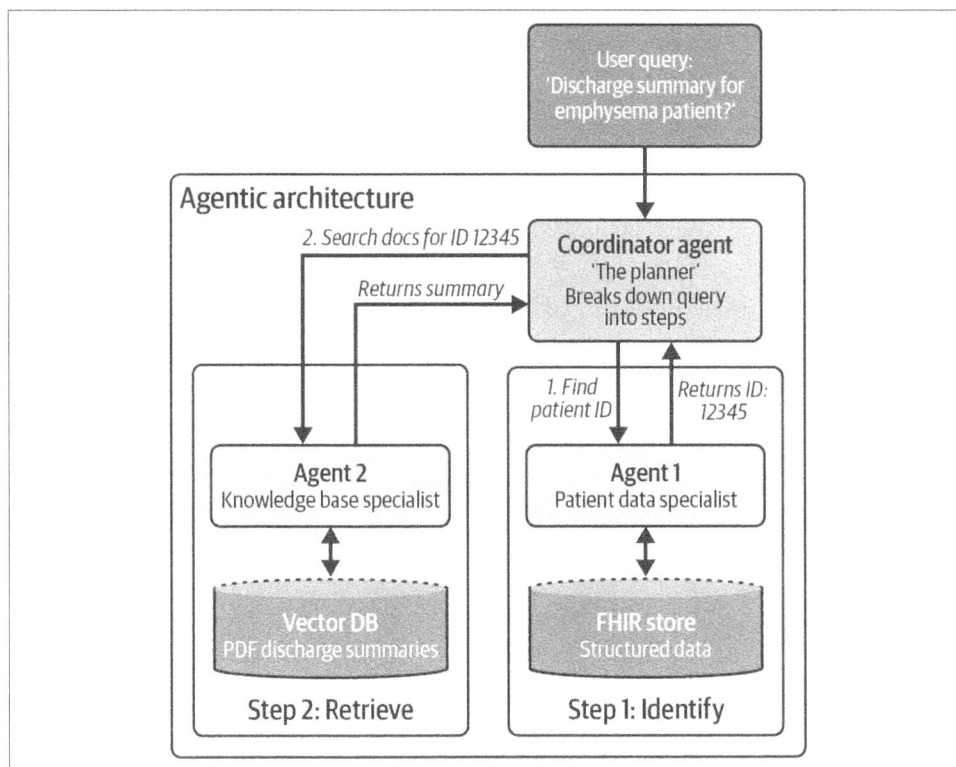

Figure 2-12. The Agentic RAG workflow, illustrating how a coordinator orchestrates specialized agents to bridge structured and unstructured data

Tying it All Together: the Enterprise RAG Knowledge Engine

This brings us to the "aha moment" that connects the entire chapter.

Let's revisit the financial services enterprise discussed at the beginning of the chapter. While a semantic layer solves structured data consistency issues like the "interest rate" confusion, the organization faces an equally critical challenge: enabling agents to reason over vast archives of unstructured knowledge, such as earnings calls and 10-K reports.

To answer complex questions like "What are BetaTech's supply chain risks?", we need a different architecture. The Enterprise RAG Knowledge Engine (Figure 2-13) is that solution. It separates the "data-readiness" work from the "agent-reasoning" work.

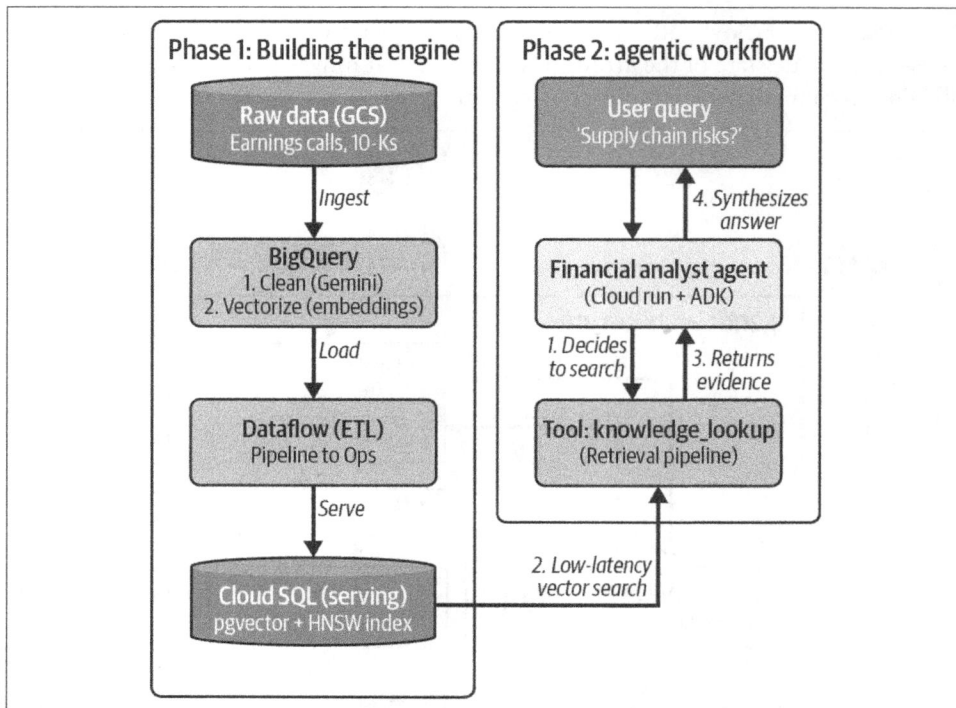

Figure 2-13. The Enterprise RAG Knowledge Engine architecture, illustrating how the data pipeline (Phase 1) is decoupled from the reasoning layer (Phase 2) to ensure that the agent accesses only curated, indexed knowledge

Phase 1: Building the Knowledge Engine (the Data Foundation)

Before the agent ever receives a query, the data engineering team builds a reliable, automated pipeline. This is the DIY RAG pipeline, but built for enterprise scale, with the following steps:

Ingestion
   Raw, unstructured data such as earnings calls, 10-K reports, and news articles are landed in their raw form in Cloud Storage.

Transformation

The data is processed within BigQuery. This is where the critical data-readiness work happens.

Extraction and transformation

Using BigQuery ML's `ML.GENERATE_TEXT` (with a Gemini model), the raw text from earnings calls is transformed into structured, clean data.

Chunking and embedding

The cleaned text is chunked and, using `ML.GENERATE_EMBEDDING`, converted into vectors all within BigQuery.

Loading (ETL)

A Dataflow (*https://oreil.ly/AlJOS*) pipeline reads this prepared, vectorized data from BigQuery and loads it into the operational serving database.

Serving (the operational DB)

The data is served from Cloud SQL (PostgreSQL), which is running the `pgvector` extension. A crucial Hierarchical Navigable Small Worlds (HNSW) index is built on the embedding column, enabling the ultra-low latency (sub-100 ms) vector search required for a production system.

Phase 2: Activating the Agentic RAG layer

Now, with a clean, fast, and reliable Knowledge Engine in place, we can deploy our Financial Analyst Agent. This is where the architecture becomes *agentic*. We don't just feed the agent context. We give it a "brain" and "tools" and let it *act* in the following way:

The agent

The agent is built using the ADK (*https://oreil.ly/3cJcY*). It's an `LlmAgent` configured with a "Senior Financial Analyst" persona, giving it the "brain" to reason about complex financial topics.

The tool

Instead of trying to know everything, the agent is given a single, powerful tool: `knowledge_lookup`. This tool encapsulates the *entire* RAG retrieval pipeline (connecting to Cloud SQL, embedding the query, running the `pgvector` HNSW search, and returning the results).

The agentic workflow

A user asks a complex question: "What are BetaTech's supply chain risks?"

The Financial Analyst agent *reasons* that it cannot answer this from its internal knowledge.

It autonomously decides to call its `knowledge_lookup` tool.

The tool executes the low-latency vector search against the Knowledge Engine and retrieves the most relevant chunks from the 10-K reports and earnings calls.

The tool returns this *evidence* to the agent.

The agent's "brain" then *synthesizes* this retrieved evidence and generates its final, expert-level analysis, complete with citations.

This completes the data readiness puzzle. While the semantic layer addressed the structured data inconsistencies (like the interest rate confusion), this architecture solves the unstructured data challenge. The specialist agent succeeds because it reasons over a *data-ready Enterprise RAG Knowledge Engine*. Deploying this architecture as a scalable API—using a managed service like Cloud Run (*https://oreil.ly/poV1B*)—bridges the final gap between a brittle prototype and a trustworthy, production-ready AI system.

Enterprise Resources

All the code samples and setup instructions for financial services enterprise scenarios are available at the Chapter 2 GitHub repository (*https://oreil.ly/gRq6D*).

Knowledge Graph
> This feature augments Gemini Enterprise (*https://oreil.ly/nD3Fi*) by mapping the dynamic relationships between people, content, and interactions. By understanding these semantic connections rather than just matching keywords, it significantly improves search relevance and context.

Architecture Patterns
> Refer to the Google Cloud Architecture center for an agent-driven architecture that uses Gemini Enterprise as a unified platform to orchestrate an end-to-end RAG dataflow (*https://oreil.ly/WXmpg*) for enterprise applications that require real-time data availability and enriched contextual search.

Data Readiness for Agent Systems

While RAG systems ground LLM responses in existing knowledge, agent systems represent a significant evolution by enabling active interaction with that knowledge. Agents not only generate text but actively take actions—calling APIs, querying databases, and making decisions based on real-time information. This transition from passive retrieval to active engagement creates entirely new data readiness considerations.

Agents fundamentally change the approach to data. With basic RAG, you're concerned with what data the model can see. With agents, you must also consider what data the system can act on, how those actions are governed, and how you maintain

---

control over increasingly autonomous systems. These considerations will become particularly relevant in Chapter 3 as we move from theory to implementation.

This evolution requires specialized data access patterns that balance flexibility with security:

Read-only interfaces
Most agent tools should provide read-only access to underlying data, with write operations limited to specific, tightly controlled scenarios. Financial services organizations, for example, typically implement strict permission hierarchies where agents can query market data freely but have limited access to client information.

Parameterized queries
Rather than allowing agents to construct arbitrary SQL, well-defined parameterized queries enable targeted data access while preventing potential injection attacks. Healthcare and financial services environments benefit particularly from this approach when agents need to access patient and client information without compromising broader clinical databases.

Authentication context
Data access should respect the requesting user's permissions, ensuring that agents can't bypass existing security controls. This becomes especially critical in environments with regulatory requirements around data access and confidentiality.

Observability
All data access through agent tools should be logged and monitored, creating an audit trail for regulatory compliance and security analysis. Comprehensive logging should capture not just what data was accessed, but the reasoning context that led to that access.

Beyond these access patterns, agents require specialized data for their reasoning and orchestration layers. The agent's "brain" relies on instructions, contextual information, and both short-term and long-term memory to plan and execute actions effectively. In a modern data platform, this "contextual information" can be dynamically sourced from a centralized service such as Dataplex Knowledge Engine, which provides agents with business context from their enterprise business data. This additional dimension requires:

Clear instructions and goals
The agent's objectives and operational boundaries must be defined through carefully structured prompts or configuration data. Unclear boundaries often lead to unexpected agent behaviors, particularly around sensitive operations.

Memory management

Agents often maintain both session-specific context and persistent knowledge across interactions. For persistent knowledge, customers can use high-performance databases such as Spanner or AlloyDB as the "operational brain" for their own agents, providing a scalable and consistent memory store. This mirrors how Google's own first-party agents, such as Looker Conversational Analytics, use Spanner as their primary context and memory store.

The combination of these specialized patterns enables agents to access enterprise data securely while maintaining appropriate governance controls. As you'll see in the next section, this expansion of AI capabilities into active system interaction makes security and governance considerations even more critical.

> This distinction between *session-specific context (short-term memory)* and *persistent knowledge (long-term memory)* is a core architectural pattern for building reliable agents. We will explore the specific implementation of these state management scopes—including temporary, user, and application state—in detail in Chapter 3.

Security and Governance: Protecting Data Throughout the LLM Lifecycle

Data security and governance take on new dimensions with LLM and agentic systems, requiring controls that work across the entire data lifecycle while maintaining utility for GenAI applications.

Data Privacy Framework

Effective protection of sensitive information in GenAI workflows requires a multilayered approach:

PII detection and handling

Cloud Data Loss Prevention (DLP (*https://oreil.ly/p7ugL*)) provides automated discovery, classification, and protection of sensitive data (PII, financial information, credentials) in both data at rest and in motion. This allows organizations to scan document repositories, implement inline masking during document processing, and validate outputs for potential leakage. For example, a healthcare organization we worked with implemented DLP scanning (*https://oreil.ly/sob5M*) of all documents before indexing, replacing patient identifiers with anonymized tokens while preserving the semantic relationships needed for accurate retrieval. See our GitHub repository (*https://oreil.ly/yRxjI*) for an extended code sample.

Dynamic data masking

BigQuery offers role-based column-level security (*https://oreil.ly/EaLt8*) via policy tags (*https://oreil.ly/EvbHM*) that can dynamically mask sensitive fields based on user permissions. This enables scenarios where different user groups see different levels of detail from the same underlying data—critical for ensuring that LLMs receive only appropriately redacted information based on the requesting user's permissions.

Encryption controls

Google-managed encryption protects data at rest by default, while customer-managed encryption keys (CMEK (*https://oreil.ly/3v3-T*)) provide additional control for sensitive data. Organizations in regulated industries typically implement CMEK for BigQuery datasets, BigLake managed open format data, and Cloud Storage buckets containing sensitive documents, ensuring cryptographic separation of different data categories.

Network and perimeter controls

Encryption secures data *at rest*, but a complete governance strategy must also secure data *in motion* and control the network perimeter. This is where Virtual Private Cloud (VPC) (*https://oreil.ly/6XDoX*) and related services become essential.

A VPC provides a private, isolated network within Google's global distributed cloud. For AI and agentic systems, this is not just a standard best practice, it's a fundamental security control. When an agent running in a serverless environment like Cloud Run or a container orchestrator like GKE needs to call a managed service like Vertex AI (for embeddings) or BigQuery (for data retrieval), you must prevent that sensitive traffic from traveling over the public internet.

This is achieved using VPC Service Controls (VPC-SC) (*https://oreil.ly/n2KFW*), which creates a secure data perimeter around your Google Cloud services. By combining this with Private Service Connect (PSC) (*https://oreil.ly/W5Z6r*), you ensure that all communication between your agent's runtime and these managed services stays entirely within Google's private global network. This isolates your entire AI workflow from the public internet, a critical requirement for any enterprise in a regulated industry. In the process, it creates a secure "bubble" for your AI applications, ensuring that sensitive data is protected at every layer.

The controls we've just discussed—DLP, CMEK, and VPC-SC—are the essential *platform-layer* guardrails for your data. In Chapter 7, we'll deep-dive on the additional *operational-layer* guardrails required to get agentic systems safely to production. We'll move from MLOps to *Agent Operations*, tackling the non-deterministic nature of agents, managing "semantic drift," and implementing the robust versioning, monitoring, and security needed to manage autonomous AI systems at scale.

Comprehensive Governance

As discussed previously, beyond security controls, effective governance ensures that data remains discoverable, trustworthy, and properly managed throughout its lifecycle:

Cataloging and discovery
    The Dataplex Universal Catalog automates the discovery and cataloging of assets not just across BigQuery and Cloud Storage, but across the entire data estate, from open formats such as Iceberg to operational databases such as Spanner and even Vertex AI models. This provides AI-driven curation and enables data discovery via natural language semantic search.

Lineage tracking
    Understanding where data originated and how it has been transformed becomes critical for GenAI applications, where outputs may combine information from multiple sources. Dataplex captures these relationships, enabling traceability from raw documents to model outputs. Modern governance now extends beyond just data to include AI assets. Platforms like Dataplex now provide AI model governance. The Dataplex Universal Catalog can discover, catalog, and manage metadata for Vertex AI models right alongside the datasets they were trained on. This unifies data and AI governance, enabling critical lineage from a raw data source all the way to the specific model version it produced.

Quality monitoring
    Defining and enforcing data quality rules ensures that LLMs work with reliable information. Dataplex Universal Catalog (*https://oreil.ly/9SScA*) lets you define and measure the quality of the data in your BigQuery tables. You can automate the data scanning, validate data against defined rules, and log alerts if your data doesn't meet quality requirements. Auto data quality lets you manage data quality rules and deployments as code, improving the integrity of data production pipelines.

Policy management
    Centralized access policies ensure consistent controls across storage layers. This is particularly important for multitier LLM architectures where the same

information may exist in multiple formats (e.g., raw documents in Google Cloud Storage [GCS], open table formats on GCS managed by BigLake, processed text in native BigQuery storage, and embeddings in Vector Search).

In Chapter 7, we'll deep-dive on additional guardrails as they relate to path-to-production for agentic systems.

Google was one of the first in the industry to publish an AI/ML Privacy Commitment (*https://oreil.ly/6crcF*), which outlines its belief that customers should have the highest level of security and control over their data that's stored in the cloud. That commitment extends to Google Cloud GenAI products. More details about how Google processes data can be found in Google's Cloud Data Processing Addendum (CDPA) (*https://oreil.ly/cNEVC*).

Practical Data Readiness Assessment

The security and governance controls we've outlined form critical components of a comprehensive data readiness framework. To move from concept to implementation, organizations need a structured approach for evaluating their current state and identifying high-priority areas for improvement.

As you prepare to implement GenAI applications, assess your organization's readiness across the key dimensions shown in the following checklist:

- **Data discovery, admin, and access control**
  - ☐ Have you established a centralized catalog of available data sources?
  - ☐ Do you have processes for exploring and understanding unstructured/multimodal content?
  - ☐ Can relevant teams access the data needed for experimentation and development?
- **Data quality and preparation**
  - ☐ Have you evaluated data quality for GenAI consumption (accuracy, completeness, formatting)?
  - ☐ Do you have processes for document processing and text extraction?
  - ☐ Have you established chunking strategies appropriate for your document types?
- **Security and governance**
  - ☐ Have you identified and classified sensitive data within your repositories?
  - ☐ Are appropriate access controls and masking policies in place?
  - ☐ Do you have processes for tracking data lineage and provenance?

☐ Have you defined read-only interfaces and parameterized queries for agent data access tools? (Critical for preventing injection attacks in agentic systems.)

- **Infrastructure and scalability**

  ☐ Can your storage and processing infrastructure handle the volume of documents needed?

  ☐ Have you evaluated vector database options based on your specific requirements?

  ☐ Are your pipelines designed to scale with growing document volumes?

  ☐ Have you provisioned high-performance operational storage (e.g., Spanner, AlloyDB) for agent memory/state? (Required for the "operational brain" discussed in the Agentic RAG section.)

  ☐ Does your data architecture support graph-based querying (e.g., Spanner Graph) for relationship retrieval? (Required for GraphRAG traversal.)

- **Integration and workflow**

  ☐ How will document updates and additions flow through your system?

  ☐ Have you defined processes for reprocessing content when needed?

  ☐ Are monitoring systems in place to detect data quality issues or drift?

This checklist represents the first step in your maturity journey—moving from "Phase 0" (ad hoc experimentation) to "Phase 1" (foundational data readiness). Answering "no" to these questions helps you identify the critical gaps you must fill to build a reliable, production-ready system. As we'll explore in Chapter 8, mastering this stage is the non-negotiable prerequisite for achieving higher-level AI maturity.

To help organizations map these requirements to specific implementation solutions, in Table 2-2 we've created reference mappings to GCP services that support LLM and agent workflows.

Table 2-2. Mapping GCP services to data readiness tasks for GenAI applications

Data readiness task	Primary GCP service(s)	Key functionality/use case for LLMs/agents
Data ingestion	Cloud Storage, BigQuery Streaming, Pub/Sub, Dataflow	Storing raw files (GCS), managing open-table formats (Iceberg, Hudi, etc.) on GCS via BigLake, loading batch data (BigQuery Load), ingesting real-time streams (Pub/Sub + Dataflow/BigQuery).
Data cleaning and transformation	Dataflow, Dataproc, BigQuery (SQL), Vertex AI Workbench, Google Cloud Serverless for Apache Spark	Large-scale batch/stream ETL (Dataflow), Spark-based processing (Dataproc), SQL transformations (BigQuery), interactive cleaning (Workbench).

Data readiness task	Primary GCP service(s)	Key functionality/use case for LLMs/agents
Structuring data (especially for RAG)	Dataflow, Dataproc, Vertex AI Workbench, Cloud Functions, BigQuery	Parsing documents, implementing chunking logic, formatting data (e.g., JSON Lines [JSONL] for fine-tuning).
Feature engineering	BigQuery (SQL), Vertex AI Workbench, Dataflow, Dataproc	Creating derived features, text processing (n-grams, etc.), embedding generation (via models called from these services).
Feature management and serving	Vertex AI Feature Store (built on BigQuery)	Centralized storage, sharing, versioning, low-latency online serving of features and embeddings, training-serving skew mitigation.
Embedding management and search	Vertex AI Feature Store (Optimized), Vertex AI Vector Search	Storing, indexing, and performing approximate nearest neighbor (ANN) search on vector embeddings for RAG retrieval, similarity search, recommendations.
Data labeling	Vertex AI Data Labeling (bring-your-own-labeler) / Partner Solutions	Managing labeling tasks and annotator workflows using your own labeling workforce or prevetted Google Cloud Partners. Used for creating labeled datasets (e.g., prompt-response pairs) for supervised fine-tuning and evaluation.
Workflow orchestration	Vertex AI Pipelines, Cloud Composer, BigQuery pipelines	Automating multistep data preparation, training, and deployment workflows.
Relationship management (GraphRAG)	Spanner Graph, Vertex AI Knowledge Graph	Modeling and querying semantic relationships between entities.
Agent state and memory	Spanner, AlloyDB, Cloud SQL, Agent Engine	Low-latency "operational brain" storage for persisting session state (short-term memory) and user history (long-term memory).
Data governance and cataloging	Dataplex, Cloud Identity and Access Management (IAM), Sensitive Data Protection, Cloud Audit Logs	Unified discovery, metadata management, lineage tracking, quality monitoring, access control, PII handling, compliance auditing.

For security and governance specifically, reference the controls in Table 2-3 to ensure that your AI data pipelines and workflows incorporate appropriate safeguards.

Table 2-3. Overview of Google Cloud security and governance controls for AI data workflows

Control area	Key GCP service(s)	How it addresses AI risks/needs
Access control	Cloud IAM, Dataplex (policy tags), Identity-Aware Proxy (IAP)	Enforces least privilege for users and service accounts accessing data, models, pipelines, and infrastructure. Manages API access.
Data discovery and classification	Dataplex (Data Catalog, Business Glossary), Sensitive Data Protection (DLP)	Automatically finds and catalogs data/AI assets, classifies sensitive data (PII, etc.), enables metadata-driven policy.
Data exfiltration prevention	VPC Service Controls, Sensitive Data Protection (DLP), IAM	Creates network perimeters to block unauthorized data movement, masks/redacts sensitive data before potential exposure, restricts export permissions.
Prompt/output security	Vertex AI AI Protection (Model Armor)	Detects/prevents prompt injection and jailbreaking, filters harmful content/URLs, sanitizes inputs/outputs, integrates DLP.

Control area	Key GCP service(s)	How it addresses AI risks/needs
Data encryption	Default encryption (at rest, in transit), customer-managed encryption keys (CMEK)	Protects data confidentiality during storage and transmission, provides customer control over keys.
Secure compute	Confidential Computing	Encrypts data during processing in memory for enhanced protection.
Model security and integrity	Vertex AI Model Registry (IAM), Artifact Registry, Binary Authorization	Controls access to models, scans custom containers for vulnerabilities, ensures that only trusted containers are deployed.
Auditing and monitoring	Cloud Audit Logs, Access Transparency, Cloud Monitoring, Cloud Logging	Records admin/data access, logs Google support access, monitors system performance and security events.
Compliance and data residency	Assured Workloads, compliance reports/certifications	Helps meet geographic data location requirements, provides evidence of adherence to standards (Health Insurance Portability and Accountability Act [HIPAA] for protected health information in the US; Federal Risk and Authorization Management Program [FedRAMP] for US federal government cloud security; International Organization for Standardization [ISO] for international standards on information security).
Unified governance	Dataplex	Centralizes metadata, lineage, quality monitoring, and policy management across distributed data and AI assets.
Threat detection and response	Security Command Center (SCC), AI Protection, Mandiant Threat Intelligence	Centralizes security posture, detects threats against AI workloads, provides threat intelligence and response recommendations.

Looking Ahead

In this chapter, we established the non-negotiable foundation of data readiness. We've moved beyond theory to define the architectural patterns, security controls, and data processing pipelines required for any production-grade AI system. We've defined the data-layer work for RAG—including preprocessing, chunking, and vector search—as the essential first step in grounding a model.

You now have your data foundation strategy for building AI and agentic systems. This foundation allows us to follow a clear evolutionary path through the rest of this book—a journey that mirrors the one you'll take in your own enterprise:

Overview of GenAI systems
    In Chapter 1, we introduced use cases for GenAI and discussed everything from foundation models to an overview of agentic frameworks for business challenges.

Grounded models (RAG)
    This chapter (Chapter 2) provided the complete data-readiness framework, evolution of data patterns, and the journey from vectors to agents.

Agents

In Chapter 3, we'll move from architecture to execution. You won't just read about agents, you'll build one. We'll construct a production-ready Customer Support Agent from scratch, equipping it with the ability to query order databases, manage persistent shopping cart state, and even analyze images of damaged products—transforming the data foundation we designed here into a fully functional AI system.

Multiagent systems

In Chapter 4, we'll scale this concept, orchestrating multiple agents to solve complex problems.

This step-by-step progression is key. As we move from theory to implementation, you'll gain practical experience with the end-to-end workflow—from the data preparation in this chapter to the full agent deployment in the next—that brings intelligent AI capabilities to life.

We've seen how different roles—data scientists, ML engineers, data engineers, and business SMEs or domain leaders—contribute their unique expertise to create a robust data foundation. We've also examined the technical patterns and implementations that convert raw information into production-ready knowledge assets for GenAI systems, from document processing to vector search.

In this chapter, we've defined the data-level requirements for a single agent: secure access patterns and a high-performance "operational brain" for memory. But the true power—and complexity—of production AI comes from orchestration.

In Chapter 4, we'll move beyond the "solo agent" and explore how to build and manage teams of specialized agents. We'll show how to connect them to databases and other tools in a secure, manageable way using emerging standards like the Model Context Protocol (MCP) (*https://oreil.ly/V_NbR*) and tackle the critical production challenges of observability (the "traceability problem") and state management that are unique to multiagent systems.

Learning Labs

To reinforce the concepts covered in this chapter and gain hands-on experience with data foundations and building RAG pipelines, we recommend exploring the learning resources available in the Chapter 2 folder of the book's GitHub repository (*https://oreil.ly/7qfi9*). Key resources you will find linked there include:

- **Hands-On Code Examples**
  - Cymbal Air (*https://oreil.ly/H-7NE*): A production-quality reference implementation for building agentic applications that use agents and RAG to query and interact with data stored in Google Cloud databases.
  - Grounding for Gemini with Vertex AI Search and DIY RAG (*https://oreil.ly/2H0d_*): A reference implementation for grounding Gemini using Vertex AI Search and DIY RAG. This solution deploys a Cloud Run application that uses Cloud SQL vector storage to enable conversational search and recommendations.
  - Build and Evaluate with Vertex RAG Engine (*https://oreil.ly/4F6oX*): A collection of notebooks demonstrating how to implement RAG pipelines using Vertex RAG Engine and third-party vector stores.
  - RAG with Cloud Run and Vector Search (*https://oreil.ly/FvNrR*): A reference architecture for deploying a RAG system using Cloud Run jobs for ingestion and Vertex AI Vector Search.
  - Agentic RAG (*https://oreil.ly/GJlz_*): A RAG agent for document retrieval and Q&A, supporting Vertex AI Search (*https://oreil.ly/G1Iq1*) and Vector Search (*https://oreil.ly/NnCg2*).
  - LlamaIndex advanced agentic RAG implementation (*https://oreil.ly/kT5ZY*): An advanced RAG system using LlamaIndex and Google Cloud Vertex AI.
- **Video Tutorials**
  - Advanced RAG techniques for developers (*https://oreil.ly/FgcD0*): Advanced RAG techniques, combining semantic and keyword search, task type embedding
  - How to prepare data for LLMs (*https://oreil.ly/yNkvt*): Developer-focused discussion on data's impact on LLM quality and security
  - Use Google BigQuery and Gemini AI for Data Analytics (*https://oreil.ly/KEclb*): Learn how Gemini models can help you generate new insights, enrich your datasets, and even analyze multimodal content including images, videos, and text
  - Grounding for Gemini with Vertex AI Search and DIY RAG (*https://oreil.ly/c5oaw*): Integrate Gemini, multimodal embeddings, and vector search to create an AI application that provides accurate, up-to-date, and relevant answers from your own data

## CHAPTER 3

Building a Multimodal Agent with the Agent Development Kit (ADK)

In Chapter 1, we explored what makes AI agents compelling: their ability to perceive, reason, and act autonomously across complex tasks. In Chapter 2, we laid the data foundations these agents require to function reliably. Now comes the crucial question: how do we actually build them?

Not every problem requires an agent. If your use case needs simple tool selection based on user queries, or deterministic RAG retrieval, you don't need the complexity of agents. These linear, stateless patterns work well for many applications.

But when your system needs to maintain context across interactions, reason about multistep solutions, self-correct when approaches fail, or proactively pursue goals, you need true agents—systems that work through problems step by step, adapting their approach based on what they learn along the way.

Building such agents well—making them reliable enough to handle production workloads, trustworthy enough for sensitive operations, and functional enough to solve real problems—can be surprisingly difficult.

The root challenge to agent development is maintaining coherence across the entire perception-reasoning-action loop (Figure 1-3). Context, state, and intent need to flow naturally from each interaction to the next. Yet in practice, information gets lost between tool calls. Errors cascade through conversations. State vanishes when sessions restart. Many frameworks leave you to figure this out through defensive programming and complex orchestration logic.

Google's Agent Development Kit (*https://oreil.ly/yB7BX*) (ADK) takes a different approach. It builds in the patterns that keep agents coherent under pressure. Conversations persist automatically, errors become information the agent can reason about, and state flows naturally between interactions. The framework anticipates and handles the complexity of real-world agent interactions from the ground up, illustrated in Figure 3-1.

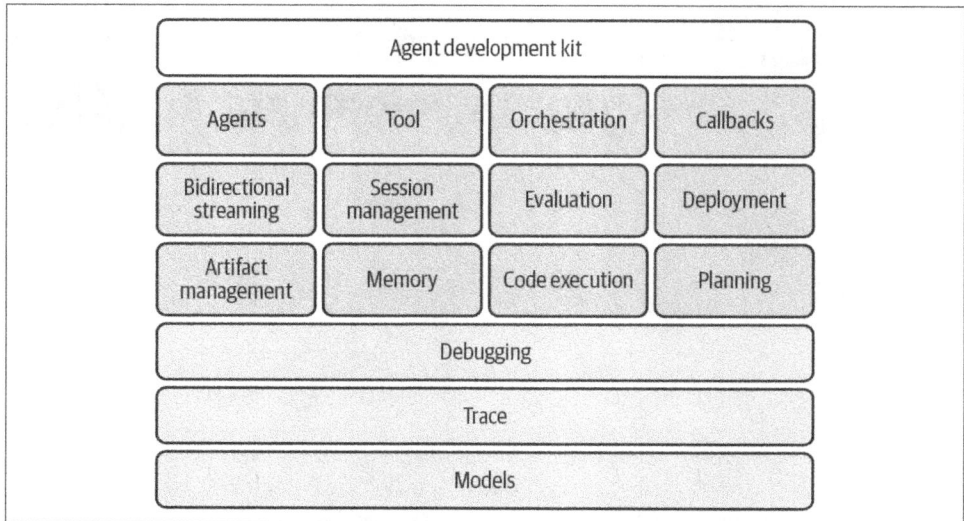

Figure 3-1. Core components of the ADK include agents (conversational units), tools (function integration), orchestration (multiagent coordination), session management (state persistence), memory (semantic knowledge), streaming (real-time interaction), artifacts (file handling), callbacks (execution hooks), and deployment options with comprehensive debugging and tracing capabilities

These design choices reflect patterns proven across Google's AI products, from handling billions of Assistant queries (*https://oreil.ly/fTLms*) to managing state in AI-powered support systems.[1] While ADK itself is new, it codifies approaches that have kept AI systems stable at scale. These are patterns that apply whether you're building a single agent or orchestrating entire teams of specialists.

In this chapter, we'll build a customer support agent using ADK. Starting with basic text interactions, we'll progressively expand to integrate tools, manage state and memory across sessions, handle multimodal inputs (images, audio, and video), and implement real-time streaming support. As we build, you'll see how the framework's design decisions translate into code that remains clean even as capabilities expand.

---

1 As of 2025, Google Assistant on mobile devices is being upgraded to Gemini, Google's AI-powered assistant that builds on Assistant's foundation while adding generative AI capabilities like multimodal conversations and advanced research features.

Google's unified AI stack offers a "no-code to high-code" continuum for agent development. On one end, the no-code *Agent Builder* console (*https://oreil.ly/f6Tt4*) allows for rapid creation of conversational agents through a visual interface. *Agent Garden* provides a library (*https://oreil.ly/JBIxM*) of prebuilt agent solutions and tools that can be customized and deployed. For production deployment, *Vertex AI Agent Engine* offers a fully managed runtime environment (*https://oreil.ly/Fabk4*) handling infrastructure, monitoring, and lifecycle management. ADK is the programmatic component of this ecosystem—an open source framework that spans from visual prototyping to full code control, letting developers rapidly experiment and build production-grade AI agents.

From Zero to Agent in Seven Lines

Every journey begins with a single step. For ADK, that step is remarkably small.

The Simplest Thing That Works

Seven lines. As shown in Example 3-1, that's all it takes to create an agent that can hold conversations, maintain context across multiple turns, and provide helpful responses. No boilerplate for session management. No event loop configuration. No state persistence setup.

Example 3-1. The minimal definition for a conversational agent using ADK's Agent class

```
from google.adk.agents import Agent

root_agent = Agent(
    name="CustomerSupportAgent",
    model="gemini-2.5-flash",
    instruction="You help customers with their SmartHome products."
)
```

This simplicity reveals ADK's fundamental philosophy: the framework should handle the logic of managing multiturn, stateful conversations so you can focus on what your agent actually does.

The ADK supports multiple language SDKs—Python (*https://oreil.ly/lpmlm*), Go (*https://oreil.ly/0EmO2*), and Typescript (*https://oreil.ly/Il9Qi*) (preview)—allowing you to build agents in the language that best fits your development environment and team expertise. The examples and code throughout this book are written exclusively using the Python SDK.

The Runtime Behind the Simplicity

The power of that simple code lies in ADK's fundamental design principle: the strict separation of an agent's logic (the "what") from its runtime (the "how"). Those seven lines define the agent's logic—its brain. They specify its purpose, instructions, and capabilities. The runtime, on the other hand, is the host application that loads and executes your agent logic, providing all the life-support systems it needs to function. For development and testing, ADK provides several command-line tools that launch interaction interfaces for this runtime: `adk run` for a simple text interface, `adk web` for a rich web UI, and `adk api_server` for exposing a direct API. You'll use `adk run` in a moment.

At the heart of the ADK runtime is a powerful "event loop" that manages the conversation lifecycle. Figure 3-2 illustrates this internal flow.

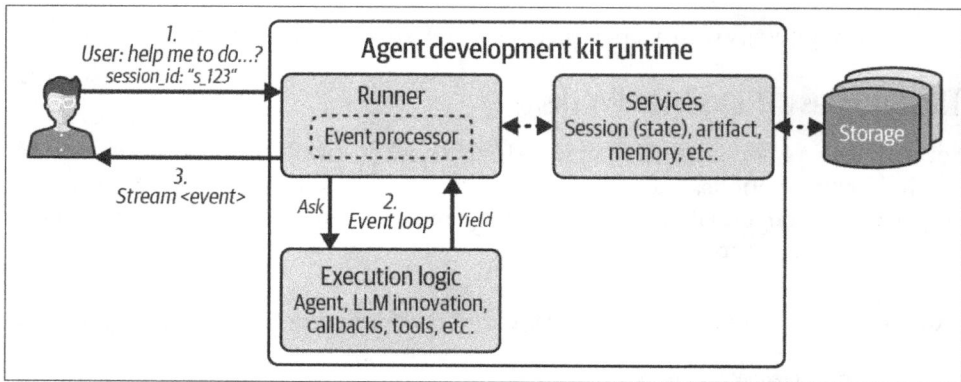

Figure 3-2. The ADK runtime Event Loop, showing the interaction between Runner, Execution Logic, and Services

When you run `adk run`, it launches the ADK runtime with a CLI. This runtime acts as a lightweight but complete host application for your agent, initializing three interconnected systems.

First, a `SessionService` creates isolated workspaces for each conversation. Every user who interacts with your agent gets their own session—a dedicated context that tracks their conversation history, maintains their state, and ensures that their information never leaks to other users. These sessions persist across interruptions, survive network failures, and can even resume after system restarts.

Second, an *event-driven system* transforms every interaction into a stream of observable occurrences. When a user types a message, it enters the event stream where it triggers a cascade: the agent begins processing, tokens stream as the response generates, and state updates as needed. This event-driven architecture enables capabilities that would be architectural nightmares in traditional request-response systems such as real-time streaming, parallel tool execution, and graceful error recovery.

Third, *state management* provides four distinct scopes with different persistence guarantees:

- Temporary state (with `temp:` prefix) handles in-flight operations.
- User state (with `user:` prefix) maintains cross-session memory.
- Application state (with `app:` prefix) manages system-wide configuration.
- Session state (no prefix) persists for the session duration. The framework handles serialization, persistence, and cleanup automatically.

Running Your First Conversation

With your agent defined and API credentials configured (see our GitHub repository (*https://oreil.ly/or9pa*) for complete setup instructions), let's start a conversation.

Example 3-2 shows a typical interaction session with the customer support agent using ADK's CLI.

Example 3-2. The [user]: prefix indicates human input, while [CustomerSupport Agent]: shows the agent's responses

```
$ adk run customer_support_agent
---
Running agent CustomerSupportAgent, type exit to exit.
[user]: Hi, my smart doorbell keeps disconnecting from wifi
[CustomerSupportAgent]: I understand how frustrating intermittent WiFi issues can
be with your smart doorbell. To help diagnose this, I need to gather a few details:

1. How often does it disconnect? (hourly, daily, randomly?)
2. When did this issue start?
3. Have you noticed any patterns (like during specific times of day)?
4. How far is the doorbell from your WiFi router?

[user]: It started about a week ago, happens every few hours
```

The agent engages naturally, gathering diagnostic information just as a human support agent would. But continue the conversation, and you'll quickly discover where it falls short.

Understanding the Limitations

Here's where it breaks down. When you ask, "What's the warranty status for my doorbell? Order #78234?", the agent might respond with something like: "I'd be happy to help you check your warranty status. While I can't access order information directly right now, I can guide you through the general warranty terms for our smart doorbells…"

The agent handles this gracefully, but it's clearly not solving the actual problem. Without access to order systems, it can offer only generic information where specific answers are needed.

Similarly, the agent can describe solutions but can't implement them. It can explain how to reset a doorbell but can't trigger the reset. It can describe the return process but can't initiate a return.

Each new conversation starts fresh: a customer who spent 20 minutes troubleshooting yesterday starts from scratch today because the agent has no memory between sessions. When customers provide serial numbers, error codes, or configuration details, the agent can only store them in conversation history. There's no structured extraction or validation.

Each of these gaps points toward a specific capability you can add. Data access limitations can be solved with tools for querying databases and APIs. Action capability requires tools that modify state and trigger processes. Cross-session memory needs user-scoped state that persists. Structured data handling demands state management with validation.

The beauty of ADK is that adding these capabilities doesn't require rewriting what you have. You can build on top of this foundation, keeping your code clean even as its capabilities expand.

In the next section, we'll address the most pressing limitation: the inability to access real data. By adding tools, we'll transform our agent from a conversational companion into an assistant that can actually solve problems.

Adding Intelligence Through Tools

The moment of truth for any customer support agent comes when a customer asks a specific question: "Where's my order?" Our conversational agent can offer sympathy and generic advice, but without access to real data, it can't provide the answer the customer actually needs. Let's fix that.

Your Agent's First Tool

Let's add our first tool—an order lookup function. Example 3-3 shows how remarkably simple this transformation is.

Example 3-3. When adding an order lookup tool to the customer support agent, the function is automatically converted to a tool by ADK when added to the tools parameter

```python
from google.adk.agents import Agent
from datetime import datetime, timedelta
import random

def look_up_order(order_id: str) -> dict:
    """Retrieves order information from our database.

    Args:
        order_id: The customer's order number

    Returns:
        Order details including status, items, and tracking info
    """
    # Simulated database lookup - in production, this would query real systems
    # Using randomization to show different scenarios

    statuses = ["shipped", "processing", "delivered"]
    status = random.choice(statuses)

    # Create realistic order data
    order_data = {
        "order_id": order_id,
        "status": status,
        "order_date": (
            datetime.now() -
            timedelta(days=random.randint(1, 7))
        ).isoformat(),
        "items": [
            {
                "name": "Smart Doorbell Pro",
                "quantity": 1,
                "price": 199.99
            }
        ],
        "total": 199.99
    }

    # Add status-specific information
    if status == "shipped":
        order_data["tracking_number"] = f"SH{random.randint(100000, 999999)}"
        order_data["estimated_delivery"] = (
            datetime.now() +
            timedelta(days=2)
```

```
        ).strftime("%B %d, %Y")
    elif status == "delivered":
        order_data["delivery_date"] = (
            datetime.now() -
            timedelta(days=1)
        ).strftime("%B %d, %Y")

    return order_data

def create_root_agent():
    return Agent(
        name="CustomerSupportAgent",
        model="gemini-2.5-flash",
        instruction="""You help customers with SmartHome products.
        Be professional, empathetic, and solution-focused.

        When customers ask about orders, use the look_up_order tool
        to get real information. Present the information clearly.""",
        tools=[look_up_order]  # Just add the function - ADK handles the rest
    )

# Create the agent instance ADK expects
root_agent = create_root_agent()
```

That's it. By adding the function to the tools parameter, we've transformed our agent from a conversationalist into a problem solver. ADK automatically extracts the function's signature and generates a tool description for the LLM, parses the docstring to understand when and how to use the tool, handles parameter validation based on type hints, and manages the execution flow when the agent decides to use the tool.

Earlier we used `adk run` to test our basic conversational agent. Now let's use `adk web` to see the tool in action with full visibility into the execution process.

The web interface provides rich insights into how our agent uses tools. Figure 3-3 shows what happens when a customer asks about their order.

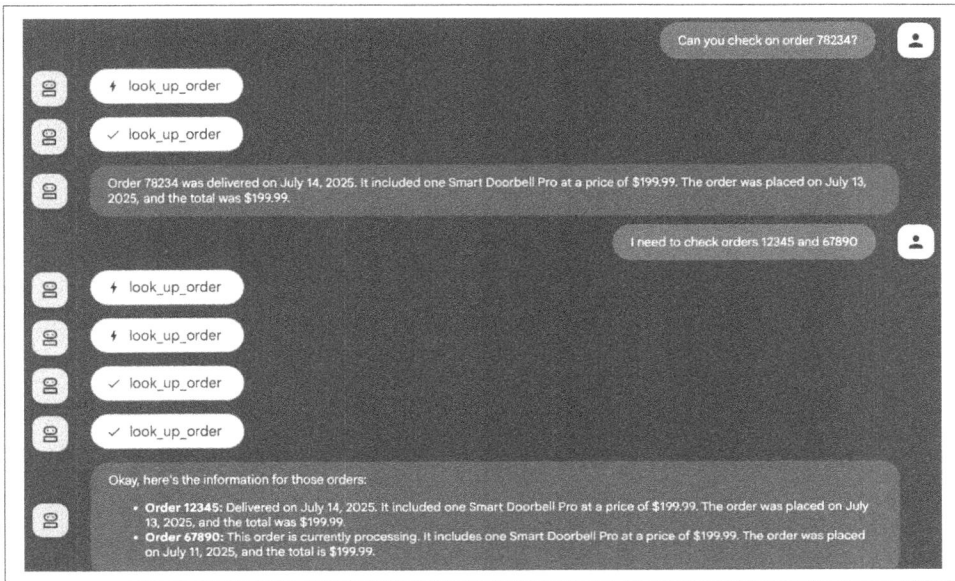

Figure 3-3. Tool execution in the ADK web interface with visual indicators for tool calls (lightning bolt icons)

The agent understood that the request required the look_up_order tool, called the function with the correct parameter, integrated the results naturally into its response, and highlighted the most important information such as status, delivery date, and tracking number. This seamless integration demonstrates ADK's tool orchestration. The framework handles all the complexity behind the scenes, letting you focus on building useful functionality.

The Event tab shown in Figure 3-4 reveals even more detail about the execution flow, showing the precise sequence of function calls and responses that power the interaction. This transparency becomes invaluable when debugging complex tool interactions or optimizing performance.

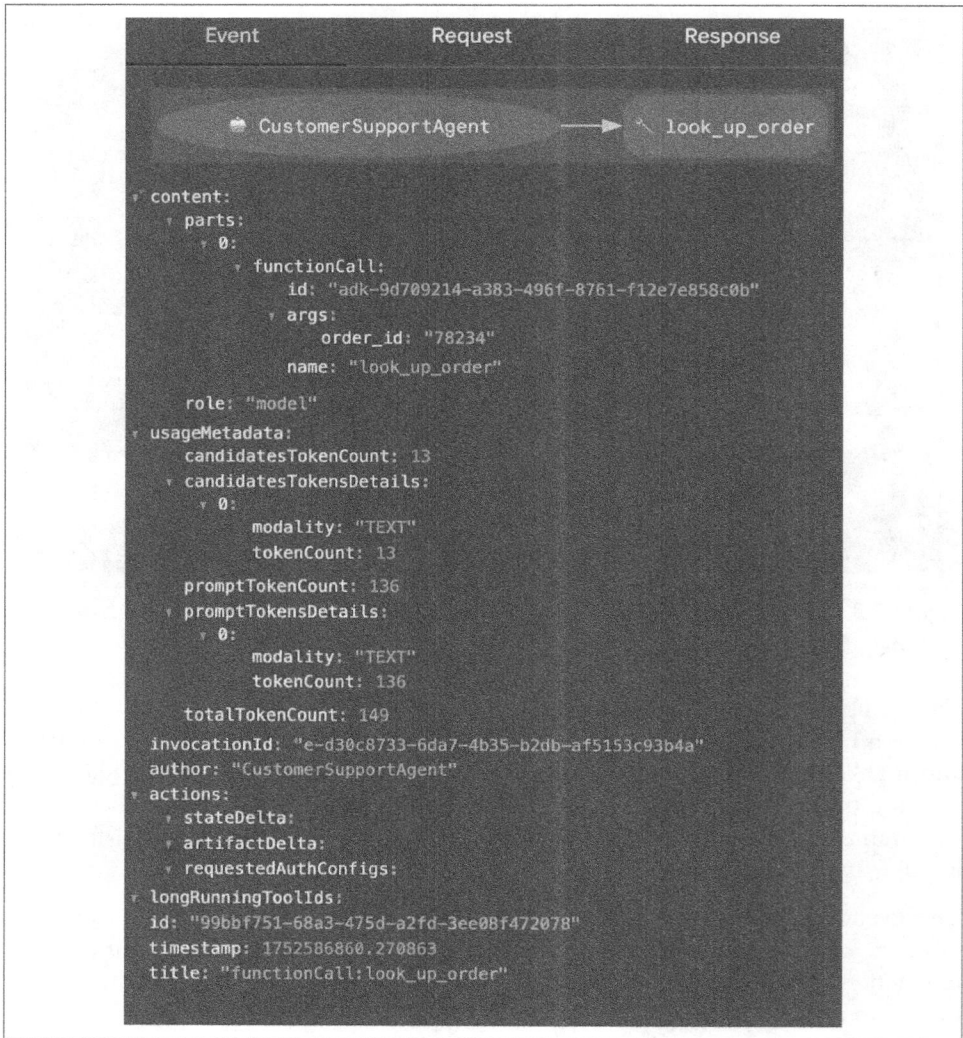

Figure 3-4. Event visualization in the ADK web interface

ADK supports several types of tools beyond simple functions. You can create long-running tools (*https://oreil.ly/y9fPt*) for operations that take time (discussed later in the chapter), use built-in tools (*https://oreil.ly/_h3ZG*), such as Google Search or code execution, or even use other agents as tools (*https://oreil.ly/kPM6n*).

Tools Versus Subagents—A Practical Decision Framework

As your agent grows more capable, you'll face a recurring architectural decision: should this new capability be a tool or a subagent? The answer shapes your system's complexity, performance, and maintainability.

You've seen how tools extend an agent's capabilities with specific functions such as looking up orders or calculating prices. ADK offers another powerful pattern: subagents. These are complete agents that your main agent can delegate to for handling entire conversations or workflows. Think of the difference this way—tools are like an agent's skills, while subagents are like specialist colleagues they can hand off to when expertise is needed.

This distinction becomes clear when we consider a common customer support scenario: handling product returns. Returns require a delicate balance of policy enforcement and customer empathy, often involving multiple steps and nuanced decision making. Let's explore how you might implement this capability.

You could start with a tool approach, as shown in Example 3-4.

Example 3-4. A simple tool implementation for processing returns—deterministic and straightforward

```
def process_return(order_id: str, reason: str, items: list) -> dict:
    """Processes a product return request."""
    # Validate order exists and is eligible
    # Create return authorization
    # Send confirmation email
    # Update order status
    return {"return_id": "RET123", "status": "approved"}
```

Or you could implement it as a subagent, as demonstrated in Example 3-5.

Example 3-5. A subagent implementation for returns—capable of nuanced conversation and complex decision making

```
returns_agent = Agent(
    name="ReturnsSpecialist",
    model="gemini-2.5-flash",
    instruction="""You are a returns specialist. Guide customers through
    the return process, ensuring they have valid reasons and helping them
    understand our policies. Be empathetic but ensure policy compliance.""",
    tools=[validate_return_eligibility, create_return_label, send_confirmation]
)

# Root agent can delegate to returns specialist
root_agent = Agent(
    name="CustomerSupportAgent",
```

```
    sub_agents=[returns_agent]
)
```

How do you choose? Here's a practical framework based on our implementation experience. The beauty of ADK is that you're not locked into your initial choice. When you find yourself writing complex conditionals or wishing the tool could ask clarifying questions, refactor it into a subagent. The framework makes this evolution natural. To help make the decision easier, Table 3-1 summarizes the key decision factors.

Table 3-1. Decision matrix for choosing between tools and subagents

Factor	Use tools	Use subagents
Operation type	Deterministic, single-purpose	Context-dependent, multistep
Reasoning required	None—clear rules suffice	Understanding, empathy, judgment needed
Interface stability	Fixed inputs/outputs	Dynamic, conversational
Performance	Fast with generally no token cost	Variable latency and token costs
Frequency	High-frequency operations	Complex, less frequent interactions
Context needs	Stateless or simple state	Maintains conversation context
Example use cases	Database lookups, calculations, API calls	Troubleshooting, negotiations, multistep workflows

Let's take an example, Example 3-6, with our use case to reinforce what we just learned.

Example 3-6. Shipping calculation as a tool—pure function with predictable outputs

```
def calculate_shipping(weight: float, destination: str) -> dict:
    """Always returns the same rate for given weight and destination."""
    # Deterministic calculation
    base_rate = weight * 0.5
    zone_multiplier = ZONE_RATES.get(destination, 1.0)
    return {"cost": base_rate * zone_multiplier}
```

Tools also shine when the task requires no reasoning. If you can write clear rules for when and how to perform an operation, it's likely a good tool candidate. Speed matters too—tool calls execute quickly with just function execution plus any network overhead. There's typically no explicit LLM inference time, token costs, or nondeterministic delays. Finally, tools work best with stable interfaces that have clear inputs and outputs that rarely change.

Often, the best solution combines both approaches, tools and subagents, as shown in Example 3-7.

Example 3-7. Hybrid architecture combining tools for deterministic operations with subagents for complex workflows

```
# Returns subagent uses specialized tools
returns_agent = Agent(
    name="ReturnsSpecialist",
    instruction="Guide return processes with empathy and policy awareness",
    tools=[
        check_return_eligibility,   # Tool: Deterministic policy check
        calculate_refund_amount,    # Tool: Financial calculation
        create_return_label         # Tool: Generate shipping label
    ]
)

# Root agent delegates complex returns to specialist
root_agent = Agent(
    name="CustomerSupportAgent",
    tools=[
        look_up_order,              # Simple tools for common tasks
        check_shipping_status
    ],
    sub_agents=[returns_agent]      # Specialist for complex workflows
)
```

Use subagents when the task requires understanding context. Return requests aren't just about processing—they require understanding why the customer is unhappy, determining whether their reason is valid, and maintaining relationship quality while enforcing policies. When a customer says, "The doorbell works but I don't like how it looks on my house," a returns specialist subagent can respond with nuance: "I understand that aesthetics are important for your home. While our standard policy covers defects, I can see this is disappointing. Let me check if we have other finish options that might better match your home's style…"

Subagents excel at coordinating multiple steps with branching logic, follow-up questions, and dynamic decision making. They can maintain specialized knowledge through their own instruction sets, tools, and even different models. This specialization improves performance without complicating your main agent. Additionally, subagents maintain their own conversation context, allowing natural multiturn interactions for complex tasks.

The patterns we're exploring here—tools for deterministic operations, subagents for complex workflows—form the foundation for building multiagent systems. In Chapter 4, we'll see how these building blocks enable teams of specialized agents to work together through coordinator and pipeline patterns.

As our customer support agent grows in the sections that follow, we'll use both patterns—tools for looking up information and performing calculations and subagents for complex workflows that benefit from specialized reasoning. This combination creates an agent that's both capable and efficient—exactly what production systems demand.

State Management That Actually Scales

While tools and subagents provide the capabilities your agent needs, there's another critical piece that determines whether your agent can handle real-world interactions: state management. Every conversation generates information that needs to persist—not just for the current exchange, but across sessions, users, and even system-wide configurations. Let's explore how ADK's state system makes this possible.

Our customer support agent can now look up orders and delegate to specialists, but it still lacks persistent memory across sessions. When a customer returns next week, the agent has no record of their preferences or previous interactions. When company policies change, there's no mechanism to propagate updates across all agent instances. These limitations stem from missing state management.

ADK provides three state scopes that solve these challenges. Let's enhance our customer support agent with a shopping cart feature to see these scopes in action.

Building a Stateful Shopping Cart

Adding shopping capabilities to our support agent introduces clarifying state challenges. Some information should exist only during the current conversation, like temporary calculations or session-specific metrics. Other data needs to persist across sessions: purchase history, customer preferences, loyalty status. And certain facts must remain consistent system-wide, such as product prices, shipping policies, and inventory rules.

Let's implement these capabilities, as shown in Example 3-8.

Example 3-8. Shopping cart implementation demonstrating state scope usage

```
from google.adk.agents import Agent
from google.adk.tools import ToolContext
from datetime import datetime

async def add_to_cart(
    product_id: str,
    tool_context: ToolContext,
    quantity: int = 1
) -> dict:
    """Adds products to cart, demonstrating state management."""
```

```python
    # User state: Cart persists across sessions
    cart = tool_context.state.get("user:cart", {"items": [], "total": 0.0})

    # Add item (simplified - assumes all products are $24.99)
    cart["items"].append({"id": product_id, "qty": quantity, "price": 24.99})
    cart["total"] = sum(item["price"] * item["qty"] for item in cart["items"])

    # Update user state
    tool_context.state["user:cart"] = cart
    tool_context.state["user:total_items"] = (
        tool_context.state.get("user:total_items", 0) + quantity
    )

    # Temp state: Session metrics
    tool_context.state["temp:last_action"] = f"Added {product_id}"
    tool_context.state["temp:session_adds"] = (
        tool_context.state.get("temp:session_adds", 0) + 1
    )

    return {"success": True, "cart_total": cart["total"]}

async def checkout(tool_context: ToolContext) -> dict:
    """Processes checkout, demonstrating state scope interactions."""
    cart = tool_context.state.get("user:cart", {"items": [], "total": 0.0})
    if not cart["items"]:
        return {"error": "Empty cart"}

    # Update user state
    tool_context.state["user:lifetime_value"] = (
        tool_context.state.get("user:lifetime_value", 0.0) + cart["total"]
    )
    tool_context.state["user:order_count"] = (
        tool_context.state.get("user:order_count", 0) + 1
    )

    # Check loyalty using app state threshold
    if (tool_context.state["user:lifetime_value"] >
        tool_context.state.get("app:loyalty_threshold", 500)):
        tool_context.state["user:is_vip"] = True

    # Clear cart
    tool_context.state["user:cart"] = {"items": [], "total": 0.0}

    return {"success": True, "order_id": f"ORD-{datetime.now():%Y%m%d%H%M%S}"}

# Create agent with simplified configuration
root_agent = Agent(
    name="CustomerSupportAgent",
    model="gemini-2.5-flash",
    instruction="""Shopping cart agent demonstrating
    temp:, user:, and app: state scopes.""",
```

```
    tools=[add_to_cart, checkout]
)
```

This condensed example shows the essential state management patterns. The complete implementation includes additional tools for viewing the cart and retrieving user preferences, along with additional error handling and product management. You can find the full code with all five tools and comprehensive functionality in our GitHub repository (*https://oreil.ly/g7k6j*).

Now let's see these state management concepts in action. Watch how state flows through an example conversation with our customer support agent in Figure 3-5. The interface displays how user state accumulates customer metrics such as order lookups, cart usage, and total items added—all of which persist across sessions. The customer begins shopping and each interaction builds on the last.

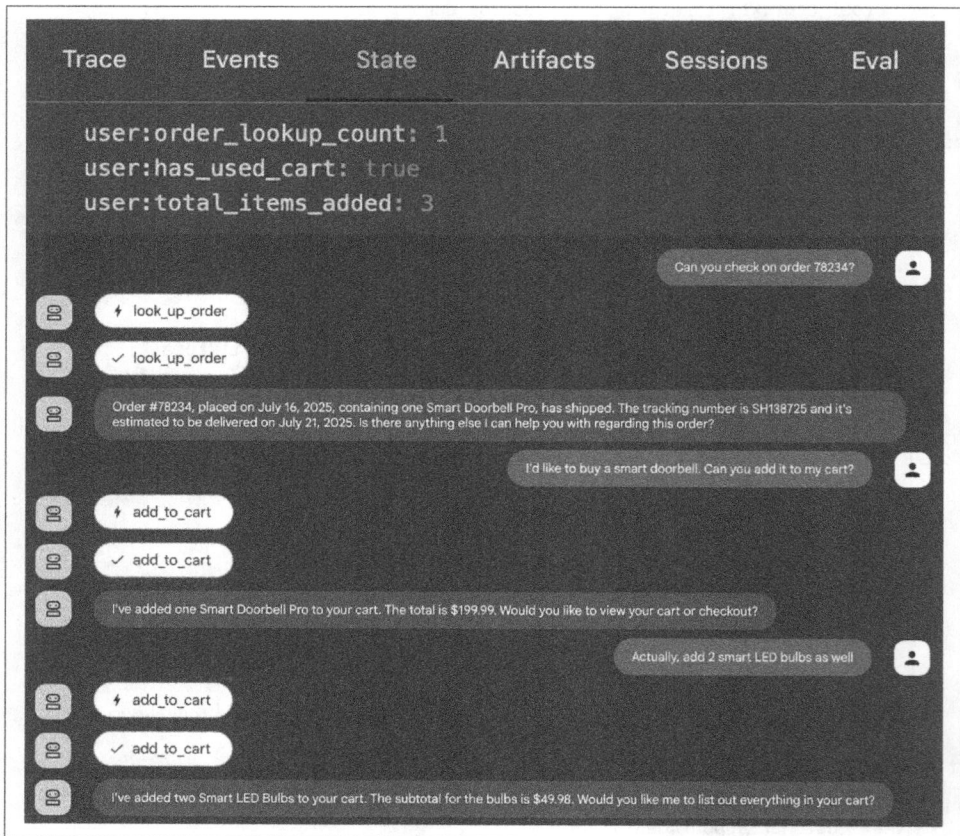

Figure 3-5. State management in the ADK web interface showing user state (user:) updating in real time

Understanding the Three Scopes

Why three different state scopes? Because what your agent needs to remember depends on context:

Temporary state (`temp:`*)*

> Lives for only the current invocation (or turn). When the agent finishes responding, this state disappears. It's perfect for in-progress form data, search filters and preferences for the current interaction, verification codes or temporary tokens, and session-specific metrics. Think of it as your agent's short-term working memory—essential for the task at hand but not worth remembering forever.

User state (`user:`*)*

> Persists across sessions for a specific user. When they come back next week, this data is still there. It's ideal for order history, preferences and settings, loyalty status and rewards, and customer-specific information. This is your agent's cross-session memory for each user—the details that make each customer feel recognized and valued.

Application state (`app:`*)*

> Applies system-wide across all users and sessions. When you update it, every agent instance sees the change. It's essential for business rules and policies, system configuration, feature flags, and global inventory levels. Consider this your agent's globally shared knowledge—the facts and rules that everyone in your organization needs to know.

Example 3-9 shows how these scopes work in practice.

Example 3-9. Temporary state holds session-specific data, user state maintains individual preferences and history, and application state contains system-wide settings

```
# Temporary state - disappears after each invocation
tool_context.state["temp:search_filters"] = {"category": "lighting", "max_price": 50}
tool_context.state["temp:verification_code"] = "123456"

# User state - persists for this user across sessions
tool_context.state["user:preferred_shipping"] = "express"
tool_context.state["user:loyalty_points"] = 1250

# Application state - shared across all users
tool_context.state["app:return_window_days"] = 30
tool_context.state["app:free_shipping_threshold"] = 50.0
```

State Scope Interactions

The real power emerges when scopes work together. Let's enhance our agent with abandoned cart recovery—a feature that showcases how different state scopes complement each other, as shown in Example 3-10.

Example 3-10. Temporary cart data moves to the user state for persistence, while the application state defines business rules such as expiration policies

```
async def save_cart_for_later(tool_context: ToolContext) -> dict:
    """Saves the current cart for later retrieval."""
    cart = tool_context.state.get("user:cart")

    if not cart or not cart["items"]:
        return {"message": "No items to save"}

    # Use temp: for actual invocation-scoped data
    tool_context.state["temp:validation_status"] = "validating"

    # Validate cart items (example intermediate step)
    if not _validate_cart_items(cart["items"]):
        tool_context.state["temp:validation_status"] = "failed"
        return {"error": "Invalid items in cart"}

    tool_context.state["temp:validation_status"] = "passed"

    # Add metadata for recovery
    cart["saved_at"] = datetime.now().isoformat()

    # Mark cart as saved in user state
    tool_context.state["user:cart_saved"] = True
    tool_context.state["user:cart_saved_date"] = cart["saved_at"]

    return {
        "success": True,
        "message": "Your cart has been saved and will be here when you return!"
    }

async def check_cart_expiry(tool_context: ToolContext) -> dict:
    """Checks if saved cart has expired based on business rules."""
    cart = tool_context.state.get("user:cart")
    cart_saved_date = tool_context.state.get("user:cart_saved_date")

    if not cart or not cart["items"] or not cart_saved_date:
        return {"status": "no_saved_cart"}

    # Check if cart is still valid
    saved_date = datetime.fromisoformat(cart_saved_date)
    days_old = (datetime.now() - saved_date).days

    # Get cart expiry policy from app state
```

```
max_days = tool_context.state.get("app:saved_cart_expiry_days", 30)

if days_old > max_days:
    # Clear expired cart
    tool_context.state["user:cart"] = {"items": [], "total": 0.0}
    del tool_context.state["user:cart_saved"]
    del tool_context.state["user:cart_saved_date"]
    return {
        "status": "expired",
        "message": f"Your saved cart has expired (older than {max_days} days)"
    }

return {
    "status": "valid",
    "message": f"Your cart from {days_old} days ago is still available",
    "days_old": days_old
}
```

State management might seem like plumbing—easily overlooked infrastructure. But with ADK's state scopes, it becomes a powerful tool for building agents that truly understand context.

Making State Persist in Production

The state management you've built handles session state, user preferences, and application configuration beautifully. Throughout this chapter, we've stored all our sessions in memory—a deliberate choice that provides instant feedback with zero configuration, perfect for development and testing.

But production applications need state that survives application restarts. When you deploy updates, scale containers, or recover from failures, your users expect their preferences and session data to persist. Let's explore ADK's persistent storage options.

Development: InMemorySessionService

The default InMemorySessionService stores everything in RAM for speed and simplicity. It's what you've been using throughout this chapter, and it excels at local development with instant feedback, rapid prototyping without configuration overhead, and testing and demonstrations.

The tradeoff is straightforward: state exists only while the application runs. Restart your process, and the state resets. This makes InMemorySessionService ideal for development but unsuitable for production deployments where users expect continuity. Example 3-11 shows the basic configuration you've been using throughout the chapter.

Example 3-11. This zero-configuration approach provides instant feedback but doesn't persist state across application restarts

```
from google.adk.runners import InMemoryRunner
from your_agent_file import root_agent

runner = InMemoryRunner(
    agent=root_agent,
    app_name="CustomerSupportAgent"
)
```

Self-managed production: DatabaseSessionService

When you need persistent state with full control over your database infrastructure, `DatabaseSessionService` connects your agent to standard relational databases such as PostgreSQL, MySQL, and SQLite. This approach works well when you have existing database infrastructure or specific compliance requirements around data storage.

Example 3-12 demonstrates a `DatabaseSessionService` configuration using PostgreSQL.

Example 3-12. This self-managed approach provides full control over database infrastructure while ensuring that state persists across application restarts

```
from google.adk.runners import Runner
from google.adk.sessions import DatabaseSessionService
from your_agent_file import root_agent

# Production configuration with Cloud SQL (PostgreSQL)
# Assumes secure connection via Cloud SQL Auth Proxy or private IP

DB_USER = "your-db-user"
DB_PASS = "your-db-password"
DB_HOST = "your-instance-private-ip"  # or 127.0.0.1 via proxy
DB_PORT = "5432"
DB_NAME = "adk_sessions_db"

db_url = f"postgresql+pg8000://{DB_USER}:{DB_PASS}@{DB_HOST}:{DB_PORT}/{DB_NAME}"

runner = Runner(
    agent=root_agent,
    app_name="CustomerSupportAgent",
    session_service=DatabaseSessionService(db_url=db_url)
)
```

Fully managed production: VertexAiSessionService

For teams deploying on Google Cloud, `VertexAiSessionService` eliminates database management entirely. Vertex AI Agent Engine handles storage, scaling, high availability, and backups automatically—representing the lowest operational overhead. The platform manages the infrastructure while you focus on agent logic. As shown in Example 3-13, the `VertexAiSessionService` configuration for fully managed state persistence is even simpler than the database approach.

Example 3-13. Vertex AI Agent Engine handles all infrastructure concerns, providing the lowest operational overhead

```
from google.adk.runners import Runner
from google.adk.sessions import VertexAiSessionService
from your_agent_file import root_agent

PROJECT_ID = "your-gcp-project-id"
LOCATION = "us-central1"
AGENT_ENGINE_ID = "your-agent-engine-id"

runner = Runner(
    agent=root_agent,
    app_name=AGENT_ENGINE_ID,  # Must match Agent Engine ID
    session_service=VertexAiSessionService(
        project=PROJECT_ID,
        location=LOCATION
    )
)
```

The choice between these implementations depends on your deployment environment, operational expertise, and infrastructure preferences, which we'll cover in more depth in Chapter 6 (infrastructure), Chapter 7 (MLOps), and Chapter 8 (AI and agentic maturity framework). Your agent code—the tools, state management patterns, and conversation logic—works identically with all three implementations. Switching between them means changing only how you initialize the runner, not rewriting the agent itself.

Beyond Structured State: Semantic Memory

The persistent state we've configured enables your agent to remember structured facts across sessions. When a customer returns weeks later, their `user:preferences`, `user:cart`, and `user:vip_status` state, for example, remain intact. This programmatic memory is powerful—it captures exactly what you choose to track.

But conversations contain knowledge that resists structure. Consider the following exchange:

> *Customer:* I finally got the doorbell working by switching to the 2.4GHz network. The 5GHz just wouldn't stay connected.
> *Agent:* That's great! I've updated your order status to resolved.

Your agent might set `user:issue_resolved = True` in state, but what about the troubleshooting insight embedded in that exchange? The fact that this customer's WiFi environment works better on 2.4GHz could help diagnose future issues with their other smart home devices. Yet it doesn't fit naturally into a state key.

This conversational nuance—the context, preferences, and tacit knowledge that emerges organically—is what semantic memory captures.

Vertex AI Agent Engine Memory Bank: Learning from Conversations

Vertex AI Agent Engine Memory Bank (*https://oreil.ly/9pW6U*), illustrated in Figure 3-6, complements structured state by automatically extracting and consolidating meaningful facts from conversation history. After each session, Memory Bank analyzes the exchange using a Gemini model to identify information worth remembering.

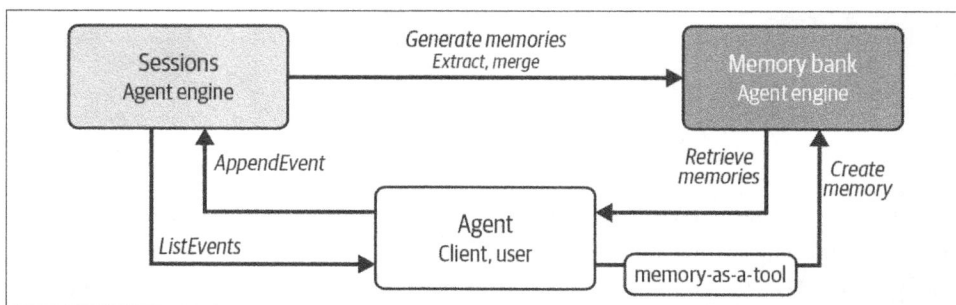

Figure 3-6. During the flow of information in Memory Bank, sessions generate memories through extraction and consolidation, which agents retrieve using semantic search

The distinction is subtle but powerful. User state requires you to decide upfront: "Store this specific piece of data." Memory Bank operates at a higher level: "what did we learn about this customer that will improve future interactions?"

Consider how these two forms of memory work together. Memory Bank extracts semantic insights such as "Customer's smart home devices perform better on 2.4GHz WiFi than 5GHz;" "Prefers detailed technical explanations over simplified summaries;" and "Concerned about shipping reliability after previous delayed order." Meanwhile, the user state tracks explicit data points such as `user:preferred_shipping = "express"`, `user:wifi_network = "2.4GHz"`, and `user:communication_preference = "email"`.

Both forms of memory enable personalization. User state provides structured facts that let your agent recognize returning customers and adapt accordingly. Memory Bank adds conversational context, creating interactions that feel genuinely attentive rather than merely informed.

Implementation

Integrating Memory Bank builds on the session persistence you've already configured. The pattern involves three steps: adding the memory service to your runner,
extracting memories from completed sessions, and equipping your agent to retrieve
relevant memories automatically.

Step 1: Add memory service to your runner

Adding VertexAiMemoryBankService to your runner requires the same configuration
elements you used for session persistence: project ID, location, and agent engine ID.

Example 3-14 shows VertexAiSessionService and VertexAiMemoryBankService
configured together.

*Example 3-14. The session service handles structured state while the memory service
captures semantic knowledge from conversations*

```
from google.adk.runners import Runner
from google.adk.sessions import VertexAiSessionService
from google.adk.memory import VertexAiMemoryBankService
from your_agent_file import root_agent

PROJECT_ID = "your-gcp-project-id"
LOCATION = "us-central1"
AGENT_ENGINE_ID = "your-agent-engine-id"

# Your existing session service for state persistence
session_service = VertexAiSessionService(
    project=PROJECT_ID,
    location=LOCATION
)

# Add memory service for semantic knowledge
memory_service = VertexAiMemoryBankService(
    project=PROJECT_ID,
    location=LOCATION,
    agent_engine_id=AGENT_ENGINE_ID
)

runner = Runner(
    agent=root_agent,
    app_name=AGENT_ENGINE_ID,
    session_service=session_service,   # Handles structured state
    memory_service=memory_service      # Handles semantic memories
)
```

Step 2: Extract memories from completed sessions

You explicitly trigger memory extraction by calling `add_session_to_memory()` on completed sessions, typically when a conversation concludes successfully. Memory Bank then automatically analyzes the conversation to identify and extract valuable knowledge, as shown in Example 3-15.

Example 3-15. When extracting memories from a completed session, Memory Bank analyzes the conversation using a Gemini model to identify and consolidate meaningful facts worth remembering

```
# Retrieve the completed session
completed_session = await runner.session_service.get_session(
    app_name=AGENT_ENGINE_ID,
    user_id="customer-user-id",
    session_id="session-id-from-conversation"
)

if completed_session:
    # Analyze conversation and extract memories
    await memory_service.add_session_to_memory(completed_session)
```

For production systems, you can automate this using an `after_agent_callback` (discussed later in this chapter) that processes sessions after successful interactions, ensuring that valuable conversations are captured without manual intervention.

Step 3: Retrieve memories automatically

ADK's `PreloadMemoryTool` performs semantic search against Memory Bank at the start of each conversation turn, injecting relevant facts into your agent's context. Example 3-16 demonstrates how to equip your agent with automatic memory retrieval.

Example 3-16. The `PreloadMemoryTool` injects relevant memories into the agent's context at the start of each turn, enriching responses with historical knowledge

```
from google.adk.agents import Agent
from google.adk.tools.preload_memory_tool import PreloadMemoryTool

root_agent = Agent(
    name="CustomerSupportAgent",
    model="gemini-2.5-flash",
    instruction="""You are a helpful customer support assistant with access
    to both current session data and relevant memories from past conversations.

    Use the retrieved memories to provide personalized support and avoid asking
    for information the customer has already shared.""",
```

```
    tools=[PreloadMemoryTool()]
)
```

The agent doesn't explicitly call memory retrieval—it simply receives enriched context for each interaction, allowing it to provide responses informed by the full conversational history with this specific customer. ADK also provides load_memory as an alternative tool that lets the agent decide when to retrieve memories.

Structured state and semantic memory working together

The combination creates a complete picture of your customer. When someone returns to your support agent, you have both operational data and conversational context. User state provides immediate, structured facts such as user:vip_status = True, user:lifetime_value = 1250.00, and user:preferred_contact = "email". Memory Bank provides contextual understanding: "Customer is price-sensitive but values reliability over cost," "Had frustrating experience with previous shipping delay," and "WiFi environment requires 2.4GHz for smart home devices."

This dual-layer approach enables agents that make smart operational decisions—applying VIP discounts and using email for notifications—while providing genuinely personalized interactions by acknowledging past shipping concerns and proactively recommending 2.4GHz-compatible products.

Your customer support agent now has memory that scales from single conversations to weeks of accumulated knowledge—exactly the foundation needed for production deployments where users expect continuity and personalization.

Expanding to Multimodal

Our customer support agent has grown considerably since the start of this chapter. It can look up orders, manage shopping carts, and remember customer preferences across sessions. But watch what happens when a customer tries to report a damaged product:

> Customer: My smart doorbell is sparking! It looks dangerous!

Our agent can respond with only generic troubleshooting steps. It can't see the sparking. It can't assess the damage. It can't generate the visual documentation needed for a warranty claim. In the real world of customer support, seeing is believing—and our text-only agent is effectively blind.

The ADK solves this limitation through three complementary capabilities. First, Gemini models natively understand images, audio, and video, allowing our agent to analyze media a customer shares. Second, the Gemini Live API (*https://oreil.ly/ wF04O*) enables real-time streaming for voice and video interactions. Third, the

Artifact Service (*https://oreil.ly/IiJUn*) provides persistent document storage, ensuring that important findings become retrievable records.

Let's enhance our customer support agent to handle these real-world scenarios. The code samples in this section show the essential patterns; for the complete implementation including WebSocket infrastructure, client-side media handling, and production-ready error handling, see our GitHub repository (*https://oreil.ly/tkjud*).

Making Our Agent See

The transformation relies on Gemini's native multimodal capabilities to "see" the damage. We add the `analyze_product_damage` tool not to process the pixels, but to capture the model's analysis—such as damage type and severity—and structure it into a formal report. Example 3-17 shows how this new multimodal damage analysis capability integrates seamlessly with our existing agent.

Example 3-17. The function processes product images, generates assessment reports, and stores them as persistent artifacts using the user: prefix for cross-session access

```
async def analyze_product_damage(
    damage_type: str,
    severity: str,
    tool_context: ToolContext
) -> dict:
    """Records the damage assessment derived from image analysis."""

    # Use the model-provided analysis values
    assessment = {
        "damage_severity": severity,
        "damage_type": damage_type,
        # In a real app, coverage logic would likely be another tool or lookup
        "warranty_coverage": "Covered - component failure",
        "recommended_action": "Warranty replacement approved"
    }

    # Generate report content
    report_content = {
        "report_type": "Damage Assessment",
        "generated_at": datetime.now().isoformat(),
        "assessment": assessment,
        "case_number": f"DMG-{datetime.now().strftime('%Y%m%d%H%M%S')}"
    }

    # Save as artifact for permanent storage
    report_json = json.dumps(report_content, indent=2)
    report_artifact = types.Part.from_bytes(
        data=report_json.encode('utf-8'),
        mime_type="application/json"
    )
```

```
    # Use user: prefix for cross-session persistence
    # Wrapped in parentheses to prevent margin breach
    filename = (f"user:damage_report_"
                f"{report_content['case_number']}.json")

    version = await tool_context.save_artifact(
        filename=filename,
        artifact=report_artifact
    )

    # Return assessment with case number
    assessment["case_number"] = report_content['case_number']
    assessment["report_saved"] = True
    assessment["report_version"] = version

    return assessment

# Update our agent to include the new capability
root_agent = Agent(
    name="CustomerSupportAgent",
    model="gemini-2.5-flash",
    # Instruction updated to explicitly tell the model to analyze first
    instruction=(
        "You help customers with SmartHome products. "
        "When customers share images, analyze the damage details and use "
        "analyze_product_damage to document the issue."
    ),
    tools=[
        look_up_order,
        add_to_cart,
        checkout,
        analyze_product_damage
    ]
)
```

With this enhancement in place, our agent can now process visual information just as naturally as text. Figure 3-7 demonstrates this multimodal capability in action, showing how the agent seamlessly combines order lookup with visual damage assessment when a customer uploads an image of their damaged doorbell.

The agent isn't just acknowledging the image—it's analyzing it, making decisions based on what it sees, and saving a formal damage report through the Artifact Service. These artifacts persist independently of conversation state, meaning customers can retrieve their case documentation weeks later for insurance claims or warranty verification.

While we've demonstrated image analysis here, the same approach works with audio and video. Customers could upload recordings of unusual sounds or videos of installation problems, with the agent analyzing the media content and capturing the findings via specific reporting tools.

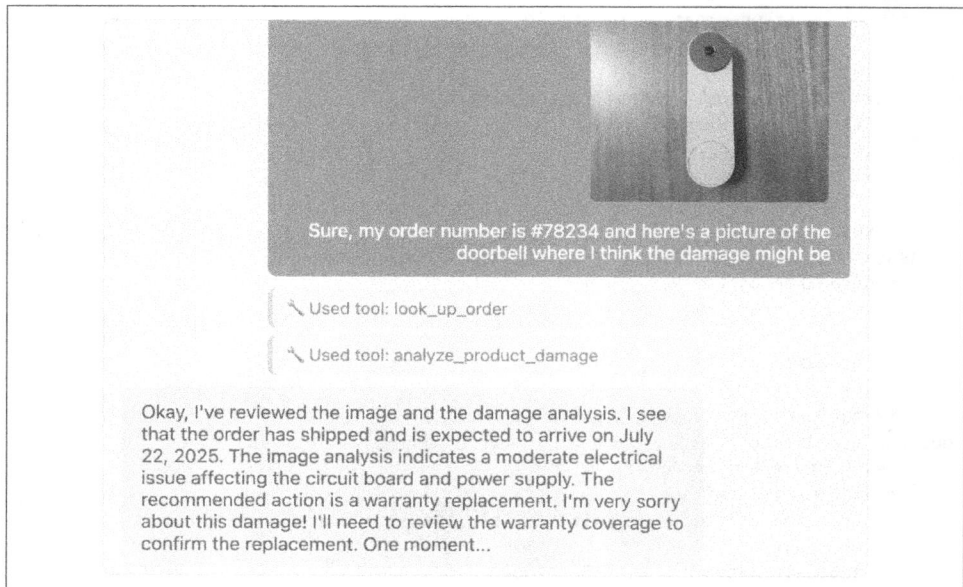

Sure, my order number is #78234 and here's a picture of the doorbell where I think the damage might be

🔍 Used tool: look_up_order

🔍 Used tool: analyze_product_damage

Okay, I've reviewed the image and the damage analysis. I see that the order has shipped and is expected to arrive on July 22, 2025. The image analysis indicates a moderate electrical issue affecting the circuit board and power supply. The recommended action is a warranty replacement. I'm very sorry about this damage! I'll need to review the warranty coverage to confirm the replacement. One moment...

Figure 3-7. The customer uploads an image of their doorbell, and the agent automatically invokes both `look_up_order` *and* `analyze_product_damage` *tools to provide comprehensive support—checking warranty status while analyzing and documenting the visible damage*

From Static Analysis to Live Support

Static media analysis solves many problems, but some situations demand real-time interaction. When a customer struggles with thermostat wiring or needs guided troubleshooting, asynchronous image sharing falls short. They need someone watching in real time, providing immediate feedback as they work.

ADK's Live API integration enables this capability through streaming interactions. Example 3-18 demonstrates how to implement real-time voice and video support.

Example 3-18. With ADK's Live API integration, the WebSocket endpoint handles bidirectional streaming, processing both audio and video inputs while streaming agent responses back to the client

```
@app.websocket("/ws-voice")
async def websocket_voice_endpoint(websocket: WebSocket):
    """Real-time voice/video support for complex troubleshooting."""
    await websocket.accept()
```

```python
session_id = f"voice_streaming_{datetime.now().timestamp()}"
user_id = "voice_user"

# Create session
session = await session_service.create_session(
    app_name="voice_streaming_demo",
    user_id=user_id,
    session_id=session_id
)

# Initialize runner with streaming agent
runner = Runner(
    agent=streaming_agent,
    app_name="voice_streaming_demo",
    session_service=session_service,
    artifact_service=artifact_service
)

# Configure for audio mode
run_config = RunConfig(
    streaming_mode=StreamingMode.BIDI,
    response_modalities=["AUDIO"],
    speech_config=types.SpeechConfig(
        voice_config=types.VoiceConfig(
            prebuilt_voice_config=types.PrebuiltVoiceConfig(
                voice_name="Aoede"
            )
        )
    ),
    input_audio_transcription=types.AudioTranscriptionConfig(),
    output_audio_transcription=types.AudioTranscriptionConfig(),
)

# Create live streaming components
live_request_queue = LiveRequestQueue()
live_events = runner.run_live(
    session=session,
    live_request_queue=live_request_queue,
    run_config=run_config
)

# Handle bidirectional streaming
async def process_client_audio():
    """Receive audio/video from client."""
    async for data in websocket.iter_json():
        if data["type"] == "audio":
            audio_bytes = base64.b64decode(data["data"])
            live_request_queue.send_realtime(
                types.Blob(
                    data=audio_bytes,
                    mime_type="audio/pcm;rate=16000"
```

```
                )
            )
        elif data["type"] == "video":
            video_bytes = base64.b64decode(data["data"])
            live_request_queue.send_realtime(
                types.Blob(
                    data=video_bytes,
                    mime_type="image/jpeg"
                )
            )

    async def stream_agent_responses():
        """Send agent audio responses to client."""
        async for event in live_events:
            if event.content and event.content.parts:
                for part in event.content.parts:
                    if hasattr(part, "inline_data") and part.inline_data:
                        # Audio response
                        audio_base64 = base64.b64encode(
                            part.inline_data.data
                        ).decode("utf-8")
                        await websocket.send_json({
                            "type": "audio",
                            "data": audio_base64
                        })

    # Run both tasks concurrently
    await asyncio.gather(
        process_client_audio(),
        stream_agent_responses()
    )
```

The complete implementation in our GitHub repository includes transcript buffering for smooth text display, comprehensive error handling and reconnection logic, client-side JavaScript for media capture and playback, and integration with the full HTML interface shown in the screenshots.

The Live API currently supports either text or audio responses (not both simultaneously). In voice mode, customers can enable their camera for visual troubleshooting while maintaining natural conversation flow.

Figure 3-8 demonstrates this live support capability in action, showing how customers can share their camera feed while receiving real-time voice guidance during complex troubleshooting scenarios.

Real-Time Streaming Chat

Connected

Mode: `Voice Mode` `Switch to Text Mode`

Oh no! Can you describe what happened with your smart doorbell?

Sure, can I show to you?

Yes, please do.

Here it is.

Okay, I see the doorbell. What seems to be the problem?

It's kind of rattling.

Rattling, got it. Does the camera still work, or is it completely unresponsive?

`Stop Voice Chat` `Disable Camera`

Listening...

Streaming Features:

- Real-time text or voice response
- Video input support (voice mode)
- Natural conversation flow
- Low latency interactions

Figure 3-8. The customer shares their camera feed while the agent provides real-time text guidance for troubleshooting—the same agent that handles text and analyzes static images now guides through live interaction

Beyond real-time interactions, our agent needs to maintain a permanent record of important customer interactions and documents.

Building Complete Interaction Memory

Beyond tracking structured data in state, your agent needs to handle actual files—images customers upload showing product damage, PDFs of receipts they want analyzed, or reports your agent generates for them to download and share. The artifact service provides persistent file storage for any binary content that needs to outlive the conversation, whether uploaded by customers or created by your agent. Example 3-19 shows how to implement comprehensive file management.

Example 3-19. The document management function retrieves and organizes all saved customer artifacts and categorizes documents by type (damage reports, receipts, installation certificates) for improved UX

```
async def list_user_documents(tool_context: ToolContext) -> dict:
    """Shows all saved documents for the customer."""
    all_artifacts = await tool_context.list_artifacts()
    user_artifacts = [f for f in all_artifacts if f.startswith("user:")]

    damage_reports = []
    receipts = []
    installation_certs = []

    for artifact in user_artifacts:
        if "damage_report" in artifact:
            damage_reports.append(artifact)
        elif "receipt" in artifact:
            receipts.append(artifact)
        elif "installation" in artifact:
            installation_certs.append(artifact)

    return {
        "damage_reports": damage_reports,
        "receipts": receipts,
        "installation_certificates": installation_certs
    }
```

The architectural consistency becomes clear when you consider the complete system. State management tracks structured data—cart contents, preferences, VIP status. The artifact service handles the actual files—damage photos, generated reports, receipts. Session persistence ensures that both survive across conversations. Together, these capabilities transform your agent from a conversational interface into a complete support system that can handle real-world customer needs from diagnosis through documentation.

Building Production-Grade Tools

The agent you've built is production-capable—it handles conversations, manages state, processes multimodal inputs, and generates documents. But enterprise deployments introduce scenarios that don't appear during development, and ADK provides patterns specifically designed for these production realities.

Real business processes often involve waiting. Approvals require manager review. Infrastructure provisioning takes minutes. External systems process requests asynchronously. Your agent needs to handle these long-running operations without blocking conversations.

Enterprise applications demand consistent security and compliance. Sensitive data needs protection across every interaction. Organizational policies must apply uniformly regardless of which agent handles the request. These requirements need systematic enforcement, not ad hoc implementation.

Production systems require visibility. When something goes wrong, you need detailed execution traces. When performance matters, you need precise metrics. When compliance asks questions, you need comprehensive audit logs. ADK's plug-in architecture provides exactly this observability.

Let's enhance our agent with these enterprise capabilities, starting with long-running operations.

Handling Asynchronous Operations

The tools we've built so far complete their operations within milliseconds or seconds. When the agent calls look_up_order or analyze_product_damage, it receives responses quickly. This works well for database lookups, API calls, and damage assessments.

Many enterprise scenarios involve multiple operations that take time. ADK handles these efficiently and runs tools in parallel when the agent requests multiple operations. If your agent needs weather data from three cities, all three API calls happen concurrently rather than sequentially. This parallel execution makes research tasks and multisource data gathering fast and responsive.

Throughout this chapter, you've been defining tools with async def rather than def. This asynchronous syntax enables ADK to run multiple tool calls concurrently when your agent requests them. When you write async def my_tool(...), you're telling Python this function can yield control while waiting for I/O operations (database queries, API calls, file operations), allowing other tools to execute simultaneously. You don't need to change how you've been writing tools—the async def pattern you've been using already enables this concurrent execution.

But some business processes are inherently singular and time-consuming: manager approvals that require human review, infrastructure provisioning that takes minutes, complex reports that process for hours. These operations can't be parallelized because they're single, long-running tasks. With standard tools, users would wait the entire duration with no acknowledgment—a poor experience when operations take minutes or hours to complete.

For these scenarios, ADK provides the `LongRunningFunctionTool` (*https://oreil.ly/oSTSq*). This specialized tool initiates long-running background operations without blocking the agent, allowing it to handle business workflows where the actual work happens asynchronously—outside the immediate request-response cycle. Figure 3-9 illustrates the interaction flow.

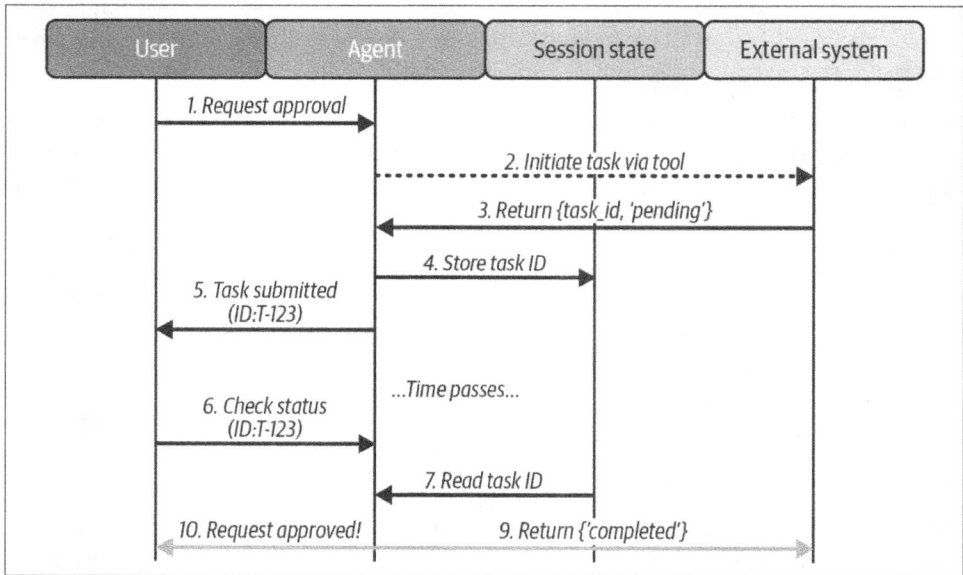

Figure 3-9. `LongRunningFunctionTool` interaction pattern showing how asynchronous operations integrate with agent execution

The interaction flow is designed to integrate seamlessly with external processes. When the agent calls a long-running tool, the tool initiates the external operation (creating an approval ticket, starting infrastructure provisioning) and stores tracking information in state—typically a task ID and status flag. The agent run completes, informing the user their request was submitted along with the task ID.

Later, when the user asks about status, the status-checking tool queries the external tracking system, discovers the current state, and updates ADK session state accordingly. If the operation has completed, the tool sets completion flags in state (such as `approval_completed:` True), allowing subsequent agents in the pipeline to proceed automatically.

Example 3-20 demonstrates implementing a manager approval workflow.

Example 3-20. Implementing asynchronous manager approval with `LongRunning FunctionTool`

```python
import random
from typing import Any
from google.adk.tools import LongRunningFunctionTool

def request_manager_approval(purpose: str, amount: float) -> dict[str, Any]:
    """Initiates a request for manager approval for an expense."""
    # In production, this would call an API to create a ticket
    # in a system like Jira or ServiceNow
    print(f"--- TOOL: Creating approval ticket for ${amount} USD "
          f"for '{purpose}' ---")

    ticket_id = f"TICKET-{random.randint(1000, 9999)}"

    # Return immediately with pending status and ticket ID
    return {
        'status': 'pending',
        'approver': 'manager@example.com',
        'ticket_id': ticket_id,
        'message': (f"Approval request submitted. Track status with "
                    f"ticket {ticket_id}")
    }

# Wrap the function with LongRunningFunctionTool
approval_tool = LongRunningFunctionTool(func=request_manager_approval)

# Add to your agent's tools list
agent = Agent(
    name="ExpenseAgent",
    tools=[approval_tool],
    instruction="Help users submit expenses for approval."
)
```

This pattern allows your agent to manage workflows that mirror real business processes, where delays and external dependencies are the norm rather than the exception.

Ensuring Safety with Human-in-the-Loop

Agents with tools that can perform sensitive or destructive actions—deleting database records, sending customer-facing emails, approving financial transactions—pose significant risk. An LLM misinterpretation could trigger an irreversible, costly mistake.

As shown in Figure 3-10, ADK provides native safety through Tool Confirmation, implementing a Human-in-the-Loop (HITL) guardrail that pauses the agent before protected tools execute.

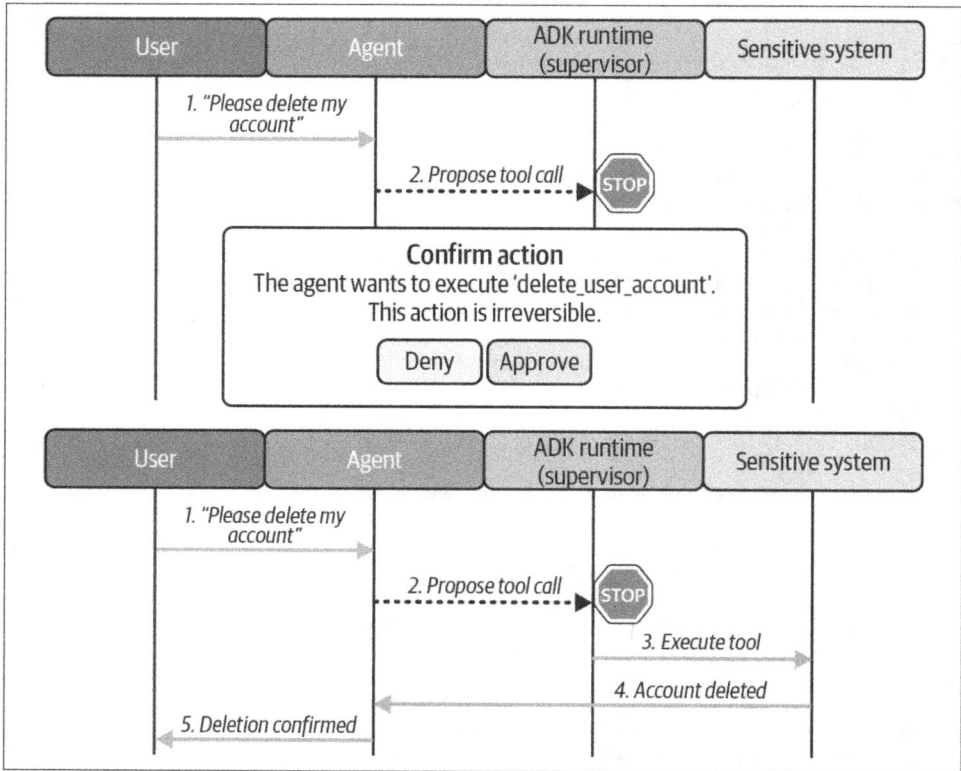

Figure 3-10. HITL confirmation flow preventing unauthorized destructive operations

For simple "yes/no" approvals, wrap a function in a `FunctionTool` and set `require_confirmation = True`, as shown in Example 3-21.

Example 3-21. Implementing HITL confirmation for sensitive operations

```
from google.adk.agents import Agent
from google.adk.tools import FunctionTool

def delete_user_account(user_id: str) -> dict:
    """
    Permanently deletes a user's account and all associated data.
    This action is irreversible and requires confirmation.
    """
    print(f"--- TOOL: Deleting account for user: {user_id} ---")
    # In production, this would call your user management API
```

```
        return {"status": "success", "message": f"User {user_id} has been deleted."}

# Wrap with confirmation requirement
delete_tool = FunctionTool(
    func=delete_user_account,
    require_confirmation=True  # Forces human approval before execution
)

safety_agent = Agent(
    name="AdminAgent",
    model="gemini-2.5-flash",
    instruction=(
        "You are an admin assistant. When asked to delete a user, "
        "use the delete_user_account tool. Always state that this is a "
        "permanent action."
    ),
    tools=[delete_tool]
)
```

When this agent runs and decides to call delete_user_account, the user sees a confirmation dialog. The tool executes only if they explicitly approve. For scenarios requiring more complex input, such as a reason for approval or multifactor authentication, use tool_context.request_confirmation() within your tool logic to request structured data from the user.

Production Monitoring and Policy Enforcement with Callbacks and Plug-ins

Throughout this chapter, we've seen callbacks (*https://oreil.ly/1cLLX*) at work behind the scenes, tracking media references, managing state transitions. But callbacks serve a critical role in production: they're one of your primary mechanisms for observability, security, and compliance.

ADK provides callback hooks at key execution points. The before_agent_callback and after_agent_callback fire when the agent run starts and ends, making them ideal for logging session metadata and tracking overall execution time. The before_model_callback and after_model_callback fire before and after LLM calls, enabling prompt inspection, output filtering, and token usage tracking. Similarly, before_tool_callback and after_tool_callback fire before and after tool execution, perfect for authorization checks, input validation, and result transformation.

While callbacks work well for agent-specific logic, production systems need consistent security policies across all agents. This is where ADK's Plugin (*https://oreil.ly/D79Um*) system becomes essential. Plug-ins are reusable, modular components that apply at the runner level, ensuring that every agent in your system follows the same security and compliance rules.

The distinction is important: use callbacks for agent-specific behavior such as custom state management, but use plug-ins for application-wide policies like PII redaction or security guardrails. ADK provides the plug-in framework through the Base Plugin class, allowing teams to build their own custom plug-ins for their specific requirements. Example 3-22 demonstrates implementing a production PII redaction plug-in.

Example 3-22. Custom PII redaction plug-in for application-wide data protection

```
from google.adk.plugins.base_plugin import BasePlugin
from google.adk.plugins.base_plugin import CallbackContext
from google.adk.models.llm_request import LlmRequest
from google.adk.models.llm_response import LlmResponse
from google.adk.tools.base_tool import BaseTool
from google.adk.tools.tool_context import ToolContext
from typing import Any, Optional
import re

class PIIRedactionPlugin(BasePlugin):
    """Custom plugin for enterprise-grade PII protection across all agents."""

    def __init__(self, redaction_patterns=None):
        """Initialize with customizable redaction patterns."""
        super().__init__(name="PIIRedactionPlugin")
        self.patterns = redaction_patterns or {
            r'\b\d{3}-\d{2}-\d{4}\b': '[SSN-REDACTED]',
            r'\b\d{3}[-.]?\d{3}[-.]?\d{4}\b': '[PHONE-REDACTED]',
            (r'\b[A-Za-z0-9._%+-]+@'
             r'[A-Za-z0-9.-]+\.[A-Z|a-z]{2,}\b'): '[EMAIL-REDACTED]',
            r'MRN\d{6,}': '[MRN-REDACTED]',  # Medical Record Numbers
            r'\b\d{4}\s?\d{4}\s?\d{4}\s?\d{4}\b': '[CREDIT-CARD-REDACTED]'
        }

    async def before_model_callback(
        self,
        callback_context: CallbackContext,
        llm_request: LlmRequest
    ) -> Optional[None]:
        """Redact PII patterns before sending to LLM."""
        if not llm_request.contents:
            return None

        for content in llm_request.contents:
            for part in content.parts:
                if hasattr(part, 'text') and part.text:
                    part.text = self._redact_text(part.text)

        return None  # Allow model call to proceed with redacted content

    async def after_model_callback(
```

```python
        self,
        callback_context: CallbackContext,
        llm_response: LlmResponse
    ) -> Optional[LlmResponse]:
        """Redact PII from LLM outputs before returning to user."""
        if not llm_response.content or not llm_response.content.parts:
            return None

        # Modify response in place
        for part in llm_response.content.parts:
            if hasattr(part, 'text') and part.text:
                part.text = self._redact_text(part.text)

        return None  # Use the modified response

    async def before_tool_callback(
        self,
        tool: BaseTool,
        tool_args: dict[str, Any],
        tool_context: ToolContext
    ) -> Optional[dict[str, Any]]:
        """Redact PII from tool arguments."""
        # Redact PII in tool arguments
        for key, value in tool_args.items():
            if isinstance(value, str):
                tool_args[key] = self._redact_text(value)

        return None  # Allow tool execution with redacted args

    def _redact_text(self, text: str) -> str:
        """Apply all redaction patterns to text."""
        for pattern, replacement in self.patterns.items():
            text = re.sub(pattern, replacement, text, flags=re.IGNORECASE)
        return text

# Production deployment: Apply plugin at runner level for all agents
from google.adk.runners import InMemoryRunner
from google.adk.runners import Runner
from google.adk.sessions import VertexAiSessionService

# Initialize your agents
healthcare_agent = Agent(
    name="HealthcareSupport",
    model="gemini-2.5-flash",
    instruction="You help patients with appointment scheduling and basic inquiries.",
    tools=[schedule_appointment, lookup_patient_info]
)

billing_agent = Agent(
    name="BillingSupport",
    model="gemini-2.5-flash",
    instruction="You help with insurance and billing questions.",
```

```
    tools=[check_coverage, process_claim]
)

# Deploy with application-wide PII protection
runner = Runner(
    agent=healthcare_agent,  # or billing_agent, or any other agent
    app_name="healthcare_system",
    session_service=VertexAiSessionService(project=PROJECT_ID, location=LOCATION),
    plugins=[
        PIIRedactionPlugin(),  # Applies to ALL agents using this runner
        # Add other custom plugins as needed
    ]
)

# For development/testing with in-memory session storage
dev_runner = InMemoryRunner(
    agent=healthcare_agent,
    app_name="healthcare_system",
    plugins=[PIIRedactionPlugin()]
)
```

This plug-in-based approach ensures that even if users accidentally share sensitive information or the model underlying the agent attempts to generate it, PII never appears in logs or responses.

These patterns—asynchronous operations, HITL controls, and systematic monitoring through custom plug-ins—transform your agent from a capable prototype into a production system ready for enterprise deployment.

Looking Ahead

Our customer support agent handles single conversations brilliantly. It processes multimodal inputs, orchestrates tools, manages state, and recovers from errors. However, what happens when problems exceed the agent's capabilities?

Real customer issues often span multiple domains. A billing problem might require technical investigation. A technical issue might have warranty implications. A warranty claim might need financial approval. Single agents, no matter how well designed, hit natural boundaries.

This is where multiagent systems become essential. Instead of building ever-more-complex single agents, we build teams of specialists that collaborate. A technical specialist deeply understands product issues and troubleshooting. A billing expert navigates financial policies and payment systems. A warranty agent interprets coverage rules and claim procedures. A coordinator routes requests and synthesizes responses across all these specialists.

Chapter 4 explores these patterns in depth. You'll discover how agents find each other's capabilities, share context without confusion, and maintain conversation coherence across handoffs. You'll learn when single agents suffice and when you need the power of agent teams.

The principles remain the same: clear state boundaries, graceful error handling, and performance focus. But the implementation shifts from monolithic to distributed, from single-threaded to concurrent, from one voice to a coordinated chorus.

Our customer support agent is complete. Next, we'll discuss how to make agents production-ready through evaluation and optimization in Chapter 5 and ensure that agents stay production ready through ML/AgentOps best practices, discussed in Chapter 7. In the next chapter, Chapter 4, you'll get a glimpse of how specialized agents can work together to solve problems no single agent could handle alone.

Learning Labs

To reinforce the ADK concepts covered in this chapter and build your own production-ready agents, we recommend exploring the learning resources available in the Chapter 3 folder in the book's GitHub repository (*https://oreil.ly/pgkpX*). Key resources you will find linked there include:

- **Hands-On Code Examples**
  - Personalized shopping agent (*https://oreil.ly/c4YIZ*): A stateful agent implementation that uses custom search and navigation tools to traverse a product catalog
  - Data Science Multiagent System (*https://oreil.ly/OK-G1*): A reference architecture that demonstrates multiagent orchestration with BigQuery and AlloyDB integration to generate analytical insights
  - Financial Advisor Multiagent System (*https://oreil.ly/4PrQm*): A reference architecture of a specialized agent team that collaborates to analyze markets, develop trading strategies, and evaluate risk
  - Weather Bot agent team tutorial (*https://oreil.ly/sAwCT*): A progressive, notebook-based journey from basic agents through multiagent delegation, state management, and safety callbacks
- **Video**
  - Getting started with Agent Development Kit (*https://oreil.ly/-ahWt*): Covers agent definition, runners, services, and local debugging with ADK's built-in tools Tutorials
  - Vibe Coding: Building ADK Agents with Gemini CLI (*https://oreil.ly/RiUEb*): An advanced workflow tutorial showing how to use "Vibe Coding" and

context engineering to rapidly scaffold and deploy production-ready ADK agents without writing boilerplate code

— Build, Test, and Deploy with ADK (*https://oreil.ly/KRl2V*): A comprehensive technical walkthrough demonstrating how to define agents, integrate tools, debug using the ADK Web UI traces, and deploy to Cloud Run

Orchestrating Intelligent Agent Teams

"My new smart thermostat is showing a wiring error, and I think it might have overcharged my last bill. Can you check if it's eligible for a warranty replacement and fix the billing issue?"

This is the kind of query that arrives every day in customer service systems. It's deceptively simple—just a brief message from a frustrated customer. But look closer, and you'll see it demands expertise from three entirely different domains: technical diagnostics for the wiring error, warranty policy interpretation for the replacement eligibility, and financial reconciliation for the billing correction.

In Chapter 3, we built a capable customer support agent using the ADK. It handled conversations gracefully, managed state across sessions, processed multimodal inputs, and executed tools reliably. For many single-domain problems, it was exactly the right solution. But throw this multidomain query at it, and you'll quickly discover the architectural limits of what we call the "monolithic agent" approach.

The Bottleneck of the Monolithic Agent

Let's examine what happens when you try to handle this query with a single LlmAgent as shown in Example 4-1.

Example 4-1. A monolithic support agent antipattern

```
# The monolithic agent antipattern
monolithic_support_agent = Agent(
    model="gemini-2.5-flash",
    name="UniversalSupportAgent",
    instruction="""You are a universal customer support agent handling:
    - Technical troubleshooting for smart home devices
    - Warranty eligibility determination and replacement processing
```

```
        - Billing inquiries, corrections, and refund processing

    When handling wiring issues, check device logs and error codes...
    When processing warranties, verify purchase date and coverage terms...
    When correcting billing, calculate prorated amounts and...
    [Instructions continue for 500+ more lines]
    """,
    tools=[
        check_device_diagnostics,
        lookup_error_codes,
        verify_warranty_status,
        process_warranty_claim,
        fetch_billing_history,
        calculate_refund,
        issue_credit,
        schedule_technician,
        order_replacement,
        send_confirmation_email,
        # ... 50 more tools
    ]
)
```

This approach creates several critical problems that become apparent only when you move beyond demos and into production use.

Conflicting Instructions

Technical troubleshooting demands a methodical, diagnostic mindset:

> "Check error logs, identify the faulty component, and recommend specific fixes."

Billing correction requires a financial compliance mindset:

> "Verify charge accuracy, calculate corrections, document adjustments for audit trails."

Warranty processing needs a policy interpretation mindset:

> "Parse coverage terms, check eligibility dates, follow replacement workflows."

Cramming all three domains into a single instruction set creates cognitive dissonance—the agent must constantly context-switch between fundamentally different ways of thinking. As instruction sets grow larger, they consume valuable context space and this can lead to confusion about which paradigm to apply (*https://oreil.ly/ h-Z9k*).

Tool Selection Paralysis

With 50+ tools at its disposal, the agent faces a combinatorial explosion in decision making. For each user query, it must evaluate which subset of tools is relevant, in what order to invoke them, and how to interpret their outputs. This "analysis paralysis" increases latency, burns tokens unnecessarily, and introduces errors as the model struggles to navigate an overwhelming decision space (*https://oreil.ly/06DeC*).

Token Limitations

Large instruction sets and extensive tool lists push token limits, forcing you to either truncate critical context or upgrade to more expensive models.

Maintenance Nightmare

When the billing team updates their refund policy, you must carefully edit the monolithic instruction set without breaking the technical troubleshooting logic. When the warranty team adds a new product line, you must add more tools and instructions without creating conflicts with existing billing rules. Every change requires understanding the entire system, testing across all domains, and hoping nothing breaks unexpectedly.

Watch what happens when this monolithic agent encounters our customer's query (Example 4-2).

Example 4-2. Breakdown of a monolithic agent

```
$ adk run customer_support_agent
---
[user]: My new smart thermostat is showing a wiring error, and I think it
might have overcharged my last bill. Can you check if it's eligible for a
warranty replacement and fix the billing issue?

[UniversalSupportAgent]: I'll help you with your thermostat issue. Let me
start by checking the device diagnostics...
[calls check_device_diagnostics]
[calls lookup_error_codes]

I see the wiring error. Before we proceed with warranty, could you clarify
what you mean by overcharged on your bill? Are you referring to your utility
bill or the purchase price?

[user]: My utility bill. It's been unusually high since I installed it.

[UniversalSupportAgent]: I understand, but I handle product warranties and
technical issues. For utility billing concerns, you would need to contact
your utility provider directly. However, let's focus on fixing the wiring error.
Please check if the C-wire is securely inserted into the terminal...
```

The agent gets lost in the complexity. It starts down the technical troubleshooting path, then realizes it needs clarification about the billing issue, but ultimately can't bridge the gap between technical diagnostics and utility billing analysis. Even worse, it doesn't recognize that the wiring error might *cause* the billing problem—a connection that requires synthesizing insights from both domains at once.

The Solution: An Agent Team

The alternative is elegantly simple: instead of building one agent that tries to do everything, build a team of specialists that each do one thing exceptionally well (Example 4-3).

Example 4-3. A multiagent approach including specialist agents and a coordinator agent

```
# The specialist approach
technical_agent = Agent(
    model="gemini-2.5-flash",
    name="TechnicalSpecialist",
    instruction="""You diagnose and resolve technical issues with smart home
    devices. Focus on device diagnostics, error codes, and repair procedures.""",
    tools=[
        check_device_diagnostics,
        lookup_error_codes,
        schedule_technician
    ]
)

warranty_agent = Agent(
    model="gemini-2.5-flash",
    name="WarrantySpecialist",
    instruction="""You determine warranty eligibility and process claims.
    Verify coverage, check dates, and initiate replacements.""",
    tools=[
        verify_warranty_status,
        process_warranty_claim,
        order_replacement
    ]
)

billing_agent = Agent(
    model="gemini-2.5-flash",
    name="BillingSpecialist",
    instruction="""You handle billing inquiries and corrections. Analyze
    charges, calculate refunds, and process credits.""",
    tools=[
        fetch_billing_history,
        calculate_refund,
        issue_credit
    ]
)
```

```
# A coordinator that routes to specialists
coordinator_agent = Agent(
    model="gemini-2.5-flash",
    name="CustomerServiceCoordinator",
    instruction="""You coordinate customer support by routing queries to
    specialist agents. Delegate technical issues to TechnicalSpecialist,
    warranty questions to WarrantySpecialist, and billing problems to
    BillingSpecialist.""",
    sub_agents=[technical_agent, warranty_agent, billing_agent]
)
```

This architecture solves all the problems we identified. Each specialist has clear, focused instructions without cognitive dissonance. Each specialist works with a small, relevant tool set without decision paralysis. Each specialist can use a smaller, faster model because its scope is narrower. Each specialist can be updated independently without touching the others.

But most importantly, the coordinator can now understand the relationships between domains because its instructions focus on orchestration. When it receives our multidomain query, it can recognize that the wiring error might cause the billing problem not because it understands thermostats or billing systems, but because it understands workflows and dependencies. It delegates to the technical specialist first to diagnose the root cause, receives a structured diagnostic report, then uses that information to help the billing specialist understand whether charges are legitimate or error-induced.

This is the essence of a multiagent system (MAS): building intelligent systems from simpler, focused components that collaborate to solve complex problems. The intelligence emerges not from a single, all-knowing agent, but from the orchestration of specialists working together.

The Roadmap: From Local Teams to Distributed Systems

Building effective multiagent systems requires mastering three progressively advanced architectural patterns, each solving a different class of problems.

First, we'll learn to compose agents *locally* using ADK's workflow agents. These are the orchestration primitives—SequentialAgent, ParallelAgent, and LoopAgent—that let you define how agents collaborate within a single application. Think of this as building a team that works together in the same office, sharing memory and context naturally. This is where most multiagent systems start, and for many applications, it's where they can stay.

Then, we'll learn to connect agents across network boundaries using the *Agent-to-Agent (A2A)* protocol and the *Model Concept Protocol (MCP)*. This is the shift from local teams to distributed systems, where agents run as independent microservices, possibly owned by different teams or even different organizations. The *BillingAgent* might run on the finance team's infrastructure, the *TechnicalAgent* on the support team's servers, and the *WarrantyAgent* as a third-party service. A2A and MCP provide the standardized communication protocols that make this distribution possible without sacrificing the seamless collaboration you achieved locally.

Finally, we'll address the critical production concerns that arise in these distributed systems. When agents communicate across network boundaries, you face challenges that don't exist in local systems: how does the BillingAgent authenticate the CoordinatorAgent? How do you trace a request that fails across multiple services? How do you ensure accountability when agents from different organizations interact? These are practical realities that determine whether your multiagent system works in production or fails under real-world conditions.

By the end of this chapter, you'll understand not just how to build multiagent systems, but how to architect them for the scale, security, and reliability that production environments demand. Let's begin with the foundation: local orchestration using workflow agents.

Local Teams

Before we can build teams of agents, we need to understand how ADK structures agent relationships. The architecture is surprisingly simple: agents form parent-child hierarchies where a coordinator agent manages specialist subagents. This hierarchical structure provides the foundation for all multiagent patterns in ADK, whether you're building local teams or distributed systems.

The Foundation: Agent Hierarchy

At the heart of every multiagent system in ADK is the sub_agents parameter, illustrated in Example 4-4. When you pass a list of agents to this parameter, you're establishing a formal parent-child relationship.

Example 4-4. The use of subagents with coordinator agent delegation

```
from google.adk.agents import Agent

# Define specialist agents
technical_agent = Agent(
    model="gemini-2.5-flash",
    name="TechnicalSpecialist",
    description="Diagnoses technical issues with smart home devices",
    instruction=("You troubleshoot device problems, interpret error codes, "
                 "and recommend solutions.")
)
```

```
warranty_agent = Agent(
    model="gemini-2.5-flash",
    name="WarrantySpecialist",
    description="Determines warranty eligibility and processes claims",
    instruction=("You verify coverage, check eligibility dates, and "
                 "initiate replacements.")
)

# Create a coordinator with specialists as subagents
coordinator = Agent(
    model="gemini-2.5-flash",
    name="SupportCoordinator",
    instruction="""You coordinate customer support by delegating to specialists.
    Route technical problems to TechnicalSpecialist and warranty questions to
    WarrantySpecialist.""",
    sub_agents=[technical_agent, warranty_agent]
)
```

This code establishes a simple hierarchy: `coordinator` is the parent and `techni cal_agent` and `warranty_agent` are its children. The parent agent doesn't need to understand technical diagnostics or warranty policies—it just needs to know when to delegate to agents that do.

The `description` parameter on each subagent is critical here. When the coordinator receives a query such as "My device won't power on," it uses these descriptions to determine which specialist can help. The LLM powering the coordinator reads the descriptions, understands the user's intent, and delegates accordingly. This is LLM-driven routing—the coordinator agent uses its language understanding to make intelligent delegation decisions.

This dynamic routing, while powerful, isn't always what you need. Sometimes you want deterministic control over execution order, timing, and flow. This is where ADK's workflow agents become essential. They provide three fundamental patterns for orchestrating agent teams with predictable, reliable behavior.

Pattern 1: The Assembly Line (SequentialAgent)

Some workflows have a natural order that must be respected. In our customer support scenario, you can't check warranty eligibility before you know what's wrong with the device. You can't process a replacement claim before verifying that the customer owns the product. These dependencies demand sequential execution—each step must complete before the next begins.

Consider the warranty claim workflow. When a customer reports a defective thermostat, you need to diagnose the issue to confirm that it's a defect and not user error, verify that the product is under warranty and the customer is eligible, and then process the replacement claim with the correct product details. Each step depends on information from the previous step, making sequential execution essential.

Here's how you implement this workflow using SequentialAgent, illustrated in Figure 4-1 and shown in Example 4-5.

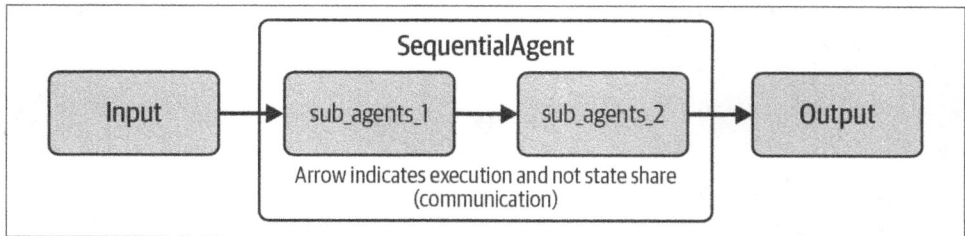

Figure 4-1. Overview of a sequential agent

Example 4-5. Implementation of a sequential agent workflow

```python
from google.adk.agents import Agent, SequentialAgent
# Step 1: Diagnose the issue
diagnostic_agent = Agent(
    model="gemini-2.5-flash",
    name="DiagnosticAgent",
    instruction="""Analyze the reported issue and determine if it's a product
    defect or user error. Save your conclusion to state.""",
    output_key="diagnosis_result",
    tools=[check_device_logs, analyze_error_patterns]
)

# Step 2: Check warranty eligibility
warranty_check_agent = Agent(
    model="gemini-2.5-flash",
    name="WarrantyCheckAgent",
    instruction="""Based on the diagnosis in {diagnosis_result}, verify if
    this issue is covered under warranty. Check purchase date and coverage terms.""",
    output_key="warranty_status",
    tools=[lookup_purchase_date, check_coverage_terms]
)

# Step 3: Process the claim
claim_processor = Agent(
    model="gemini-2.5-flash",
    name="ClaimProcessor",
    instruction="""If {warranty_status} indicates coverage, process the
    replacement claim. Use details from {diagnosis_result}.""",
    tools=[initiate_replacement, send_confirmation]
)

# Orchestrate the sequence
warranty_claim_workflow = SequentialAgent(
    name="WarrantyClaimWorkflow",
    sub_agents=[diagnostic_agent, warranty_check_agent, claim_processor]
)
```

The `SequentialAgent` executes these specialists in strict order: first, `diagnostic_agent`, then `warranty_check_agent`, then `claim_processor`. But notice the intelligence in how they communicate. The `diagnostic_agent` saves its conclusion to `state["diagnosis_result"]` using the `output_key` parameter. The `warranty_check_agent` then reads this value directly from the state using the `{diagnosis_result}` placeholder in its instruction. This state-based communication is how sequential agents pass information forward through the pipeline.

The power of this pattern lies in its predictability. You know exactly when each agent runs, what information it receives, and where it stores its output. This deterministic behavior makes sequential workflows easy to debug, test, and reason about. When a warranty claim fails, you can trace through the sequence step by step to find exactly where and why it broke.

Behind the scenes, the `SequentialAgent` passes the same `InvocationContext` to each subagent. This shared context means they all access the same session state, making data flow effortless. The first agent writes to state, the second agent reads from it, the third agent builds on both—all happening naturally through the shared context.

Pattern 2: The Independent Taskforce (ParallelAgent)

Not all tasks have dependencies. Sometimes you need multiple pieces of information that can be gathered simultaneously. When a customer asks about their thermostat's energy usage, you might need to fetch their purchase history from the order database, retrieve the product manual from the documentation system, and pull their usage data from the telemetry service. None of these tasks depends on the others—they can all happen at once.

This is where `ParallelAgent`, illustrated in Figure 4-2, transforms performance. Instead of waiting for each operation to complete sequentially, it executes all subagents concurrently, as shown in Example 4-6.

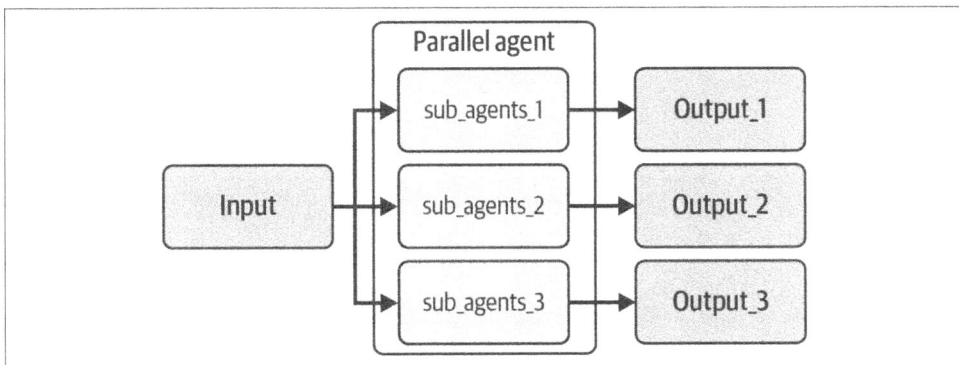

Figure 4-2. Overview of a parallel agent

Example 4-6. Implementation of a parallel agent workflow

```python
from google.adk.agents import Agent, ParallelAgent
# Independent information gathering agents
purchase_history_agent = Agent(
    model="gemini-2.5-flash",
    name="PurchaseHistoryAgent",
    instruction="Fetch and summarize the customer's purchase history.",
    output_key="purchase_data",
    tools=[query_order_database]
)

manual_lookup_agent = Agent(
    model="gemini-2.5-flash",
    name="ManualLookupAgent",
    instruction="Retrieve the product manual and relevant troubleshooting guides.",
    output_key="manual_content",
    tools=[fetch_product_manual, get_troubleshooting_guides]
)

usage_analysis_agent = Agent(
    model="gemini-2.5-flash",
    name="UsageAnalysisAgent",
    instruction="Analyze the device's usage patterns and energy consumption.",
    output_key="usage_data",
    tools=[query_telemetry_service, calculate_energy_metrics]
)

# Execute all information gathering concurrently
info_gathering_taskforce = ParallelAgent(
    name="InformationGathering",
    sub_agents=[purchase_history_agent, manual_lookup_agent, usage_analysis_agent]
)

# A synthesis agent processes the combined results
synthesis_agent = Agent(
    model="gemini-2.5-flash",
    name="SynthesisAgent",
    instruction="""Combine information from {purchase_data}, {manual_content},
    and {usage_data} to provide comprehensive support."""
)

# Complete workflow: gather in parallel, then synthesize
support_workflow = SequentialAgent(
    name="ComprehensiveSupport",
    sub_agents=[info_gathering_taskforce, synthesis_agent]
)
```

When `info_gathering_taskforce` executes, all three subagents run simultaneously. The `ParallelAgent` launches them concurrently and collects their results as they complete. Each agent still uses `output_key` to save its findings to state, but now these writes happen in parallel rather than sequence. The workflow waits for all three to finish before invoking the synthesis_agent to process the combined information.

The performance benefit is substantial. If each information-gathering operation takes two seconds, sequential execution requires approximately six seconds total. Parallel execution completes in approximately two seconds—the duration of the slowest operation. For workflows involving multiple API calls, database queries, or external service requests, this concurrent execution can reduce latency by an order of magnitude.

One important consideration: parallel agents must be truly independent. They can all read from the shared state, but if they try to modify the same state keys, you'll encounter race conditions. This is why each agent in our example writes to a distinct output_key. The framework provides the concurrent execution infrastructure, but you must design your agents to avoid conflicts.

Pattern 3: The Iterative Refiner (LoopAgent)

Some problems can't be solved in a single pass. When a customer describes an intermittent issue—"My thermostat sometimes shows the wrong temperature"—you need an iterative approach: suggest a potential fix, ask the customer to test it, evaluate the results, and repeat if necessary. This iterative refinement is the domain of LoopAgent, illustrated in Figure 4-3.

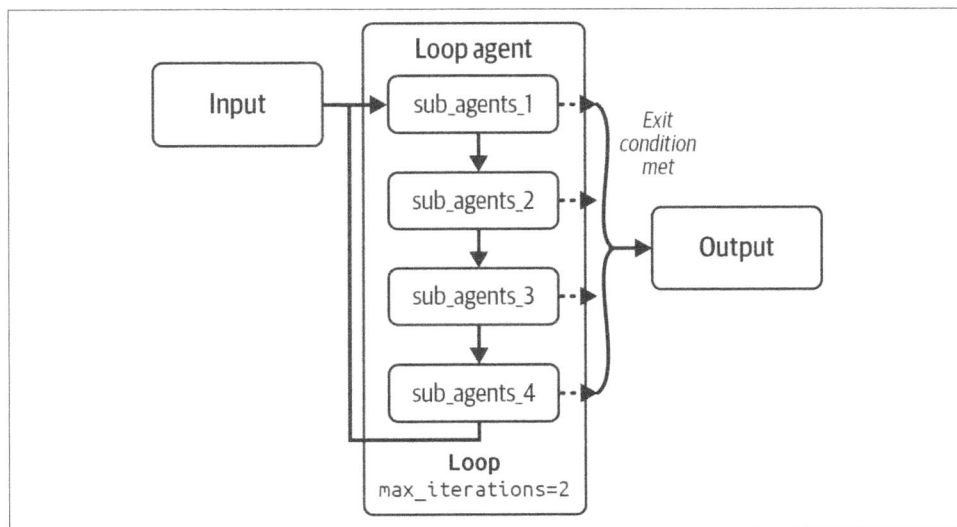

Figure 4-3. Overview of a loop agent

Consider a troubleshooting workflow shown in Example 4-7, where you want to try progressively more involved solutions until the problem resolves.

Example 4-7. Implementation of a loop agent workflow

```python
from google.adk.agents import Agent, LoopAgent

# Agent that suggests a solution
solution_agent = Agent(
    model="gemini-2.5-flash",
    name="SolutionAgent",
    # Assumes 'issue_description' was populated by a previous agent/callback
    instruction=(
        "Based on {issue_description} and {previous_attempts} and the "
        "previously suggested solution '{suggested_solution}', if any, "
        "suggest the next troubleshooting step. Start with simple "
        "solutions and progress to more complex ones."
    ),
    output_key="suggested_solution",
    tools=[lookup_troubleshooting_steps, check_known_issues]
)

# Agent that validates if the solution worked
validation_agent = Agent(
    model="gemini-2.5-flash",
    name="ValidationAgent",
    instruction=(
        "Ask the customer to test {suggested_solution} and report "
        "results. Determine if the issue is resolved."
    ),
    output_key="solution_status",
    tools=[prompt_user_for_feedback, analyze_test_results, check_resolution]
)

# Loop until resolved or max attempts reached
troubleshooting_loop = LoopAgent(
    name="TroubleshootingLoop",
    sub_agents=[solution_agent, validation_agent],
    max_iterations=5
)
```

The LoopAgent executes its subagents repeatedly. Each iteration runs solution_agent and then validation_agent in sequence. The state persists across iterations— previous_attempts (incremented by a callback or tool) accumulates, allowing solution_agent to avoid suggesting the same fix twice and progress to more advanced solutions.

The loop terminates in two ways. First, if it reaches max_iterations (five attempts in this example), it stops to prevent infinite loops. Second, any subagent can signal success by returning an event with escalate=True in its actions. When validation_agent determines the issue is resolved, it escalates to terminate the loop early, as shown in Example 4-8.

Example 4-8. Validation step of a loop agent workflow

```
from google.adk.agents import Agent
from google.adk.events import Event, EventActions

validation_agent = Agent(
    model="gemini-2.5-flash",
    name="ValidationAgent",
    instruction="""Ask the customer to test {suggested_solution}. If they
    report the issue is resolved, you MUST indicate success.""",
    output_key="solution_status"
)

# In practice, you'd implement this logic in a custom tool or callback
# that checks the solution_status and returns an escalating event when resolved
async def check_resolution(tool_context):
    status = tool_context.state.get("solution_status", "")
    if "resolved" in status.lower() or "fixed" in status.lower():
        tool_context.actions.escalate = True
    return {}
```

This termination mechanism is crucial. Without it, your loop would always run the maximum number of iterations, wasting time and tokens on unnecessary attempts after the problem is already solved. With it, your agent responds efficiently, stopping as soon as success is achieved while still having a safety limit to prevent infinite execution.

The LoopAgent is particularly valuable for workflows that involve trial and error, progressive refinement, or iterative improvement. Troubleshooting, content revision, parameter optimization—any process where you can't determine the right solution upfront but can evaluate proposed solutions iteratively benefits from this pattern.

These three workflow agents—SequentialAgent, ParallelAgent, and LoopAgent—provide the building blocks for orchestrating agent teams locally. You can compose them hierarchically: a SequentialAgent might contain a ParallelAgent as one step, or a LoopAgent might include a SequentialAgent in its iteration. This composability lets you build complex workflows from simple, predictable components.

These patterns all assume your agents run within the same application, sharing memory and state naturally. What happens when your agents need to run as independent services, possibly on different infrastructure or even owned by different organizations? That's where we move from local orchestration to distributed collaboration.

Distributed Collaboration

The workflow agents we've built work beautifully—as long as all your agents live in the same application. The `SequentialAgent` passes state seamlessly because everything shares the same memory. The `ParallelAgent` coordinates concurrent execution because all subagents run in the same process. This local orchestration is simple, fast, and requires minimal network overhead.

This pattern serves many production use cases well. But some scenarios require agents to run as independent services, particularly when organizational boundaries come into play.

The Organizational "Why"

Let's revisit our `BillingAgent`. In our examples so far, we've treated it as just another specialist agent—a Python object instantiated alongside the `TechnicalAgent` and `WarrantyAgent`, all running in the same customer support application.

In many organizations, billing lives in a separate domain. The finance team often maintains their own systems, databases, and compliance requirements. The billing logic isn't a simple function you can import—it's a complex service that handles payment processing, refund calculations, tax compliance, fraud detection, and audit trails. This service typically runs on infrastructure the finance team controls, using databases only they can access, following security policies only they enforce.

When the customer support team needs billing information, they can't just instantiate a `BillingAgent` object in their Python code. The billing service exists as an independent microservice, running on separate servers, maintained by a different team with different deployment schedules and different service-level agreements (SLAs). This pattern—specialized capabilities living in specialized services—is common in enterprise architecture.

You'll see similar patterns, illustrated in Figure 4-4, throughout organizations.

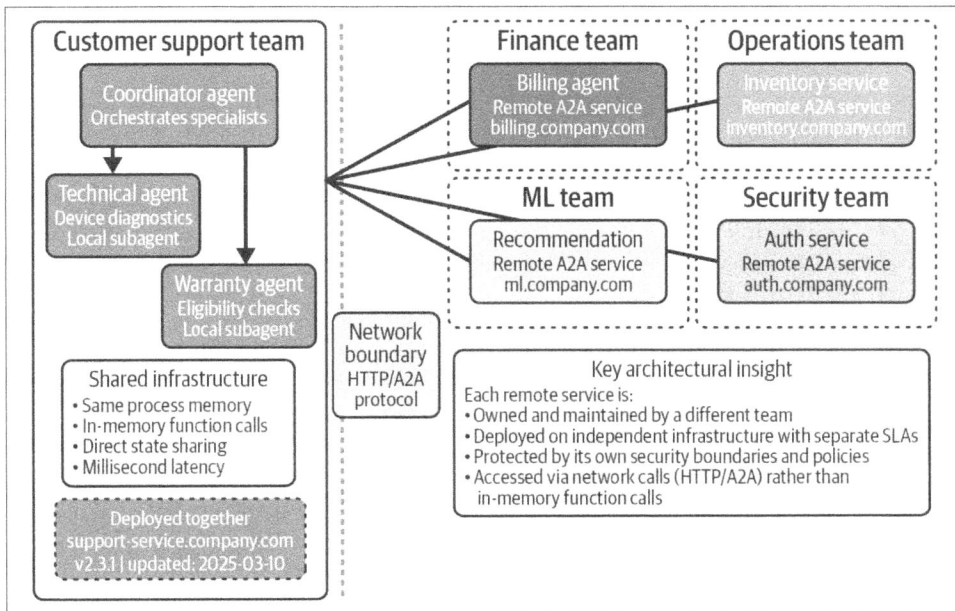

Figure 4-4. Common organization boundaries in enterprise multiagent architecture

The inventory system runs as a service owned by operations. The recommendation engine runs as a service owned by the ML team. The authentication service runs on infrastructure managed by the security team. Each team builds, deploys, and maintains their service independently. Your customer support agent needs to work with all of them, but none of them exist as local code you can import.

This shift from local modules to independent services introduces a fundamental architectural change. You're no longer orchestrating agents within a single application—you're coordinating agents across network boundaries, where each agent is a service with its own lifecycle, its own infrastructure, and its own team of maintainers.

This is the problem that the A2A Protocol (*https://oreil.ly/O9aqk*) and MCP (*https://oreil.ly/C7TSS*) solve. They provide standardized ways for agents to discover, communicate with, and invoke other agents and tools across these organizational and network boundaries. Before we dive into how these protocols work, we need to understand the distinction between the two patterns we're discussing.

Local agents are what we've been building so far. These are agent instances that exist within your application's code. When you create a SequentialAgent with subagents, those subagents are Python objects (or Java objects or Go structs—depending on your ADK language) instantiated in your process memory. They share the same InvocationContext, access the same session state, and communicate through direct function calls. This is internal code organization—different classes working together within a single application boundary.

Remote agents are independent services. They run in separate processes, possibly on different servers, possibly managed by different teams or organizations. They have their own memory space, their own state management, their own security boundaries. When your agent needs to work with a remote agent, it makes network calls over HTTP, following standardized protocols that both sides understand. This is distributed systems architecture—independent services collaborating across organizational and network boundaries.

The distinction might seem academic until you consider what it means in practice. With local subagents, when your CoordinatorAgent delegates to the BillingAgent, it's an in-memory agent invocation that completes in near real time. The state is already in memory. There's no network latency, no serialization overhead, no authentication required. With remote agents, that same delegation becomes an HTTP request that might take hundreds of milliseconds. The request must be serialized, transmitted over the network, authenticated, processed by a separate service, and the response transmitted back. If the billing service is down or slow, your coordinator agent must handle that failure gracefully.

This distinction shapes everything about how you build your system. Local subagents let you move fast—you can refactor freely, share state easily, and debug by stepping through code. Remote agents require you to think carefully about boundaries—you design explicit contracts, handle network failures, implement authentication, and monitor distributed traces. Neither approach is better; they solve different problems. The art is knowing when to use each.

Here's a simple heuristic: if two agents need to share the same organizational context—same team, deployment, database, security boundary—keep them local. Use workflow agents to orchestrate them within a single application. But when agents cross organizational boundaries, when they're maintained by different teams with different lifecycles, make them remote and use A2A or MCP to connect them.

In our customer support example, the TechnicalAgent and WarrantyAgent might stay local—both are owned by the customer support team, deployed together, and share the same customer database. The BillingAgent becomes remote because it's owned by Finance, runs on its infrastructure, and accesses its protected financial systems. The coordinator agent orchestrates the local specialists directly while communicating with the remote billing service through a standardized protocol.

This is where A2A and MCP enter the picture. They provide the standardized protocols that make remote agent communication possible without requiring custom integration code for every service.

The agent communication landscape is still evolving, and several protocols exist for enabling distributed agent systems. While we focus on A2A and MCP in this chapter, you may encounter other frameworks in the wild—such as IBM's Agent Communication Protocol (*https://oreil.ly/UX47q*) (ACP) or various proprietary solutions from other vendors. We've chosen to focus on A2A and MCP because they represent the most widely adopted open standards, with strong community support and active development. However, the community hasn't fully centralized on a single standard yet, and the patterns and architectural principles we discuss here apply regardless of which protocol you ultimately choose.

Let's examine each protocol and understand when to use which.

MCP: The Language of Tools

When your agent needs to query a database, call an API, or execute a specific function on a remote system, you don't need another stateful agent. You need a tool—a stateless request-response interaction that takes inputs, performs a defined action, and returns results. This is the domain of the MCP, illustrated in Figure 4-5.

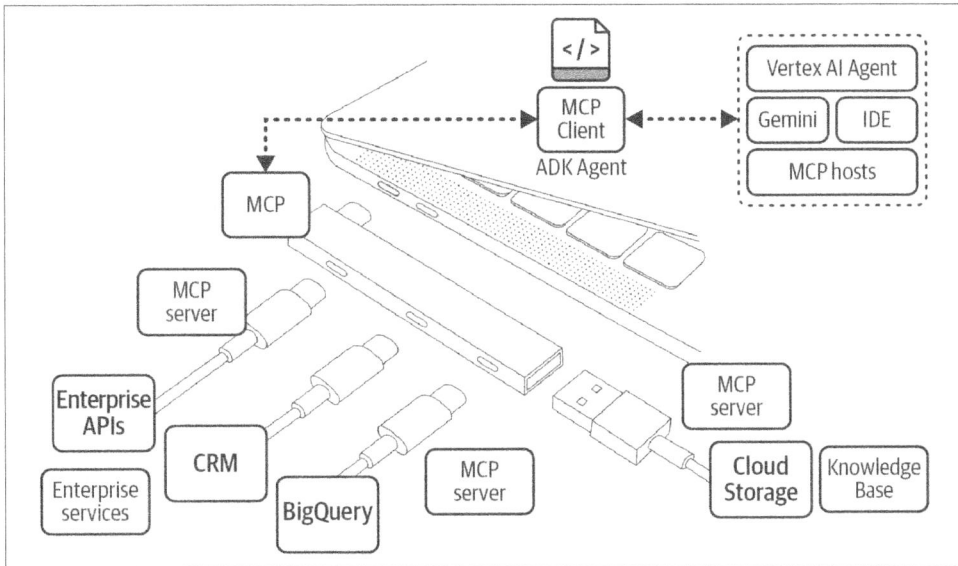

Figure 4-5. The "USB for AI" analogy: connecting models to diverse data sources via a standard protocol

MCP is an open standard for exposing resources—databases, APIs, filesystems, external services—as tools that any LLM-powered agent can discover and use. Think of it as a universal adapter that turns diverse backend systems into a standardized tool interface. Instead of writing custom integration code for every database or API your agent needs to access, you connect to an MCP server that already speaks the protocol.

The protocol is deliberately simple. An MCP server exposes a catalog of available tools, each with a clear schema defining its inputs and outputs. Your agent queries the server to discover what tools exist, reads their schemas to understand how to use them, then invokes them like any other function. The server handles the actual interaction with the underlying resource—executing SQL queries, making REST API calls, reading files—and returns structured results your agent can process.

ADK makes working with MCP servers straightforward through the MCPToolset. Example 4-9 shows how you might connect your customer support agent to a database of customer information.

Example 4-9. Connecting an agent to an external database with MCPToolset

```
from google.adk.tools import MCPToolset
from google.adk.tools.mcp_tool.mcp_session_manager import SseConnectionParams

# Connect to an MCP server that exposes your customer database
customer_db_tools = McpToolset(
    connection_params=SseConnectionParams(
        url="http://customer-db-mcp.internal:8080"
    ),
    tool_name_prefix="CustomerDatabase"
)

# Your agent can now use these tools
support_agent = Agent(
    model="gemini-2.5-flash",
    name="SupportAgent",
    instruction=(
        "You help customers with their orders. Use CustomerDatabase tools "
        "to look up order details."
    ),
    tools=[customer_db_tools]
)
```

The agent doesn't need to know SQL or understand the database schema. The MCP server exposes high-level operations like lookup_customer_by_email or get_order_history, handling the underlying database complexity. Your agent simply calls these tools as needed, passing parameters and receiving structured results.

While less common than the conversational agent pattern we'll discuss next, some architectures expose agent operations through MCP. For instance, if your `BillingAgent` performs discrete, well-defined operations (`check_billing_status`, `process_refund`), you could expose these as stateless MCP tools rather than as a conversational agent. This works well when operations are atomic and independent, trading flexibility for simplicity and predictability.

For teams building agents that need to work with diverse data sources, Google provides the MCP Toolbox for Databases (*https://oreil.ly/JZfn8*)—a production-ready MCP server that exposes common databases (PostgreSQL, MySQL, BigQuery, Firestore, and many others) as ready-to-use tools. Instead of building custom database access layers, you deploy the MCP Toolbox, configure it with your database connections, and immediately get a standardized tool interface your agents can use.

Beyond generic database access, Google provides industry-specific MCP toolboxes that handle complex domain protocols. For example, the Cloud Healthcare API Toolbox (*https://oreil.ly/vD2oI*) exposes FHIR patient records and DICOM medical imaging through standardized MCP tools, allowing healthcare agents to search patient data or retrieve medical images without understanding the underlying FHIR or DICOM specifications. This same pattern applies across industries—finance, legal, manufacturing—where domain-specific toolboxes can expose specialized systems through the universal MCP interface.

The value becomes clear when you consider maintenance. When your database schema changes, you update the MCP server configuration—not every agent that uses the database. When you add a new data source, you extend the MCP server—not every application that needs access. The protocol provides a clean separation between data access logic and agent logic, letting each evolve independently.

Taking this a step further, Google Cloud offers fully managed remote MCP servers (*https://oreil.ly/-_SjJ*) for its core services. Instead of deploying and hosting your own MCP intermediate layer, you can connect your agents directly to global, enterprise-ready endpoints for services like BigQuery, Google Maps, and Google Kubernetes Engine (GKE). These managed endpoints handle the translation between MCP and the service API automatically, enforcing IAM permissions and providing built-in observability without any infrastructure management on your part.

Regardless of whether the server is managed or self-hosted, MCP has a natural boundary: it works beautifully for stateless operations where you have a clear input-output relationship. Query a database, get results. Call an API, receive a response. These are function-like operations that complete quickly and deterministically. When you need something more intelligent—when you want to delegate an entire goal to another intelligent system that can reason, plan, and adapt—you need a different protocol.

A2A: The Language of Delegation

A2A enables agents to delegate complex, multiturn goals to other agents, illustrated in Figure 4-6. Unlike MCP's request-response pattern, A2A supports stateful interactions where an agent can ask clarifying questions, reason through problems, and adapt its approach based on what it learns.

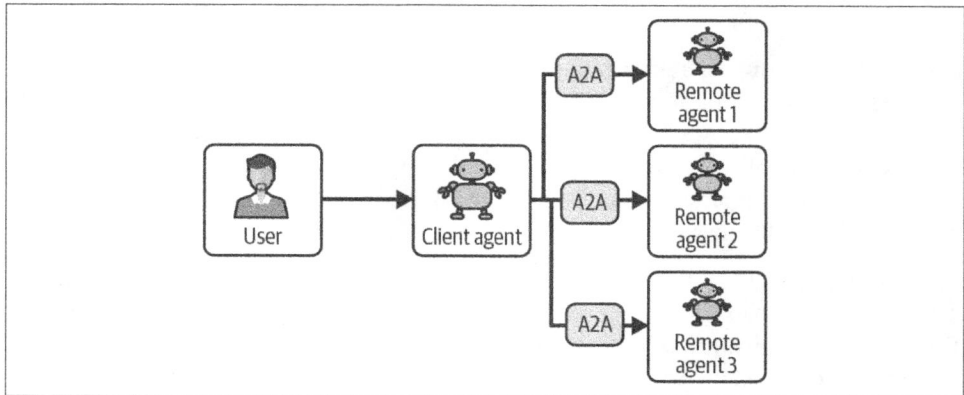

Figure 4-6. Overview of A2A delegation among agents

Consider billing scenarios that require judgment and context. When a customer reports "I was overcharged after installing a faulty thermostat," the support agent needs to delegate a complex investigation—explain the full situation to a billing specialist, have them analyze it in context, possibly ask clarifying questions, apply policy judgment, and reach a conclusion. This conversational, context-rich delegation is what A2A enables.

Just as MCP standardizes tool interactions, A2A standardizes agent-to-agent delegation. It defines how agents discover each other's capabilities, communicate their needs, and exchange results. Unlike MCP, A2A maintains state across multiple conversational turns, enabling the collaborative intelligence needed for ambiguous, judgment-heavy tasks.

Let's see how this works in practice by building a realistic example: our customer service coordinator working with a remote billing agent owned by the finance team.

Exposing a specialist agent: the finance team's perspective

The finance team maintains their billing service. They've built a comprehensive agent that understands billing policies, processes refunds, handles disputes, and ensures compliance with financial regulations. Now they want to make this agent available to other teams—customer support, sales, operations—without giving direct access to their internal systems or databases.

ADK makes this remarkably simple through the to_a2a() utility. Example 4-10 shows how the finance team exposes their billing agent.

Example 4-10. Exposing an agent as an A2A service with to_a2a()

```
# billing_service/agent.py - The finance team's billing agent
from google.adk.agents import Agent
from google.adk.a2a.utils.agent_to_a2a import to_a2a

# The billing agent itself - comprehensive logic for financial operations
billing_agent = Agent(
    model="gemini-2.5-flash",
    name="BillingAgent",
    instruction="""You are a billing specialist. You analyze charges, process
    refunds, handle billing disputes, and ensure compliance with financial policies.

    When analyzing billing issues:
    1. Review the customer's billing history
    2. Identify any anomalies or incorrect charges
    3. Calculate appropriate refunds or credits
    4. Explain your reasoning clearly
    5. Process approved adjustments
    """,
    tools=[
        query_billing_history,
        calculate_refund_amount,
        check_payment_status,
        process_credit,
        generate_invoice
    ]
)

# Expose this agent via A2A - generates AgentCard automatically
a2a_app = to_a2a(billing_agent, port=8001)
```

That's it. The to_a2a() function wraps the agent in an A2A-compatible server that handles all the protocol details. It automatically generates an AgentCard as illustrated in Figure 4-7.

An Agent Card is a public descriptor that explains what the agent does, its capabilities, and how to communicate with it. This card gets published at a well-known URL (/.well-known/agent-card.json), where other agents can discover it.

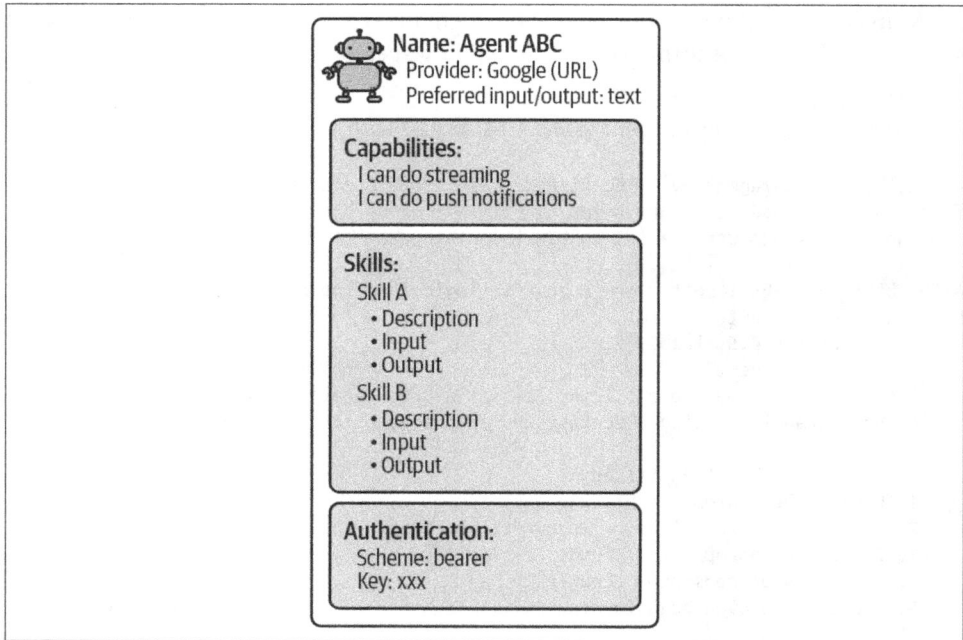

Figure 4-7. Illustration of an Agent Card

The finance team then deploys this service to their infrastructure, as shown in Example 4-11.

Example 4-11. Deploying an A2A agent service with uvicorn

```
# Start the A2A server
uvicorn billing_service.agent:a2a_app --host 0.0.0.0 --port 8001
```

Now the billing agent runs as an independent microservice. It has its own infrastructure, its own security boundary, its own deployment lifecycle. The finance team can update it without coordinating with customer support. They can scale it independently. They can enforce their own authentication and authorization policies.

From the outside, it looks like any other A2A agent—discoverable, describable, and invokable through the standard protocol. This is illustrated in Figure 4-8.

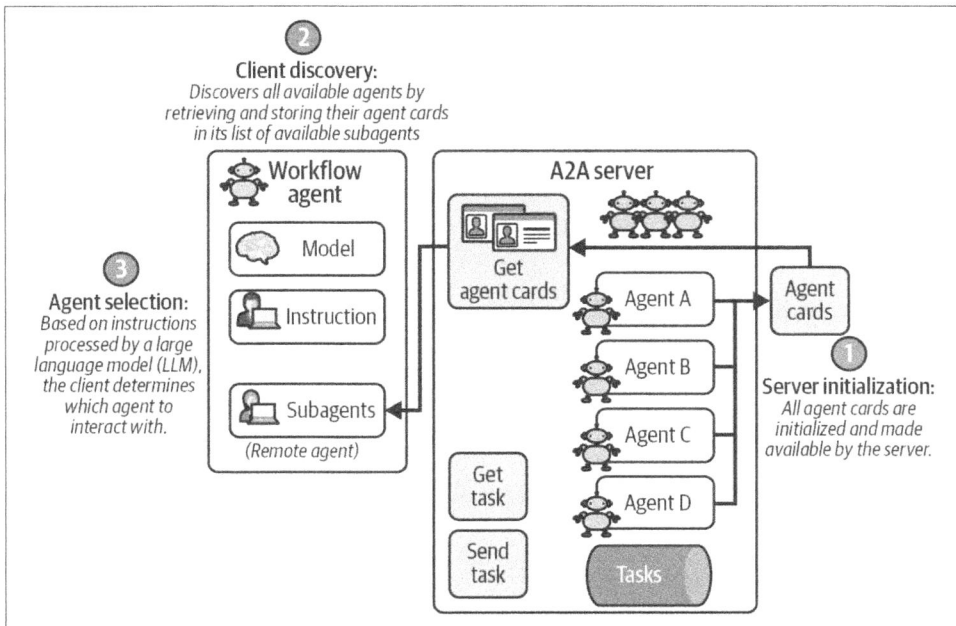

Figure 4-8. *A2A initialization, discovery, and selection process*

Consuming the specialist agent: the customer support team's perspective

Now let's switch perspectives to the customer support team. They need billing expertise, but they don't want to maintain billing logic, understand financial regulations, or access sensitive financial databases. They just want to delegate billing questions to the finance team's specialist.

ADK's `RemoteA2aAgent` makes this delegation feel local, as shown in Example 4-12.

Example 4-12. *Consuming a remote A2A agent with* `RemoteA2aAgent`

```
# support_service/agent.py - The customer support coordinator
from google.adk.agents import Agent
from google.adk.agents.remote_a2a_agent import RemoteA2aAgent

# Connect to the remote billing agent via its AgentCard
billing_agent = RemoteA2aAgent(
    name="BillingAgent",
    description="Specialist for billing inquiries, refunds, and payment issues",
    agent_card="http://billing-service.internal:8001/.well-known/agent-card.json"
)

# Use it like any other subagent
coordinator = Agent(
    model="gemini-2.5-flash",
```

```
    name="CustomerServiceCoordinator",
    instruction=(
        "You coordinate customer support by delegating to specialists.\n\n"
        "For billing questions, refund requests, or payment issues, "
        "delegate to BillingAgent. For technical problems, handle them "
        "yourself using diagnostic tools."
    ),
    sub_agents=[billing_agent],
    tools=[check_device_status, lookup_error_codes]
)
```

From the coordinator's perspective, `billing_agent` looks just like a local subagent. The coordinator can delegate to it, the billing agent processes the request with full context, and the results come back seamlessly. The customer support team doesn't see HTTP requests, JSON serialization, or network calls—they just see delegation working exactly as it does with local agents.

But under the hood, something substantial is happening. When the coordinator delegates to `billing_agent`, ADK does the following:

1. Serializes the current conversation context and the delegation request.

2. Makes an HTTP request to the billing service's A2A endpoint.

3. The billing service receives the context, spins up its agent, and processes the request.

4. The billing agent can ask clarifying questions, use its tools, and reason through the problem.

5. Once complete, it returns the result back to the coordinator.

6. The coordinator receives this as if it came from a local subagent.

The conversation remains coherent across this network boundary. The billing agent has access to the relevant context—what the customer asked, what's been discussed so far—without needing direct access to the customer support system's database or state.

Putting It All Together: A Hybrid Agent Team

Most production systems aren't purely local or purely remote—they're hybrid. Some specialists live locally, others are remote services. Let's build a realistic example, illustrated in Example 4-13, that shows this hybrid architecture in action.

Example 4-13. Hybrid agent team combining local agents, remote A2A agents, and MCP tools

```
from google.adk.agents import Agent, SequentialAgent
from google.adk.agents.remote_a2a_agent import RemoteA2aAgent
from google.adk.tools import MCPToolset
```

```python
from google.adk.tools.mcp_tool.mcp_session_manager import SseConnectionParams

# Local specialist: Technical diagnostics
technical_agent = Agent(
    model="gemini-2.5-flash",
    name="TechnicalAgent",
    description="Diagnoses technical issues with smart home devices",
    instruction="""You troubleshoot device problems. Analyze error codes,
    check device logs, and recommend solutions.""",
    output_key="technical_diagnosis",
    tools=[
        check_device_diagnostics,
        analyze_error_patterns,
        lookup_known_issues
    ]
)

# Remote specialist: Billing (owned by finance team)
billing_agent = RemoteA2aAgent(
    name="BillingAgent",
    description="Handles billing inquiries, refunds, and payment processing",
    agent_card="http://billing-service.internal:8001/.well-known/agent-card.json"
)

# MCP tools: Customer database access
customer_db = McpToolset(
    connection_params=SseConnectionParams(
        url="http://customer-db-mcp.internal:8080"
    ),
    tool_name_prefix="CustomerDatabase"
)

# The coordinator orchestrates everything
coordinator = Agent(
    model="gemini-2.5-flash",
    name="CustomerServiceCoordinator",
    instruction="""You coordinate customer support by intelligently routing
    requests and combining expertise from multiple specialists.

    For our multi-domain thermostat query:
    1. First, delegate to TechnicalAgent to diagnose the wiring error
    2. Use CustomerDB to verify the customer's purchase and usage history
    3. If the diagnosis suggests the device is defective and causing excess
       energy usage, delegate to BillingAgent to analyze if charges are
       legitimate and process any necessary credits

    Synthesize all findings into a comprehensive response.""",
    sub_agents=[technical_agent, billing_agent],
    tools=[customer_db]
)
```

Let's trace through what happens when our coordinator receives the complex query "My new smart thermostat is showing a wiring error, and I think it might have overcharged my last bill. Can you check if it's eligible for a warranty replacement and fix the billing issue?"

First, the coordinator recognizes that this needs technical expertise and delegates to the local `technical_agent`. This happens in-process, fast and simple. The technical agent uses its tools to diagnose the wiring error, determines it's a defective component, and saves its conclusion to `state["technical_diagnosis"]`.

Second, the coordinator queries the `customer_db` using MCP tools. It retrieves the purchase date, warranty status, and historical usage data. These are stateless queries—fetch data, return results. MCP handles the database interaction while keeping the agent code clean.

Third, armed with the technical diagnosis and usage history, the coordinator delegates to the remote `billing_agent`. This crosses the network boundary to the finance team's service. The billing agent receives the full context—the wiring error diagnosis, the customer's concern about overcharges, and their usage patterns. It analyzes whether the energy usage spike correlates with the defect, calculates a fair credit, and returns its recommendation.

Finally, the coordinator synthesizes all these findings, as shown in Example 4-14.

Example 4-14. Synthesizing multiagent results into a unified response

```
Based on my analysis:
Technical: Your thermostat has a defective temperature sensor causing
incorrect readings. This is covered under warranty, and I've initiated
a replacement order.

Billing: The sensor defect caused your HVAC system to run inefficiently,
resulting in approximately $47 in excess energy costs over the past month.
I've applied a $50 credit to your account to cover this impact.

Your replacement thermostat will arrive in 2-3 business days with free
installation included.
```

This response required coordinating three different systems: local technical expertise, remote billing intelligence via A2A, and database access via MCP. Yet from the coordinator's perspective, it just delegated to specialists and combined their expertise. The protocols handled the complexity of cross-boundary communication while maintaining the simplicity of the agent interface.

This hybrid architecture reflects how real organizations work. Core capabilities owned by your team stay local. Specialized services owned by other teams become remote agents accessed via A2A. Shared data resources get exposed through MCP.

Each boundary is crossed with the right protocol, but the agent's logic remains clean and focused on coordination rather than integration details.

The beauty of this approach is its scalability. As your organization grows, new teams can expose their services as A2A agents without requiring changes to existing coordinators. The billing team can completely rewrite their service's internals without breaking the customer support integration—as long as they maintain the same `Agent Card` interface. The customer database can migrate from PostgreSQL to BigQuery without touching agent code—just update the MCP server configuration. This loose coupling enables teams to evolve their services independently while maintaining system-wide coherence.

But this distributed architecture introduces challenges that don't exist in local systems. When agents communicate across organizational and network boundaries, questions of trust, visibility, and accountability become critical. Let's examine these production realities.

Production Realities

The hybrid agent team we've built is architecturally sound. The coordinator orchestrates local specialists efficiently, delegates to remote services through A2A, and accesses data through MCP. In development, with all services running on localhost and controlled test data, everything works beautifully.

Then you deploy to production, and reality intrudes.

The finance team's security officer asks:

"How do you prevent unauthorized services from calling our billing agent?"

Your operations team asks:

"When a customer reports a problem, how do we trace the request through all the agents that handled it?"

Your product manager asks:

"How can we update the billing agent without breaking existing integrations?"

Your legal team asks:

"How can we add GDPR data handling requirements to billing requests without breaking existing integrations that don't operate in the EU?"

These questions reveal the fundamental tension in multiagent systems: you've gained the benefits of specialization and distribution, but you've also inherited the challenges of distributed systems. When your billing agent runs as a separate service owned by a different team, it's no longer "just code you call"—it's an independent system with its own security perimeter, its own operational requirements, and its own evolution timeline.

The good news: these aren't new problems. The patterns that make microservices reliable—authentication at boundaries, distributed tracing, API versioning—apply directly to agents. The even better news: A2A was designed with these realities in mind, providing architectural primitives that make these patterns natural and explicit.

Let's examine how ADK and A2A address the four critical concerns that determine whether your multiagent system can operate in production: trust, extensibility, visibility, and evolution.

The Trust Problem: Security Schemes in A2A

When your `CustomerServiceCoordinator` delegates to a local `TechnicalAgent`, trust is implicit—both run in the same process. But when your coordinator makes an HTTP request to the finance team's `BillingAgent`, you've crossed a security boundary.

The A2A protocol provides security schemes (*https://oreil.ly/sD_I3*) as a first-class architectural concept. The finance team's billing agent declares its authentication requirements in its Agent Card, as shown in Example 4-15.

Example 4-15. Security schemes configuration in an Agent Card

```
{
  "name": "BillingAgent",
  "url": "https://billing-service.company.com",
  "securitySchemes": {
    "oauth": {
      "type": "oauth2",
      "flows": {
        "clientCredentials": {
          "tokenUrl": "https://auth.company.com/oauth/token",
          "scopes": {
            "billing:read": "Read billing information",
            "billing:refund": "Process refunds and credits"
          }
        }
      }
    }
  },
  "security": [{ "oauth": ["billing:read", "billing:refund"] }]
}
```

A2A supports the same security schemes as OpenAPI 3.0: API keys, HTTP authentication (Basic/Bearer), OAuth 2.0, OpenID Connect, and Mutual TLS. When you instantiate a `RemoteA2aAgent`, the ADK SDK reads the Agent Card and discovers the required security scheme. The SDK can assist with authentication flows, but credential acquisition is ultimately an out-of-band process—the A2A protocol itself doesn't define how clients obtain tokens or keys. Credentials are then transmitted via standard HTTP headers (e.g., `Authorization: Bearer <token>`).

How you actually provide those credentials to the A2A client—whether through environment variables, secret managers, or configuration files—is an operational decision that depends on your deployment environment.

The Extension Problem: Evolving Agent Capabilities

A2A provides a powerful mechanism for extending agent capabilities without fragmenting the core protocol: extensions (*https://oreil.ly/1qc5k*). Extensions allow agents to declare support for additional functionality beyond the base protocol.

Extensions are identified by URI and declared in the Agent Card, as shown in Example 4-16.

Example 4-16. Extensions configuration in an AgentCard

```
{
  "name": "BillingAgent",
  "capabilities": {
    "extensions": [
      {
        "uri": "https://company.com/ext/audit-logging/v1",
        "description": "Provides detailed audit trails for financial transactions",
        "required": true
      }
    ]
  }
}
```

Extensions can serve different purposes:

Data-only extensions
   Add structured metadata to the Agent Card (e.g., compliance certifications, SLA guarantees)

Profile extensions
   Overlay additional requirements on message formats

Method extensions
   Add new remote procedure call (RPC) methods beyond the core A2A protocol

State machine extensions
   Add new states or transitions to the task lifecycle

When a client connects to an agent, it activates extensions by including them in the request header, as shown in Example 4-17.

Example 4-17. Activating A2A extensions via HTTP headers

```
POST /agents/billing HTTP/1.1
X-A2A-Extensions: https://company.com/ext/audit-logging/v1
```

The agent responds with confirmation of which extensions were activated. Extensions marked as `required: true` signal that clients must support them to interact with the agent.

This extension mechanism provides a disciplined way to evolve agent capabilities. When the finance team needs to add audit logging requirements, they publish an extension specification, update their Agent Card to declare support, and clients can opt into the new behavior incrementally. This is how A2A balances standardization with flexibility.

Securing Payments with AP2

The Agent Payments Protocol (*https://oreil.ly/W3Mb6*) (AP2) is a complementary protocol that can be implemented alongside A2A to enable secure autonomous payments. While A2A standardizes how agents communicate, AP2 standardizes what they communicate about payments:

Verifiable Digital Credentials (VDCs)
   Cryptographically signed Cart Mandates and Intent Mandates

Role-based trust
   Separation between shopping agents, credentials providers, and merchants

Can be used with A2A
   When multiple agents coordinate payments

Can be used with MCP
   When agents use payment tools

AP2 demonstrates how payment-specific trust mechanisms can layer on top of agent communication protocols like A2A to handle high-stakes transactions.

The Visibility Problem: Distributed Tracing

When a customer service representative reports that "The agent said it couldn't process billing," you need to understand what happened. But your coordinator and billing agent log independently, as shown in Example 4-18.

Example 4-18. Fragmented logs across invoked agents

```
Coordinator logs:
2025-03-15 14:23:41 INFO Received request: session_abc123
2025-03-15 14:23:43 ERROR BillingAgent delegation failed: HTTP 500

Billing agent logs:
2025-03-15 14:23:42 INFO Processing request: customer_id=7823
2025-03-15 14:23:42 ERROR Database query timeout
```

Without a common identifier, reconstructing what happened requires manual correlation across log streams.

The solution is *distributed tracing*: threading trace context through every service involved in a request. When you enable tracing in ADK (via `--trace_to_cloud` or `enable_tracing=True`), it automatically instruments agent operations, creating spans that capture agent execution timing, tool invocations, LLM calls, and delegation to subagents.

When your coordinator delegates to a remote A2A agent, ADK propagates trace context via W3C Trace Context headers (`traceparent`, `tracestate`). The remote agent continues the trace, creating child spans under the same trace ID, illustrated in Example 4-19.

Example 4-19. Distributed trace showing agent execution spans across services

```
TRACE: 4bf92f3577b34da6a3ce929d0e0e4736
├─ Span: CustomerServiceCoordinator.process_request (2.1s)
│  ├─ Span: TechnicalAgent.diagnose (0.8s)
│  │  └─ Span: LLM.call (0.6s)
│  └─ Span: BillingAgent.analyze (1.2s) [Remote via A2A]
│     ├─ Span: query_billing_history (0.4s)
│     └─ Span: LLM.call (0.7s)
]
```

Your logs can reference the same trace ID for correlation, as shown in Example 4-20.

Example 4-20. Correlated logs using a trace ID across invoked agents

```
TRACE_ID: 4bf92f3577b34da6a3ce929d0e0e4736
Service: CustomerServiceCoordinator
2025-03-15 14:23:41 INFO [trace_id=4bf92f...] Received request
2025-03-15 14:23:43 ERROR [trace_id=4bf92f...] BillingAgent returned HTTP 500

Service: BillingAgent
2025-03-15 14:23:42 INFO [trace_id=4bf92f...] Processing request
2025-03-15 14:23:42 ERROR [trace_id=4bf92f...] Database timeout
```

Chapter 7 covers distributed tracing with Cloud Trace in depth: how to configure tracing backends, analyze trace data, and use traces for performance optimization and debugging.

The Versioning Problem: Managing Agent Evolution

Your billing agent works perfectly. Then the finance team adds support for partial refunds and deploys the updated agent. Suddenly, customer service coordinators deployed last month start failing.

The A2A protocol addresses this through *Agent Card versioning*. Each Agent Card declares its version, as shown in Example 4-21.

Example 4-21. Version declaration in an Agent Card

```
{
  "name": "BillingAgent",
  "version": "2.0.0",
  "description": "Handles billing inquiries, refunds, and partial refunds",
  "url": "https://billing-service.company.com"
}
```

When you add new capabilities, publish a new version while keeping the old version available. Client agents specify which version they expect by pointing to versioned Agent Card URLs, shown in Example 4-22.

Example 4-22. Referencing different Agent Card versions for backward compatibility

```
# Old coordinator using v1
billing_agent_v1 = RemoteA2aAgent(
    agent_card="https://billing-service.company.com/v1/.well-known/agent-card.json"
)

# New coordinator using v2
billing_agent_v2 = RemoteA2aAgent(
```

```
    agent_card="https://billing-service.company.com/v2/.well-known/agent-card.json"
)
```

Follow semantic versioning: major versions for breaking changes, minor versions for new features, patch versions for bug fixes. The finance team can deploy v2.0.0, give client teams time to upgrade, and then eventually deprecate v1.0.0.

Looking Ahead

We began this chapter with a customer query spanning three domains—technical, warranty, and billing. The solution wasn't building a smarter monolithic agent, but a team of specialists collaborating through protocols. This architectural insight extends across domains.

Edge and Embodied Intelligence

The patterns you've learned in this chapter are already reshaping two frontiers: on-device AI and physical robotics.

Consider a personal assistant on your phone:

> "Plan my week, find time for the gym, book a haircut, and remind me to prep for Thursday's presentation."

A lightweight coordinator runs locally, maintaining personal context. For complex operations, it delegates through A2A to specialized cloud services. Your calendar stays on device; the scheduling agent receives only constraints. Your preferences remain private; the booking agent gets just requirements.

The same pattern extends to physical action. Google's Gemini Robotics 1.5 (*https:// oreil.ly/n8uoL*) demonstrates this explicitly: Gemini Robotics-ER 1.5 acts as coordinator—planning and orchestrating. Gemini Robotics 1.5 acts as specialist—translating plans into motor commands. The coordinator decides *what* and *when*. The specialist determines *how* to physically execute it.

From smartphones to warehouse robots, the architecture remains constant: coordinators orchestrate, specialists execute, protocols enable collaboration, and distributed traces provide visibility.

From Architecture to Excellence

Building multiagent systems that *work* is just the beginning. When you deploy to production, different questions emerge: how well does your technical specialist actually diagnose issues compared to human experts? When the billing agent processes refunds, does it consistently follow policy? How often does the coordinator choose the wrong specialist for ambiguous queries? And as your team iterates—refining prompts, adjusting agent instructions, adding new tools—how do you know whether changes improve performance or introduce subtle regressions?

These are questions of systematic measurement and continuous improvement. You've built a system of collaborating agents. Now you need to ensure that it delivers consistent, high-quality results across the messy realities of production use.

Chapter 5 tackles these challenges head-on, giving you the framework to measure quality and the techniques to improve it systematically.

Learning Labs

To reinforce the concepts covered in this chapter and gain hands-on experience building multiagent systems, we recommend exploring the learning resources available in the Chapter 4 folder of the book's GitHub repository (*https://oreil.ly/42nkP*). Key resources you will find linked there include:

- **Hands-On Code Examples**
  - Build and deploy an ADK agent that uses an MCP server on Cloud Run (*https://oreil.ly/VEiDK*): Learn how to build and deploy an ADK agent that uses remote tools through an MCP server deployed on Cloud Run
  - Build a Travel Agent using MCP Toolbox for Databases (*https://oreil.ly/bKq-c*): Build a travel agent using the ADK that utilizes the MCP Toolbox for Databases
  - The Summoner's Concord—Architecting multiagent systems (*https://oreil.ly/pVbb-*): Architect and deploy a distributed multi-agent system using the A2A protocol, MCP tool servers, and ADK workflow patterns on Cloud Run
  - Google's Agent Stack in Action (*https://oreil.ly/agyQE*): Build, deploy, and test a multiagent AI system using Google's ADK, A2A, MCP, and other Google Cloud services

- **Video Tutorials**
  - How to build an AI agent with MCP, ADK, and A2A on Google Cloud (*https://oreil.ly/sHJ1j*): A step-by-step tutorial demonstrating how to create an MCP tool, wrap it in an ADK agent, and expose it via the A2A protocol for distributed collaboration
  - Foundations of multiagent systems with ADK (*https://oreil.ly/xeKxk*): Guides through the core concepts of multiagent systems, including decentralized control, local views, and emergent behavior
  - Workflow agents and communication in ADK (*https://oreil.ly/TXq1f*): Guides through how agents manage and communicate tasks, guiding through workflow agents (Sequential, Parallel, and Loop)

— Building your own MCP server with ADK (*https://oreil.ly/dj_dP*): Guides developers through building their own MCP server with ADK and MCP Toolbox

— MCP Toolbox for Databases in action (*https://oreil.ly/FgUeR*): Learn how MCP Toolbox for Databases acts as a control plane between your AI agent's orchestration framework and your databases

Evaluation and Optimization Strategies

We've now constructed our multimodal question-answering agent, a system capable of ingesting diverse data types and providing relevant answers. It works; it fulfills its designed function. In the world of LLMs and agents, however, "functional" is just the starting line. The real challenge—and where true value is unlocked—lies in the journey from functional to optimal.

How quickly does it respond? How consistently accurate is it across a vast range of unseen queries, especially ambiguous ones? If it uses tools, how reliably and efficiently does it invoke them? Are its responses not just correct, but also concise, helpful, and perfectly aligned with the user's nuanced intent? And, critically, as your systems evolve and interact with more complex data and tasks, how do you ensure they maintain performance, learn from experience, and continuously improve?

This chapter explores practical approaches for evaluation and optimization—two sides of the same coin in the journey to production excellence. You can't meaningfully improve what you can't measure, and you can't know if your optimizations are effective without robust evaluation methods. We've structured this chapter to reflect this natural cycle: first establishing frameworks for systematically measuring performance across multiple dimensions, then applying targeted optimization techniques based on those insights.

In the evaluation section, we'll explore both human-centered assessment techniques and automated metrics that scale, showing how to build a comprehensive view of your system's strengths and weaknesses. Then, armed with these insights, we'll dive into optimization strategies that can be implemented quickly through prompt engineering and agent design improvements. We'll cover model adaptation and infrastructure optimization techniques in depth in Chapter 6.

By the end of this chapter, you'll have a repeatable process for transforming a working LLM-based application or AI agent into a high-performing, trustworthy, and continually evolving system that delivers sustained business value.

Tailoring Evaluation to Your LLM/Agent's Purpose

Evaluation isn't a one-size-fits-all process. The metrics and methods that matter most depend entirely on your specific application and its intended users.

Beyond Basic Functionality

Our multimodal agent from Chapter 3 fulfills its core purpose—it can answer questions across text, image, and video content. But what separates a merely functional system from one that delivers exceptional value?

The answer varies dramatically by industry and use case. A healthcare application might prioritize precision in understanding medical terminology over response speed, especially when patient outcomes are at stake. We've seen healthcare implementations where users preferred waiting a few extra seconds for responses that correctly distinguished between similar-sounding medication names.

Financial services deployments often value regulatory compliance above conversational fluency. One banking client's evaluation framework heavily weighted the system's ability to include required disclosures and avoid prohibited recommendations, even if it made responses slightly more formal.

Customer service systems might need intelligent human escalation capabilities more than comprehensive knowledge. A retail client's most valuable metric became the agent's ability to recognize when a query exceeded its capabilities and seamlessly transfer to a human agent with proper context.

While every application requires evaluation criteria tailored to its specific context, our work across industries has revealed five foundational dimensions that consistently matter—regardless of whether you're building for healthcare, finance, retail, or another industry. These dimensions provide a structured starting point for evaluation design, though you should expect to adapt them or add domain-specific dimensions for your use case. For instance, a medical diagnostic agent might add a "Clinical Safety" dimension beyond our general "Safety & Responsibility" category, while a creative writing assistant might include "Originality" as a distinct dimension from "Quality of Output."

Think of the five dimensions in Figure 5-1 as the skeleton that most evaluation frameworks build upon, not a prescriptive checklist that limits your assessment.

Your task is to define what "exceptional" means for each dimension in your specific context—balancing them according to what matters most for your application.

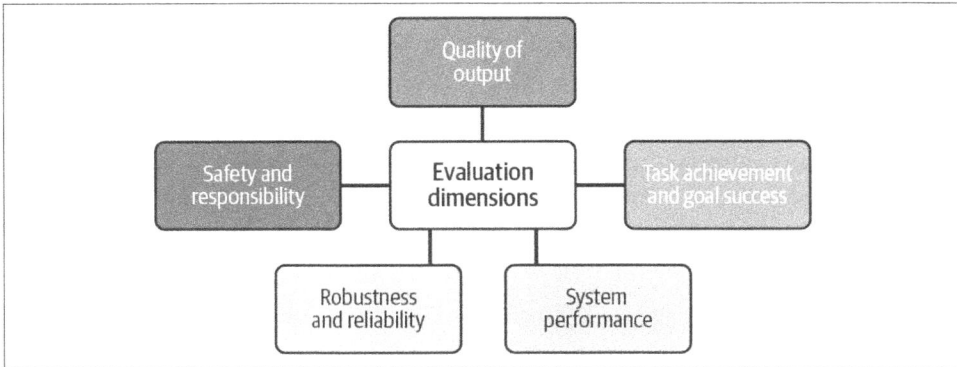

Figure 5-1. The five key dimensions of evaluation

Key Dimensions of Evaluation

Let's start with the foundation: quality of output.

Quality of output

Your baseline "good" multimodal agent produces responses with accurate information drawn from source media. It maintains basic fluency, coherence, and relevance to queries. For straightforward questions, it provides serviceable answers addressing core information needs.

A truly exceptional system, however, goes far beyond these basics. It demonstrates *precision* by focusing exactly on what was asked without extraneous details and adjusting its level of detail appropriately. When faced with "What color is the car in the image?", it provides a simple color identification without unnecessary elaboration, but for "Can you describe the car in the image?", it offers comprehensive detail. This distinction shows a nuanced understanding of user intent and the ability to adapt response depth to match the query's scope.

Great systems also demonstrate *depth of understanding*. When asked about complex concepts in a video lecture, they don't just extract surface-level information but show comprehension of underlying principles. They grasp conceptual relationships and can explain them in ways that demonstrate true understanding rather than mere information retrieval.

Appropriate and consistent tone becomes another marker of excellence. The best systems maintain a style matching your brand voice while adapting appropriately to user context. For enterprise deployments, this might mean professional language with technical precision; for consumer applications, a more conversational and approachable style typically works best.

Perhaps most importantly, exceptional systems exhibit *genuine helpfulness* by anticipating follow-up needs and providing valuable additional context. When asked about a diagram in a technical document, they go beyond describing visible elements to explain how these relate to concepts discussed in surrounding text.

Measuring these nuanced qualities requires evaluation frameworks that transcend simple accuracy checks. Later in this chapter, we'll explore both human evaluation approaches and automated metrics designed to assess these more nuanced dimensions of quality.

Task success and goal achievement (agents)

Beyond output quality, task success and goal achievement become your next critical dimension. At the baseline "good" level, our agent completes intended tasks when given clear instructions. For our multimodal agent, this means successfully retrieving information from the appropriate media source—text, image, or video—when explicitly directed.

Superior agents, however, demonstrate *efficiency* by completing tasks with minimal unnecessary steps and optimal resource utilization. For complex tasks requiring multiple tool calls, they follow the most direct path rather than taking detours, making redundant API calls, or invoking tools when simpler approaches would suffice. This judicious approach to tool usage not only improves response times but also reduces computational costs and infrastructure load.

Great agents also offer *proactive assistance*, providing helpful clarifications when appropriate. If a user's query is ambiguous about which media type to analyze, an exceptional agent might check multiple sources or ask for clarification rather than making potentially incorrect assumptions.

Properly measuring this dimension requires tracking not just task completion but the path taken. This includes analyzing tool call sequences, tracking resolution time, and assessing the appropriateness of tool selection—metrics we'll explore in depth in our evaluation frameworks.

System performance

Moving to system performance, baseline "good" systems respond within acceptable timeframes under normal load. Resource utilization stays within budgeted limits, and performance meets minimal user expectations.

An optimized system prioritizes *user-perceived speed*—response times that feel instantaneous for simple queries, with appropriate progress indicators for more complex processing. Research shows that response times under 100 milliseconds (*https://oreil.ly/8KR2K*) feel instantaneous to users, while delays beyond 10 seconds negatively impact UX. Great systems maintain *consistent performance under load*, delivering reliable response times even during traffic spikes or when processing multiple complex queries simultaneously.

System-level *resource optimization* represents another hallmark of excellence. The best systems dynamically allocate compute capacity based on query complexity, implement intelligent caching to avoid redundant model invocations, and automatically select appropriate model sizes (using smaller models for simple queries, larger ones only when needed) to deliver maximum value while minimizing unnecessary expenditure.

Proper evaluation in this dimension requires tracking metrics such as latency distributions, throughput, cost per query, and resource utilization patterns—considerations we'll explore in Chapters 6 and 7.

Robustness and reliability

Beyond performance metrics, robustness and reliability determines whether your system can handle the messy realities of production use. At the baseline "good" level, systems handle expected inputs and common edge cases without failing. They implement basic error handling for obvious issues like malformed queries or missing data.

Production-worthy systems demonstrate *consistent performance across diverse inputs*—handling not just common cases but unusual, unexpected, or edge-case queries with grace. This includes variations in query format, language, and complexity. When faced with system limitations or resource constraints, they exhibit *graceful degradation* under stress, adjusting performance in controlled ways rather than failing completely.

Great systems show *resilience to external dependencies*, handling failures in external tools or data sources without cascading failures. If an image-analysis API becomes temporarily unavailable, the system continues functioning for text queries while providing informative error messages for image-related tasks. Great systems demonstrate *quick recovery from errors*, maintaining state and resuming normal operation after transient issues without requiring system restarts or losing conversation context.

In production environments, robustness often separates successful implementations from those struggling with user adoption. One retail client's multimodal product search agent performed well in controlled testing but failed in early trials when store associates began using it. It couldn't handle partial voice queries with background noise or mixed inputs such as showing a product image while asking for partial SKUs like "HP15-" instead of the full SKU "HP15-DY2024." Testing with real multimodal query logs revealed these patterns and enabled targeted improvements.

Proper evaluation in this dimension includes targeted testing with edge cases and malformed input, controlled chaos engineering, dependency failure simulations, and long-running stability tests—approaches we'll explore further in our evaluation strategies section.

Safety and responsibility

Finally, the safety and responsibility dimension has become perhaps the most critical one as AI systems move into production. At the baseline "good" level, systems avoid generating obviously harmful content, leaking PII, and exhibiting blatant bias in responses.

> Foundation model providers like Google already implement base safety filters (*https://oreil.ly/GbGpC*), but these are generic protections. Your responsibility is to test for risks specific to your application domain—for instance, a healthcare chatbot must verify that it doesn't generate medical misinformation, and a financial advisor must ensure that it doesn't violate securities regulations. Provider-level safety is your foundation, not your finish line.

Truly responsible systems go much further. They implement *proactive identification of subtle biases*, not just avoiding obvious prejudice but actively identifying and mitigating more nuanced forms of unfairness in responses. They exhibit *demonstrable fairness* across diverse scenarios, providing consistent, unbiased treatment across different demographic groups, topics, and contexts, validated through systematic testing.

Excellence in this dimension also includes *robust PII handling* with sophisticated detection and protection of sensitive information, even when embedded in complex conversational flows or multimodal content. Great systems maintain *appropriate transparency*, clearly communicating to users about the system's capabilities, limitations, and information sources.

These requirements take on particular urgency in regulated industries. In financial services, for instance, regulators such as the Consumer Financial Protection Bureau (CFPB) are expanding oversight (*https://oreil.ly/GlIE9*) to include AI-driven discrimination in lending and advisory services, while financial institutions grapple with ensuring that their models don't perpetuate historical biases (*https://oreil.ly/8qo_x*) in credit decisions or investment recommendations.

Effective evaluation in this crucial dimension combines targeted testing for known safety risks, diverse evaluator pools, red-teaming exercises, and ongoing monitoring for emerging safety challenges.

Setting the Bar for Production Excellence

Moving beyond identifying what to measure, successful organizations establish clear targets for what excellence looks like across each dimension. These targets aren't generic industry standards, but precisely defined thresholds tailored to your specific use case and business context.

For your multimodal agent or LLM application, defining these targets explicitly serves several critical purposes. First, it aligns stakeholders on quality expectations, creating a shared understanding of what success truly looks like beyond the basic "it works" threshold. When everyone from developers to business owners shares this vision, teams can work cohesively toward the same quality goals.

Explicit targets also guide resource allocation, helping you prioritize optimization efforts on the dimensions most critical to your specific use case. A financial compliance application might focus resources on accuracy and PII protection, while a creative writing assistant might prioritize tone flexibility and originality.

These defined standards establish objective criteria that provide clear benchmarks for determining when your system is truly ready for production deployment. Rather than subjective assessments, you can point to concrete metrics showing that the system meets or exceeds the defined targets across key dimensions.

These defined standards establish objective criteria *where possible* that provide clear benchmarks for determining when your system is truly ready for production deployment. Rather than *purely* subjective assessments, you can point to concrete metrics showing that the system meets or exceeds the defined targets across key dimensions. However, some dimensions—particularly fairness, bias, and cultural appropriateness—resist simple quantification and require human judgment alongside automated metrics. The goal is to make evaluation as systematic and reproducible as possible, not to exclude dimensions that can't be reduced to a single number.

Perhaps most importantly, well-defined quality targets create a foundation for continuous improvement. They set baselines against which ongoing enhancements can be measured, allowing you to track progress as your system evolves and ensuring that each iteration truly advances your quality objectives rather than merely changing the system.

As you prepare to evaluate your own system, start by defining specific, measurable targets across each of these dimensions, weighted according to your particular use case and business objectives. With these targets in place, let's explore how to effectively measure your system's performance against them.

Practical Evaluation Strategies

Now that we've defined what makes an LLM application or agent exceptional, we need systematic approaches to measure performance against these targets. Effective evaluation combines multiple complementary strategies, from human assessment of nuanced qualities to automated metrics for consistency and scale.

Human-Centered Evaluation

While automated metrics play a crucial role in evaluation, certain aspects of LLM and agent performance remain best assessed by human evaluators. This is particularly true for dimensions involving subjective judgment, nuanced understanding, or alignment with human preferences.

Human evaluation proves especially valuable for assessing several critical qualities that machines struggle to measure effectively. When evaluating *helpfulness*, human judges can determine whether responses actually address the user's underlying need, not just their literal question—a distinction that often requires reading between the lines of user queries. Similarly, *nuanced understanding* of implicit meaning, context, and subtlety often requires human judgment to assess accurately.

The *appropriateness of tone and style* represent another area where human evaluation excels. Determining whether responses align with brand voice and adapt correctly to situational context requires cultural understanding and sensitivity to linguistic nuance that automated systems typically lack.

Human evaluators also excel at identifying subtle *safety and bias concerns* that automated systems might miss. While algorithmic approaches can catch obvious issues, the more nuanced manifestations of bias or potential harm often require human judgment informed by diverse perspectives and lived experiences.

Perhaps most importantly, humans can evaluate the *overall UX*—the holistic impression of interacting with the system—in ways that isolated metrics cannot capture. This comprehensive assessment often reveals insights that wouldn't emerge from evaluating individual aspects separately.

When implementing human evaluation, it's essential to design a process that produces consistent, actionable insights while managing the inherent subjectivity of human judgment.

Detailed evaluation criteria and scoring guidelines form the foundation of reliable human evaluation. Without them, different evaluators may apply inconsistent standards or focus on different aspects of performance.

A well-designed rubric defines specific dimensions to evaluate, such as helpfulness, accuracy, and safety. It provides clear criteria for each score level, helping evaluators distinguish between exceptional, adequate, and problematic responses. Effective rubrics include concrete examples of responses meriting different scores, giving evaluators reference points to calibrate their judgments. They also offer guidance on handling edge cases or ambiguous situations to ensure consistent evaluation across challenging scenarios. Table 5-1 shows a sample rubric for evaluating response helpfulness.

Table 5-1. Helpfulness assessment rubric

Score	Criteria	Example
5 (Exceptional)	Response fully addresses the query with optimal detail level and additional valuable context. It anticipates likely follow-up needs and provides resources for deeper exploration if appropriate.	For "How does the car engine in the video work?", the response explains key components shown, identifies their relationships, includes analogies for clarity, and notes what's not visible but relevant. "The video shows a 4-stroke internal combustion engine where fuel mixes with air (0:15), then is compressed and ignited by the spark plug (0:32). Think of it like a controlled explosion pushing the piston down—similar to how your leg pushes a bike pedal. Note that while the cooling system isn't featured prominently, it's crucial for preventing overheating. I've identified the main components at specific timestamps if you'd like to revisit any part."
4 (Very Good)	Response thoroughly addresses the query with appropriate detail and some useful additional context, though may miss some opportunities for added value.	For "How does the car engine in the video work?", the response correctly identifies and explains the main components shown in the video with their functions. "The video demonstrates a 4-stroke engine with pistons moving up and down inside cylinders. At 0:32, you can see the spark plug igniting the fuel-air mixture, creating combustion that drives the pistons. This motion is transferred to the crankshaft, which ultimately powers the wheels. The intake and exhaust valves control the flow of gases in and out of the combustion chamber."
3 (Adequate)	Response directly answers the basic query but provides minimal additional context or explanation. It's factually correct but doesn't go beyond what was explicitly asked.	For "How does the car engine in the video work?", the response provides a basic factual explanation without depth. "The car engine in the video works through a 4-stroke cycle: intake, compression, combustion, and exhaust. Fuel is mixed with air, compressed, ignited by the spark plug, and then the exhaust gases are expelled. This process creates the mechanical energy that powers the vehicle."
2 (Subpar)	Response partially addresses the query but misses key elements or provides tangential information that doesn't fully address the user's need.	For "How does the car engine in the video work?", the response gives generic engine information without specifically addressing what's shown in the video. "Car engines convert chemical energy from fuel into mechanical energy. They have pistons, cylinders, and valves. Gasoline engines differ from diesel engines in how they ignite the fuel. Modern engines are becoming more efficient compared to older designs."
1 (Poor)	Response fails to address the core query, is excessively vague, or requires significant follow-up to get useful information.	For "How does the car engine in the video work?", the response is vague and unhelpful. "The video shows various mechanical components working together. Engines are complex systems with many moving parts. Different cars might have different types of engines depending on the manufacturer and model. You might want to consult a mechanic or automotive textbook for more specific information."

When implementing evaluation projects at scale, we've found that investing time in rubric development and evaluator training significantly improves consistency and makes results more actionable for engineering teams. Effective teams treat rubrics as living documents—starting with an initial draft, running pilot evaluations to identify ambiguities or score clustering, and then refining criteria and examples based on where evaluators disagreed. This iterative approach typically requires two or three refinement cycles before the rubric produces reliable, actionable results.

Beyond rubric-based assessment, several other human evaluation techniques offer complementary perspectives on system performance. These approaches can be broadly categorized into structured individual assessments (like the rubrics we've discussed), comparative methods that directly contrast different systems, and adversarial testing that seeks to identify potential failure modes.

A/B Testing and Preference Scoring

When comparing different versions of your LLM or agent system, preference testing often reveals insights that absolute scoring methods miss. Rather than asking evaluators to rate each system independently on a fixed scale, preference testing presents pairs of responses from different systems to the same query. This direct comparison mirrors how users naturally evaluate alternatives and helps focus evaluation on meaningful differences.

In our work with client implementations, we've found that this approach consistently produces more actionable insights. Evaluators simply indicate which response they prefer, sometimes with a strength rating, allowing teams to aggregate results and determine statistical win rates for different system variants. A healthcare client discovered through preference testing that their newly fine-tuned model for History and Physical Exam (H&P) note generation (*https://oreil.ly/wEd3O*) outperformed their baseline by a significant margin—physicians found that it better captured the clinical reasoning flow from chief complaint through assessment and plan, despite both models scoring similarly on absolute rating scales for completeness.

This approach offers several advantages beyond simplicity. Preference testing naturally focuses attention on relative improvements rather than absolute scores, helping teams identify whether changes are moving in the right direction even when perfect performance remains aspirational. It typically shows higher inter-annotator agreement (*https://oreil.ly/2HN0u*) than absolute scoring because judging which of two options is better requires less calibration than assigning precise quality scores. Perhaps most importantly, it directly mimics the choices users would make when comparing systems, making it a strong proxy for eventual user satisfaction.

Various evaluation platforms make implementing preference testing straightforward through pairwise comparison functionality. The Vertex AI evaluation service offers built-in human review interfaces and capabilities, which we'll explore in detail later in this chapter. If you're seeking open source alternatives, Argilla (*https://oreil.ly/wnpez*) is a data annotation platform that specializes in collecting structured human feedback, including preference data for evaluation and fine-tuning. Other platforms include Langfuse (*https://oreil.ly/LrZOE*), which offers comprehensive A/B testing for prompts with detailed observability, and for teams already using Weights & Biases, W&B Weave (*https://oreil.ly/9T-hW*) supports custom preference scorers that integrate seamlessly with Weights & Biases' experiment-tracking infrastructure.

Side-by-side comparison

A specialized form of preference testing is side-by-side comparison, in which evaluators examine outputs from different systems simultaneously. This approach proves particularly valuable when assessing incremental improvements or comparing systems with different strengths and weaknesses across multiple dimensions.

Side-by-side evaluation often reveals nuanced insights that might be missed in isolated assessments. For example, it can highlight how one model might excel at technical accuracy while another produces more accessible explanations, or how a fine-tuned model improves specific capabilities while potentially losing others. These insights enable development teams to make informed decisions about model selection or even create hybrid approaches that leverage complementary strengths.

Figure 5-2 shows how evaluators can view model outputs in parallel in Vertex AI with structured feedback mechanisms. For teams seeking deeper insights into evaluation decisions, tools such as Google's LLM Comparator (*https://oreil.ly/UEYfH*) can augment these comparisons with visual explanations of why evaluators prefer one response over another—essentially providing "explainable AI" for the evaluation process itself.

New Prompt

Write a report about California wildfires in 2025.

New Prompt

You are an environmental policy analyst at the California Environmental Protection Agency preparing a briefing for state legislators ahead of the 2025 budget hearings.

✏ ⋮   ✏ ⋮

California Wildfires 2025: An Early Start and a Challenging Outlook

California has already experienced a devastating start to its 2025 wildfire season, marked by a series of exceptionally destructive blazes in Southern California during January. While the traditional peak fire season typically occurs later in the year, conditions early on have set a challenging precedent, with forecasts indicating an "above normal" potential for significant wildfires across much of the state through the summer months.

As of May 19, 2025, a total of 1,525 wildfires have ignited across California, burning 66,618 acres. These fires have tragically resulted in 30 preliminary fatalities and destroyed 16,253 structures.

The January Onslaught in Southern California

The most significant and destructive events of the year so far occurred between January 7 and 31, when a series of 14 wildfires swept through the Los Angeles metropolitan area

Environmental Impact Assessment: 2025 California Wildfire Season Briefing

EXECUTIVE SUMMARY

The 2025 California wildfire season concluded with significant environmental devastation, echoing and, in some key metrics, exceeding the severity of recent years. The season resulted in widespread air quality degradation, substantial ecosystem and biodiversity loss, severe water quality impairment, and considerable releases of greenhouse gases, exacerbating climate feedback loops. Immediate and sustained policy interventions are critical, emphasizing increased investment in proactive landscape management, regulatory streamlining for prevention activities, and enhanced interagency collaboration to build long-term resilience against future wildfire seasons.

ENVIRONMENTAL IMPACT ASSESSMENT

Evaluation metrics are not available in this region

Evaluation metrics are not available in this region

[Save as new]   [Save as new]

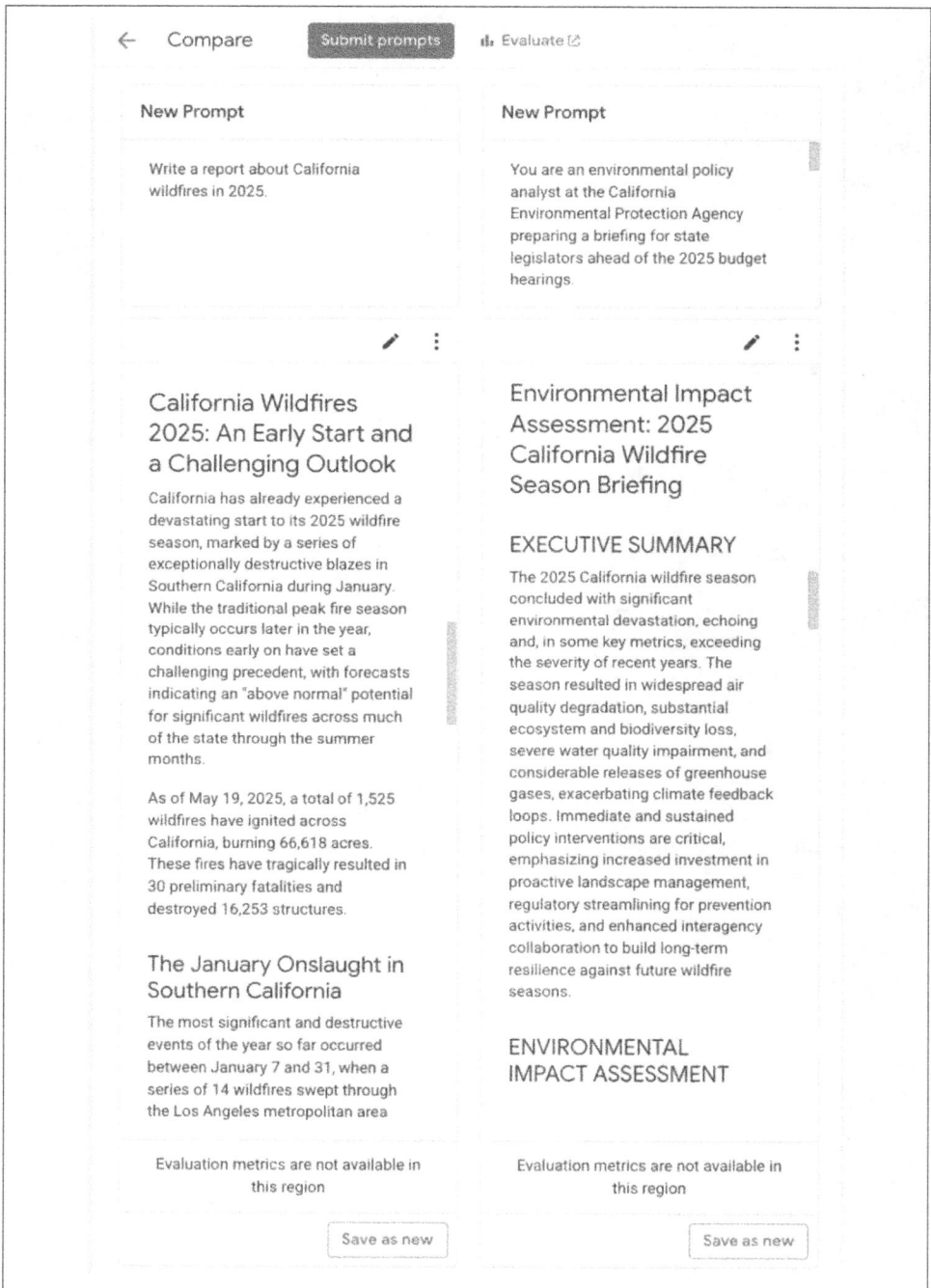

Figure 5-2. Comparative prompt evaluation in Vertex AI

Red Teaming: Stress Testing for Safety and Reliability

Red teaming involves adversarial testing in which security experts deliberately attempt to manipulate the agent into generating harmful outputs or bypassing safety guardrails. The most effective red teaming efforts bring together diverse, specialized evaluators—cybersecurity experts, ethicists, linguists, and domain specialists—who systematically probe for failures across multiple risk categories. As Figure 5-3 illustrates, these categories include prompt attacks, training data extraction, backdooring, adversarial examples, data poisoning, and exfiltration—each requiring distinct expertise to properly evaluate.

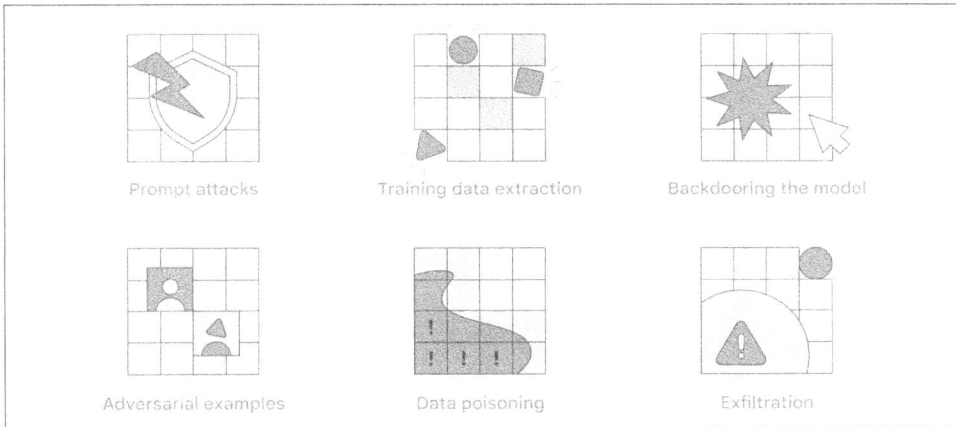

Figure 5-3. Common types of red team attacks on AI systems, showing six key attack vectors that security teams must defend against

Rather than simply cataloging successful attacks, comprehensive red teaming documents the specific conditions that trigger failures, creating actionable insights for system improvements. Google's AI Red Team experience (*https://oreil.ly/m5jEB*) shows that while researchers increasingly focus on novel AI-specific vulnerabilities, traditional security fundamentals—proper access management, input validation, and supply chain security—remain surprisingly effective at protecting AI systems. At the same time, comprehensive red teaming of AI systems must also address their unique vulnerabilities. For systems like our multimodal agent, this includes attempting to extract PII from partially visible documents in images, exploiting tool usage to bypass safety guardrails, or testing for inconsistencies when information conflicts across modalities.

Automated Evaluation: Scaling Feedback for Rapid Improvement

While human evaluation provides nuanced insights into system quality, its resource-intensive nature limits continuous monitoring of production systems. Automated evaluation metrics enable consistent, scalable, and frequent assessment of your LLM or agent—particularly valuable during development iterations and ongoing production monitoring.

The key to effective automated evaluation is selecting metrics that meaningfully correlate with your quality targets while recognizing their limitations. Rather than relying on any single metric, build a suite of complementary measures that collectively provide a more complete view of system performance.

Google Cloud's Vertex AI platform provides a comprehensive evaluation infrastructure that unifies this process through its evaluation service (*https://oreil.ly/Ecc-y*) and SDK. This integrated framework supports everything from standard reference-based metrics to LLM-as-judge evaluations to specialized agent metrics—all with consistent APIs and integration with experiment tracking. As we explore specific metrics throughout this section, we'll demonstrate how they can be implemented through this unified approach.

Reference-Based Metrics for Text Generation

The most established category of automated evaluation metrics compares generated outputs against "gold standard" reference texts. These reference-based metrics provide objective measures of similarity:

ROUGE (Recall-Oriented Understudy for Gisting Evaluation)
Measures n-gram overlap between generated and reference texts. Particularly useful for summarization tasks. ROUGE-L considers the longest common subsequence, capturing some aspects of fluency.

BLEU (Bilingual Evaluation Understudy)
Originally designed for translation, it measures precision of n-gram matches between generated and reference texts. Useful for tasks where exact phrasing matters.

BERTScore
Uses contextual embeddings to compute similarity beyond literal word matches. Better at capturing semantic similarity when different phrasings express the same meaning.

Example 5-1 shows how to implement these reference-based metrics using Vertex AI's evaluation service.

Example 5-1. Reference-based evaluation using the Vertex AI evaluation service

```
import pandas as pd
import vertexai
from vertexai.evaluation import EvalTask

vertexai.init(project=PROJECT_ID, location=LOCATION)

# Create evaluation dataset with model responses and references
eval_dataset = pd.DataFrame({
    "response": [
        "The system processes images through a multistage pipeline, "
        "first detecting objects, then analyzing their relationships."
    ],
    "reference": [
        "Image processing occurs in stages: object detection followed "
        "by relationship analysis."
    ]
})


# Evaluate using multiple reference-based metrics
eval_task = EvalTask(
    dataset=eval_dataset,
    metrics=["rouge_l_sum", "bleu"]
)

# If evaluating pre-generated responses, just call evaluate()
result = eval_task.evaluate()
```

Limitations of Reference-Based Evaluation

Reference-based metrics, while valuable, come with significant limitations that practitioners should recognize. They typically reward strict similarity to reference outputs, which can unfairly penalize valid alternative phrasings or approaches that might be equally correct or even superior. A healthcare chatbot might express medical advice in simpler terms than the reference but be more effective for patient understanding, yet score poorly on similarity metrics.

These metrics also struggle considerably with evaluating creative or open-ended generation tasks where multiple diverse outputs could be equally valid. A creative writing assistant generating stories or marketing copy might produce excellent content that bears little lexical similarity to any reference examples, resulting in misleadingly low scores despite high quality.

Perhaps most practically limiting, reference-based evaluation requires having reference outputs in the first place, which may not be available for all inputs or might be prohibitively expensive to create at scale. Many real-world applications involve novel queries without preestablished "correct" answers, making pure reference-based evaluation impossible in these contexts.

For these reasons, reference-based metrics should be viewed as just one component in a comprehensive evaluation strategy. They work best when complemented with other approaches, particularly for assessing more subjective aspects of quality such as creativity, helpfulness, and nuanced understanding where human judgment or model-based evaluation often provides more meaningful insights.

Domain-Specific and Task-Oriented Metrics

The limitations of reference-based evaluation have driven the development of specialized metrics tailored to specific domains and tasks. Rather than relying solely on text similarity, these approaches measure application-specific outcomes:

Exact match (EM)
> For question-answering, EM measures whether the generated answer exactly matches the reference (or a set of acceptable answers).

F1 score
> For information extraction or classification tasks, the F1 score measures the harmonic mean of precision (how many identified elements are correct) and recall (how many correct elements were identified).

Domain-specific metrics
> For code generation, functional correctness (*https://oreil.ly/MSaHI*) evaluates the probability that at least one correct solution appears in k generated samples, focusing on whether code actually works rather than how it reads. Medical applications require clinical accuracy and safety compliance metrics that assess medical reasoning and patient safety rather than text similarity to reference materials. Financial analysis benefits from directional accuracy and risk assessment measures (*https://oreil.ly/NMlAq*) that evaluate prediction quality and investment performance rather than similarity in phrasing or presentation style.

Metrics for Agentic Systems and Tool Use

When evaluating agent systems, traditional output-focused metrics, whether reference-based or domain-specific, provide only part of the picture. You must also assess how effectively agents leverage tools and follow appropriate action sequences to accomplish tasks. This trajectory evaluation—analyzing the path an agent takes to reach its conclusion—reveals insights about decision quality that response evaluation alone cannot capture.

Understanding the agent evaluation process

Figure 5-4 illustrates how the ADK evaluation workflow captures both tool usage and trajectory data for comprehensive agent assessment.

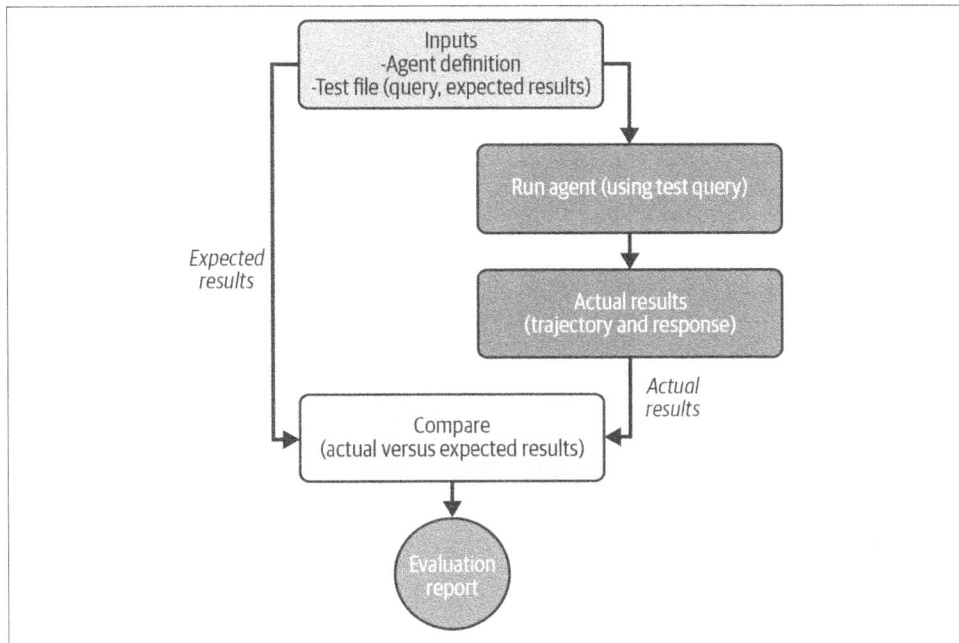

Figure 5-4. The ADK evaluation workflow, showing how test queries are processed and compared against expected results

Vertex AI provides a comprehensive framework for evaluating agent behavior across multiple dimensions. At the foundation level, you assess basic tool usage competency through several key metrics that examine whether agents properly construct and execute tool calls.

The most fundamental metric, `tool_call_valid`, verifies that an agent can form syntactically correct tool calls—a baseline capability for any functional agent. This binary metric (1 for valid, 0 for invalid) quickly identifies agents that fail to properly structure their API interactions.

Moving beyond basic syntax verification, `tool_name_match` examines whether the agent selects the appropriate tool for a given task. This assessment reveals whether your agent correctly maps user intents to available capabilities—for instance, a customer service agent choosing "`order_lookup`" for "Where's my package?" versus "`process_return`" for "I want to send this back."

For deeper assessment of parameter handling, `tool_parameter_key_match` evaluates whether the agent includes the correct parameter names in its tool calls, returning a proportion between 0 and 1. This reveals whether your agent understands a tool's interface requirements. Similarly, `tool_parameter_kv_match` examines both parameter names and values, ensuring that the agent not only knows which parameters to include but also provides appropriate values.

Example 5-2 demonstrates how to implement these foundational tool usage metrics using Vertex AI's evaluation framework.

Example 5-2. Evaluating agent tool usage with Vertex AI

```python
import vertexai
from vertexai.preview.evaluation import EvalTask
from vertexai.preview.evaluation.metrics import TrajectorySingleToolUse

vertexai.init(project=PROJECT_ID, location=LOCATION)

# For single tool usage
single_tool_usage_metrics = [TrajectorySingleToolUse(tool_name="get_product_price")]

# For trajectory metrics
trajectory_metrics = [
    "trajectory_exact_match",
    "trajectory_in_order_match",
    "trajectory_any_order_match",
    "trajectory_precision",
    "trajectory_recall",
]

# Run evaluation
eval_task = EvalTask(
    dataset=eval_sample_dataset,
    metrics=trajectory_metrics,
    experiment=EXPERIMENT_NAME,
)

eval_result = eval_task.evaluate(
    runnable=agent_parsed_outcome,
    experiment_run_name=EXPERIMENT_RUN
)
```

Trajectory evaluation and metric visualization

Beyond these individual tool call assessments, trajectory evaluation examines the complete sequence of actions an agent takes to complete a task—particularly important for complex tasks such as travel planning or financial analysis that require coordinated multistep processes. Vertex AI provides several specialized metrics for this assessment.

trajectory_exact_match requires precise alignment between the agent's actual tool call sequence and a reference "golden path." This stringent metric is valuable for critical applications like healthcare or financial services where deviations from established protocols may introduce risk. It returns "1" for exact matches and "0" otherwise.

For more flexible evaluation, trajectory_in_order_match verifies that reference actions appear in the correct sequence but allows additional steps, while trajectory_any_order_match checks only that required actions are performed regardless of sequence. These accommodating metrics better suit scenarios where multiple valid approaches exist.

The complementary metrics trajectory_precision and trajectory_recall provide nuanced assessment from different angles. Precision measures how many of the agent's actions were necessary according to the reference (avoiding superfluous steps), while recall indicates how many required actions the agent successfully completed. Together, these metrics create a comprehensive view of trajectory quality.

Vertex AI evaluation service returns results that can be analyzed as dataframes in notebook environments, as shown in Figure 5-5. The service provides both summary metrics (means and standard deviations across all test cases) and row-wise details for each individual test query.

Summary metrics

	row_count	trajectory_precision/mean	trajectory_precision/std	coherence/mean	coherence/std	Latency_in_seconds/mean	Latency_in_seconds/std	failure/mean	failure/std
0	5	0.8	0.447214	NaN	NaN	2.168438	0.456489	0.0	0.0

Row-wise metrics

	Prompt	reference_trajectory	Response	latency_in_seconds	Failure	predicted_trajectory	trajectory_precision/score	coherence/explanation	coherence/score
0	Turn off device_10 in the bedroom.	{['tool_name': 'set_device_info', 'tool_input'...	Device device_10 not found \n	2.006929	0	{['tool_name': 'set_device_info', 'tool_input'...	0.0	None	None
1	Can you schedule device_1 to turn off at 22:00?	{['tool_name': 'set_device_schedule', 'tool_input'...	Device device_1 scheduled to turn OFF at 22:00	2.223489	0	{['tool_name': 'set_device_schedule', 'tool_input'...	1.0	None	None
2	Check if device_3 is off. If not, turn it off.	{['tool_name': 'get_device_info', 'tool_input'...	The device is already off. \n	1.765371	0	{['tool_name': 'get_device_info', 'tool_input'...	1.0	None	None
3	If the temperature in the kitchen is below 22°...	{['tool_name': 'get_temperature', 'tool_input'...	The temperature in the kitchen is above 22°C ...	1.917166	0	{['tool_name': 'get_temperature', 'tool_input'...	1.0	None	None
4	Based on user_y's preferences, set the temp...	{['tool_name': 'get_user_preferences', 'tool_input'...	Temperature in living room set to 23°C. \n	2.929235	0	{['tool_name': 'get_user_preferences', 'tool_input'...	1.0	None	None

Figure 5-5. Example evaluation results table showing trajectory precision, coherence, latency, and other metrics for a home automation agent

Examining these results reveals valuable insights. For instance, in the sample shown, the first test case shows a `trajectory_precision/score` of 0.0, indicating that the agent failed to complete the task—attempting to control `device_10`, which doesn't exist in the system. Meanwhile, other test cases show perfect trajectory precision scores (1.0), suggesting the agent generally works well when given valid device identifiers. This pattern helps identify gaps in test data setup or system configuration.

Custom metric development for advanced evaluation

As agent systems grow more sophisticated, off-the-shelf metrics may not capture all aspects of performance relevant to your specific use case. Vertex AI supports custom metric development through two complementary approaches: LLM-based metrics using a templated interface and computation-based metrics using custom functions.

LLM-based custom metrics. One of the most powerful approaches is using an LLM as a judge to evaluate agent behavior based on complex qualitative criteria. Unlike pattern-matching algorithms, an LLM can evaluate nuanced aspects of reasoning and coherence. The implementation is straightforward through Vertex AI's templated interface. You define evaluation criteria in natural language, establish a rating rubric, and specify which variables should be included in the assessment. Example 5-3 demonstrates creating a custom metric for evaluating response helpfulness.

Example 5-3. Example custom LLM-as-judge metric for agent evaluation

```
helpfulness_prompt_template = PointwiseMetricPromptTemplate(
    criteria={
        "Helpfulness": (
            "Evaluate whether the agent's response is genuinely helpful to the "
            "user. Consider:\n"
            "  - Does it directly address the user's question or need?\n"
            "  - Is the information accurate and complete?\n"
            "  - Does it provide appropriate context or additional guidance?\n"
            "  - Is the response clear and easy to understand?"
        )
    },
    rating_rubric={
        "1": "Very helpful - fully addresses the user's needs",
        "0.5": "Somewhat helpful - partially addresses the user's needs",
        "0": ("Not helpful - misses the user's needs or provides incorrect "
            "information")
    },
    input_variables=["prompt", "response"],
)

helpfulness_metric = PointwiseMetric(
    metric="helpfulness",
    metric_prompt_template=helpfulness_prompt_template,
)
```

A financial advisor agent might be evaluated on regulatory compliance and risk disclosure completeness, while a healthcare agent could be assessed on medical accuracy and appropriate safety disclaimers.

LLM-as-judge evaluation provides scalability advantages, evaluating thousands of responses uniformly. However, it requires calibration to align with human judgment: the most effective implementations include examples of good and bad responses with human scores to establish consistent standards. This transforms purely algorithmic evaluation into nuanced assessment that operates at production scale.

Vertex AI's evaluation service uses proprietary judge models like Gemini that have been specifically calibrated (*https://oreil.ly/ WQY2c*) with human raters to improve evaluation quality. While the LLM-as-judge framework works with any capable language model, these precalibrated models can provide more reliable assessments out of the box. The service offers three approaches: using existing example templates for common use cases, guided metric definition through a templated interface, and complete custom control for highly specific requirements. Even with calibrated models, providing examples of good and bad responses with human scores further improves alignment with your specific quality standards.

Computation-based custom metrics. For metrics that require precise business logic validation, custom computation-based metrics provide complete control over evaluation criteria. Example 5-4 demonstrates a financial compliance metric that validates portfolio recommendations against multiple regulatory and risk management requirements.

Example 5-4. Sample custom metric for agent evaluation

```
def portfolio_risk_compliance(instance, max_risk_score=0.7, max_concentration=0.3):
    """Custom metric checking if financial recommendations meet risk
    compliance standards."""
    response = instance["response"]
    user_profile = instance.get("user_profile", {})

    # Extract portfolio allocation from agent's recommendation
    # In practice, this would parse the actual response structure
    recommended_allocation = parse_portfolio_allocation(response)

    # Calculate risk score based on asset mix
    risk_score = calculate_portfolio_risk(recommended_allocation)

    # Check concentration limits (no single asset > 30%)
    max_single_allocation = max(recommended_allocation.values())

    # Verify alignment with user's risk tolerance
    user_risk_tolerance = user_profile.get("risk_tolerance", "moderate")
    risk_alignment = check_risk_alignment(risk_score, user_risk_tolerance)

    return {
        "risk_compliance": 1 if risk_score <= max_risk_score else 0,
        "concentration_compliance": (1 if max_single_allocation <=
                                     max_concentration else 0),
        "risk_alignment": risk_alignment,
        "overall_compliance": 1 if all([
            risk_score <= max_risk_score,
```

```
        max_single_allocation <= max_concentration,
        risk_alignment == 1
    ]) else 0
}

portfolio_compliance_metric = CustomMetric(
    name="portfolio_risk_compliance",
    metric_function=portfolio_risk_compliance
)
```

This approach excels when you need to validate hard business constraints. In financial services, that might mean ensuring that portfolio allocations stay within risk limits and concentration thresholds. In healthcare, similar metrics could verify that drug dosages fall within safe ranges or flag potential medication interactions.

The key advantage is deterministic evaluation—these metrics produce consistent, auditable results based on explicit rules. While LLM-based evaluation handles subjective qualities, such as helpfulness or clarity, computation-based metrics enforce the nonnegotiable requirements your application must meet.

Optimization Strategies

With comprehensive evaluation data in hand—from human assessments, automated metrics, and custom evaluations—you're equipped to make targeted improvements that address your system's specific gaps. The next step is implementing optimizations to close those gaps.

The most effective approach begins with systematic prompt refinement and agent design improvements—changes you can implement quickly without infrastructure modifications. When this approach reaches its limits, more advanced techniques involving model adaptation and infrastructure optimization (covered comprehensively in Chapter 6) may be necessary.

Refining Prompts

Prompt engineering often provides the quickest wins for improving LLM and agent performance. Rather than ad hoc tweaking, successful teams approach this as a systematic process. They identify specific improvement targets based on evaluation results, hypothesize which prompt elements could address those issues, implement variations to test different approaches, then evaluate results both quantitatively and qualitatively before iterating based on findings.

Several patterns have proven particularly effective across different applications. Explicit *role and context definition* works by priming the model's attention mechanisms to activate domain-specific knowledge representations, essentially creating a specialized context window that emphasizes relevant training patterns while de-emphasizing generic responses. In mixture of experts (*https://oreil.ly/4bOHk*) (MoE) architectures, this context priming helps route processing through the most relevant expert networks. Task decomposition breaks complex tasks into explicit steps, guiding the model through structured reasoning processes that reduce errors and improve consistency.

Few-shot examples provide concrete demonstrations of desired inputs and outputs, essentially teaching the model through examples rather than abstract instructions. *Output structuring* explicitly defines the desired response format, ensuring consistency across interactions. *Thinking process guidance* directs the model's reasoning approach, encouraging it to consider multiple perspectives and potential conflicts before responding.

For our multimodal agent, if evaluation showed weaknesses in visual detail extraction, we might test prompts with more explicit instructions about image analysis depth. The key is connecting specific evaluation insights to targeted prompt improvements rather than making generic adjustments.

Vertex AI's Prompt Optimizer service (*https://oreil.ly/yNumF*) can automate much of this experimentation, systematically testing prompt variations and identifying the most effective approaches based on your evaluation criteria. You can optimize the instruction component (role and system instructions), the demonstration component (few-shot examples), or both simultaneously, allowing you to focus optimization efforts where your evaluation identifies the most significant gaps. Figure 5-6 shows the workflow of how the Prompt Optimizer transforms your original prompt template into an optimized version through systematic testing. For most applications, prompt engineering should be your first optimization approach due to its simplicity and rapid iteration cycle.

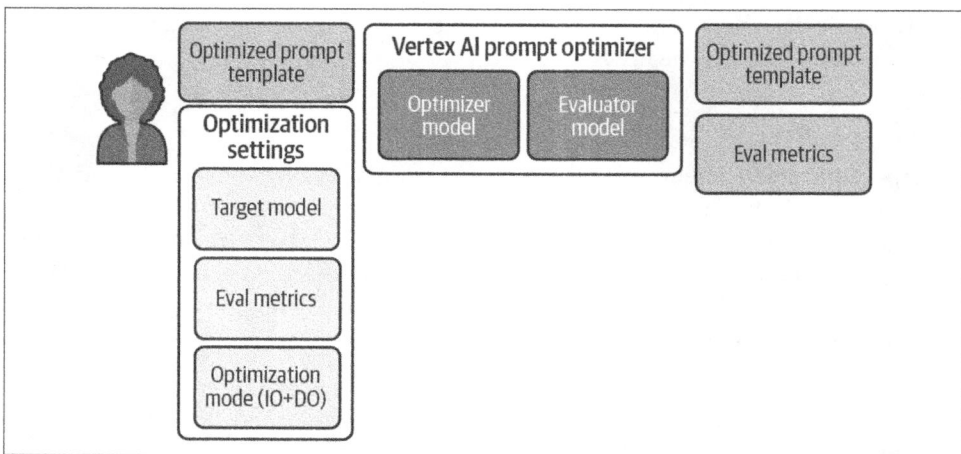

Figure 5-6. Vertex AI Prompt Optimizer inputs and outputs

Elevating Agent Performance

Agents add another layer of complexity to LLM applications by incorporating tool use, planning, and multistep reasoning. The most successful agent optimizations focus on designing robust tools and improving agent-reasoning capabilities, often extending into advanced multiagent architectures for complex domains.

Designing robust tools

Tools form the interface between your agent and external systems, making their optimization crucial for reliability and usability. The most robust tools provide clear specifications with detailed descriptions, parameter definitions, and usage examples that help the LLM understand when and how to use each tool. They implement thorough input validation to catch and handle invalid inputs gracefully, preventing cascading failures that can bring down entire agent workflows.

Modern protocols like MCP (Model Context Protocol) and A2A (Agent-to-Agent communication), which we explore in Chapter 4, standardize how tools expose their capabilities and enable dynamic tool discovery, eliminating the need to hardcode tool specifications into agent prompts.

Effective tools are designed to fail gracefully with informative error messages the agent can understand and act upon. Where possible, they're built to be *idempotent*, meaning multiple identical calls produce the same result, making agents more resilient to repeated tool invocations. They minimize state dependencies between tool calls to reduce complexity and potential failure modes.

Well-designed tools include retry logic for handling temporary failures, structure their results for optimal LLM consumption rather than human readability, and provide actionable error messages when failures occur. They limit response sizes to prevent overwhelming the model with excessive information while ensuring that essential data remains accessible. Strong type checking with frameworks such as Pydantic (*https://oreil.ly/XIxzB*) helps catch parameter errors before they reach external APIs, while comprehensive error handling ensures that agents receive useful feedback when operations fail.

Improving agent reasoning and planning

Beyond tools, optimizing how agents make decisions and plan multistep processes proves critical for complex tasks. Modern agent architectures employ several reasoning techniques.

Chain-of-thought prompting provides the foundation, explicitly instructing agents to reason step by step before taking actions. Leading implementations enhance this with structured frameworks like *ReAct* (reasoning and acting), which alternates between thought and action steps, allowing agents to observe results and adjust their approach mid-task. *Tree of Thoughts* (ToT) extends this further by exploring multiple reasoning paths in parallel before committing to actions, which is particularly valuable for complex problems with uncertain solution paths.

Modern agents also employ *dynamic planning* that adjusts based on intermediate results. Rather than following rigid sequences, they maintain goal hierarchies and can reformulate subgoals when initial approaches fail. This includes techniques such as plan-and-execute patterns (*https://oreil.ly/e8uH3*) where agents first create high-level plans, as shown in Figure 5-7, then decompose them into executable steps, monitoring progress and adjusting as needed.

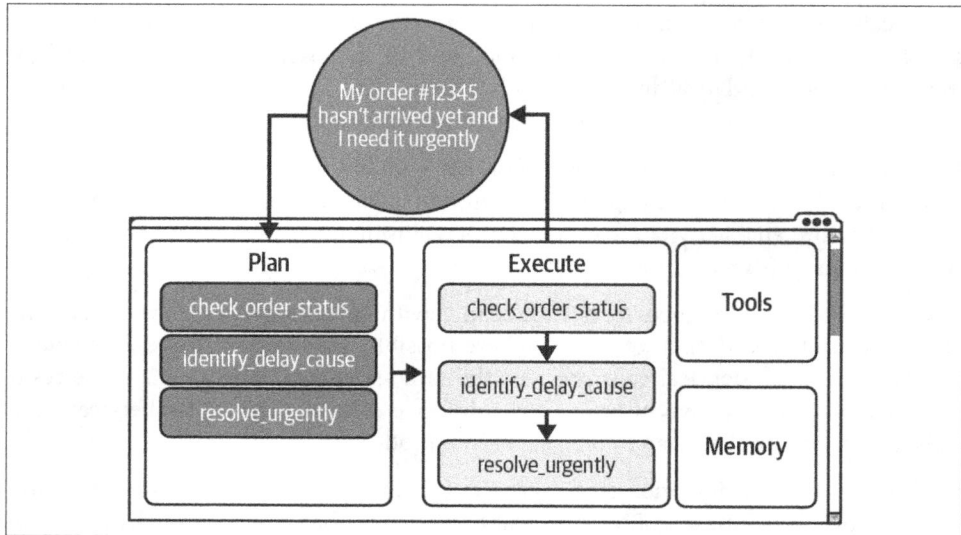

Figure 5-7. Dynamic planning in action—an agent creates a plan to resolve an urgent order issue, then adapts its execution based on findings at each step

For enhanced decision making, agents maintain both *working memory* (current task context) and *episodic memory* (past experiences) to inform decisions. Working memory typically leverages session state for immediate context, while episodic memory—the ability to recall similar past scenarios and learn from previous interactions—often requires infrastructure choices. Simple implementations might use in-memory storage for prototyping, but production systems typically need persistent solutions such as vector databases or managed services (*https://oreil.ly/Y9eo3*) to maintain knowledge across sessions and system restarts. This memory isn't just passive storage—it's actively used to weight decisions and predict likely outcomes of different action sequences.

When it comes to self-improvement, advanced reflection mechanisms go beyond simple validation. Agents can engage in *multilevel reflection*: immediate reflection on tool outputs ("Is this result reasonable?"), strategic reflection on approach ("Am I making progress toward the goal?"), and meta-reflection on their own reasoning process ("Am I overthinking this?"). Some implementations include *adversarial self-critique*, where the agent deliberately challenges its own assumptions before proceeding.

Finally, when deployed in multiagent systems (detailed in Chapter 4), agents can engage in *collaborative reasoning*—consulting with specialized agents for domain expertise, validating decisions through peer review, or even engaging in structured debates to explore different perspectives before reaching conclusions.

These reasoning techniques transform agents from simple tool-callers into adaptive problem-solvers that can handle ambiguity, recover from errors, and continuously improve their performance.

Multiagent optimization patterns

While Chapter 4 provides comprehensive coverage of multiagent systems, certain optimization patterns deserve mention here because they directly impact individual agent performance within larger systems.

The choice between *role specialization* and *generalization* significantly impacts optimization strategies. Specialized agents can be more deeply optimized for their specific domains, with focused prompts, curated tools, and targeted evaluation metrics. However, this must be balanced against the coordination overhead and the risk of over-specialization that limits flexibility.

In multiagent systems, optimizing *inter-agent communication* becomes crucial. This includes developing efficient message formats, implementing *smart routing* to avoid unnecessary communication loops, and managing conversation state across agent boundaries. Effective communication patterns can reduce latency, prevent information loss, and ensure that specialized agents can collaborate seamlessly.

Multiagent systems can also exhibit emergent behaviors—both beneficial and problematic. Optimization strategies must account for these system-level effects, including implementing *circuit breakers* to prevent cascade failures, designing feedback mechanisms that promote beneficial emergence, and creating *governance structures* that maintain system coherence without stifling innovation.

Beyond Prompt and Agent Optimizations

While prompt engineering and agent design improvements can deliver significant gains, some optimization challenges require deeper technical interventions. When you've exhausted these configuration-level approaches, you may need to consider model adaptation through fine-tuning techniques such as Low-Rank Adaptation (LoRA) and Quantized Low-Rank Adaptation (QLoRA), which allow you to specialize models for your specific domain while managing computational costs. Infrastructure optimizations for latency and cost reduction become crucial as your application scales, requiring decisions about quantization, model compression, and efficient serving strategies. Advanced deployment approaches, including edge computing and specialized hardware acceleration, may be necessary for applications with stringent performance requirements or unique deployment constraints.

These advanced optimization strategies require careful planning and often significant computational resources. They also introduce new complexity around model versioning, A/B testing infrastructure, and performance monitoring. Chapter 6 provides comprehensive coverage of these tuning and infrastructure considerations, helping you determine when they're necessary and how to implement them effectively for your specific use case. The key is knowing when you've reached the limits of prompt and agent optimizations—typically when you're seeing diminishing returns despite systematic experimentation, domain-specific requirements demand specialized model behavior, or scaling requirements necessitate infrastructure-level changes.

Looking Ahead

In this chapter, we've established a comprehensive framework for evaluating and optimizing LLM applications. We explored how to define excellence across multiple dimensions—from output quality and task success to efficiency and safety—and equipped you with both human-centered and automated evaluation strategies to measure performance against these targets.

We then demonstrated how evaluation insights drive targeted optimization through prompt engineering and agent design patterns. While certain capabilities—particularly persistent memory systems and multiagent coordination—may require infrastructure considerations, many enhancements such as reasoning frameworks, reflection mechanisms, and basic tool optimization can be implemented within your existing setup.

While we've focused on the initial evaluation and optimization process, production systems require ongoing attention. Regular reevaluation helps detect performance drift, changing user needs, and emerging edge cases. Chapter 7 will show you how to operationalize this process within a comprehensive MLOps framework, transforming these one-time improvements into systematic, continuous enhancement that keeps your system aligned with evolving user needs and business objectives.

In Chapter 6, "Tuning and Infrastructure," we'll explore the model adaptation and infrastructure optimization techniques we briefly touched upon here. You'll learn when fine-tuning becomes necessary, how to implement techniques like LoRA and QLoRA, and how to build serving infrastructure that balances performance with cost as your application scales.

Learning Labs

To reinforce the concepts covered in this chapter and deepen your understanding of evaluation frameworks and optimization strategies, we recommend exploring the learning resources available in the Chapter 5 folder of the book's GitHub repository (*https://oreil.ly/0bnlQ*). Key resources you will find linked there include:

- **Hands-On Code Examples**
  - Getting Started with Vertex AI Gen AI Evaluation Service SDK (*https://oreil.ly/t_n_r*): Comprehensive introduction to model-based evaluation with the Vertex AI Python SDK
  - Build and Evaluate BigQuery Agents using ADK and GenAI Eval Service (*https://oreil.ly/oeL9G*): A codelab demonstrating BigQuery agent evaluation against golden responses
  - Zero-Shot Prompt Optimizer (*https://oreil.ly/JaicF*): Real-time prompt optimization without labeled data
  - Data-Driven Prompt Optimizer (*https://oreil.ly/YaVBk*): Prompt optimization using labeled samples and evaluation metrics
- **Video Tutorials**
  - How to evaluate your GenAI models with Vertex AI (*https://oreil.ly/pR7Ny*): A practical guide to using the Vertex AI evaluation service to assess model performance with both pre-built and custom metrics
  - The Agent Evaluation Revolution (*https://oreil.ly/bpl_m*): Explores why traditional software testing fails for autonomous agents and introduces a "full-stack" system-level testing approach for evaluating planning, tool use, and memory
  - Evaluating and Debugging Non-Deterministic AI Agents (*https://oreil.ly/FdG01*): A clear explanation of why AI systems behave unpredictably and how to design evaluation strategies that account for this inherent variability

## CHAPTER 6

Tuning and Infrastructure

You built a capable customer service agent in Chapters 3 and 4. It handles requests across text, images, and video, and routes complex queries to specialist agents when needed. You followed Chapter 5's evaluation framework, measuring performance, iterating on prompts, and refining coordination patterns. The system works.

But as you prepare for production, new questions emerge. What if response times need to drop by 50%? What if the request volume scales to millions per day? What if your domain vocabulary—the specific terminology and patterns unique to your business—proves too specialized for the base model to handle reliably? When prompt engineering and agent design reach their limits, what comes next?

This chapter explores the deeper interventions that become necessary at scale. We'll examine when fine-tuning justifies its costs, how to implement it efficiently, and how to build inference infrastructure that balances performance, cost, and operational complexity.

The Tuning Decision

These questions about latency, scale, and domain specialization don't all have the same answer. Some point toward fine-tuning. Others don't. To see why, consider a financial services client whose agent struggled with two problems. First, it missed fraud signals, failing to recognize when routine-sounding inquiries were actually red flags for account takeover. The client had tried detailed prompts describing fraud patterns, but even with regular updates, the model treated these as rigid rules rather than adaptable heuristics. It would flag obvious cases but miss variations like new phishing approaches or slight changes in social engineering tactics.

Second, it couldn't match the conversational nuances that helped customers feel heard and guided toward resolution. They had refined prompts for empathetic language, but the agent would apply them mechanically, following the rules while missing the contextual judgment that distinguished experienced customer service representatives from those following a script. With configuration-level optimizations exhausted and thousands of successful human interactions logged, fine-tuning seemed like the logical next step for both problems.

It wasn't—at least not for both. The fraud detection issue could be solved by connecting the agent to their existing security infrastructure. Rather than teaching the model to recognize fraud patterns through fine-tuning, the agent could query real-time risk scoring systems when evaluating transactions—systems that were already processing millions of transactions and updating continuously based on emerging threats. The conversational nuances, however, required a different approach. Prompting could describe these patterns such as "be empathetic when customers are frustrated" but couldn't encode the learned associations between conversational signals and appropriate responses. When does a customer's one-word answer signal frustration versus simple efficiency? These patterns require contextual comprehension that emerges from statistical regularities across thousands of interactions. Fine-tuning on their call transcripts allowed the model to develop this comprehension—learning, for instance, that silence following a complaint paired with terse responses often signals the need to slow down and validate feelings rather than push toward resolution. Prompting gives rules; fine-tuning builds understanding of when and how to apply them.

Before committing to fine-tuning, map each capability requirement to these questions: can real-time data solve this (e.g., fraud detection via security APIs)? Does this require learned intuition from patterns (e.g., conversational judgment from interaction histories)? Could prompt engineering bridge 80% of the gap? This financial services case study demonstrates that even seemingly obvious candidates for fine-tuning may have simpler solutions. The question becomes: how do you make this evaluation systematically?

The Fine-Tuning Decision Framework

Five key decision criteria for this evaluation have emerged from production deployments. Table 6-1 summarizes the framework.

Table 6-1. Fine-tuning decision framework

Fine-tuning criterion	When to apply	Example use case	Key signal
Reasoning and intuition	Model must synthesize information, not just retrieve it	Medical diagnosis from patient records	External tools provide facts, but judgment requires learned patterns
Domain specialization	Domain vocabulary/concepts poorly represented in base model	Radiology terminology, contract clause structures	Specialized jargon or niche industry knowledge

Fine-tuning criterion	When to apply	Example use case	Key signal
Style and consistency	Specific communication patterns required	Legal document generation matching firm style	Prompting produces correct content but inconsistent tone/structure
Response latency	Real-time requirements or limited connectivity	Factory floor quality inspection	Round-trip API calls exceed operational requirements
Economics of scale	High-volume requests with retrieval costs	Millions of customer service interactions	Per-request RAG/API costs exceed fine-tuning investment

Consider fine-tuning when your task requires the model to develop *intuition* rather than just access information. A medical diagnosis agent might connect to an MCP server that serves patient records and lab results, but the ability to synthesize these into differential diagnoses—understanding subtle patterns and interactions—benefits from fine-tuning on case histories. The external tools provide the facts; the fine-tuned model provides the reasoning.

Fine-tuning becomes essential when your domain uses *specialized* vocabulary, concepts, or knowledge poorly represented in foundation model training data. Medical imaging models analyzing radiology scans need to learn subtle visual patterns and technical terminology that general vision-language models haven't encountered. Legal document systems must understand jurisdiction-specific contract language and clause structures. Manufacturing quality inspection agents need to internalize proprietary defect classifications and industry standards. When your domain's core concepts are niche or specialized, fine-tuning bridges the knowledge gap that prompting and retrieval alone can't.

Beyond knowledge gaps, fine-tuning also addresses how models express what they know. *Style and consistency requirements* often justify fine-tuning even when the information could be accessed externally. A legal document generation agent we worked with could pull clause templates from a database, but fine-tuning was necessary to ensure that the connecting language, transitions, and overall document flow matched the firm's house style. Every attempt to achieve this through prompting alone resulted in subtle inconsistencies that trained lawyers immediately spotted.

Operational constraints introduce additional considerations. *Response latency* creates another compelling case, particularly for edge deployments or environments with limited connectivity. Consider quality inspection on a factory floor: models need to analyze images in milliseconds to keep production lines moving. The round-trip time to a remote server—uploading high-resolution images, processing, and receiving results—often exceeds operational requirements. Add intermittent factory WiFi or security restrictions on external connections, and local inference becomes essential. Fine-tuning smaller models like Gemma 3n (*https://oreil.ly/s7VuH*)—which can run directly on edge devices with relevant visual patterns internalized—becomes the most viable approach.

Finally, the *economics of scale* often tip the balance toward fine-tuning. When you're processing millions of requests, the cumulative cost of retrieving context—whether through RAG, MCP servers, or API calls—can exceed fine-tuning costs within weeks. This calculation becomes even more stark when using closed model APIs where each request incurs pay-as-you-go token charges. A fine-tuned open model running on your own infrastructure might have higher upfront costs but eliminates per-request pricing that can spiral at scale. Of course, fine-tuned models aren't "train once and forget"—they require periodic retraining as data distributions shift or domain knowledge evolves, turning a one-time training cost into an ongoing operational commitment. The key is understanding whether your use case justifies these lifecycle costs versus configuration-level approaches such as prompt engineering, tool integration, and retrieval systems, which can be refined and deployed without retraining cycles.

> Certain industries have adopted fine-tuning as standard practice due to recurring patterns in these criteria. Ad tech agencies routinely fine-tune image and video generation models for proprietary brand aesthetics (style and consistency + domain specialization). Healthcare organizations fine-tune for specialized medical terminology and diagnostic reasoning (domain specialization + reasoning and intuition). Financial services fine-tune for regulatory compliance language and risk assessment patterns (style and consistency + reasoning and intuition). If your industry isn't listed here, don't assume fine-tuning is unnecessary—use the framework to evaluate your specific requirements.

Fine-Tuning Strategies: From Full Training to Efficient Adaptations

The framework tells you whether to fine-tune. But deciding "yes" opens a new set of questions: what will this actually cost in production? Should you use a managed platform or build custom infrastructure? How do modern parameter-efficient methods change the implementation calculus? The gap between "We should fine-tune" and "We're serving a fine-tuned model in production" is where many projects stumble—in fact, a 2023 industry survey (*https://oreil.ly/NTJVt*) found that 30% of organizations cite customization and fine-tuning as a top challenge when deploying LLMs.

The Real Cost of Fine-Tuning

Economics offers one lens into these challenges. The true costs of fine-tuning often bear little resemblance to initial estimates.

Consider a SaaS company fine-tuning a 7B (7-billion-parameter) model for its customer service agent. The company needs the model to match its brand voice, understand its product ecosystem, and handle domain-specific troubleshooting. The company estimated $800 in compute costs and 2 weeks of engineering time. The reality proved far more demanding: 7 training iterations across 3 months, more than $3,500 in compute costs, and 400 hours of engineering time. That time broke down into four weeks for data preparation (cleaning, formatting, balancing), three weeks for infrastructure setup (training pipelines, evaluation metrics, integration), and three weeks for experiment management (analyzing results, adjusting hyperparameters, iterating on approaches).

This pattern repeats across projects. The direct training costs appear modest—processing millions of tokens and several hours of GPU time might total a few hundred dollars per run. However, production-ready fine-tuning rarely happens in one shot. In practice, teams typically need three to seven iterations to achieve their quality targets, each involving data curation improvements, hyperparameter adjustments, and evaluation refinements. Those iterations quickly multiply the initial cost.

The compute costs, while significant, typically pale in comparison to the engineering investment. Then come the ongoing operational costs that transform a "one-time investment" into a recurring expense: model versioning and storage, A/B testing infrastructure, performance monitoring, and periodic retraining as data distributions shift or domain knowledge evolves. The SaaS company now retrains its model monthly, each iteration requiring data updates, quality validation, and careful deployment. What seemed like a project became an ongoing operational commitment.

Implementation Approaches

The costs are understood. The commitment is made. Now comes the practical question: how do you actually implement fine-tuning?

Fine-tuning requires loading your model into GPU memory, along with your training data and the optimizer (the training algorithm that calculates how to adjust parameters). For example, a 7B parameter model in 16-bit precision requires 14 GB just to load into memory. During training, the process gets more expensive. The training algorithm must track not just the model weights themselves, but also the gradients (the calculations showing which direction to adjust each weight) and optimizer states (information about past adjustments that helps training converge faster). These additional requirements add roughly three times the model size. That's 42 GB of training overhead on top of the 14 GB model—56 GB total before accounting for the actual data being processed. Consider a typical development GPU with 24 GB of memory, common in hardware like a NVIDIA RTX 4090 (*https://oreil.ly/b2o3D*) or L4 (*https://oreil.ly/1cQ7r*). The 56 GB requirement makes full fine-tuning impossible on a single accelerator.

Parameter-efficient methods such as LoRA (*https://oreil.ly/1EMeS*) (Low-Rank Adaptation) solve this by changing what gets updated during training. As illustrated in Figure 6-1, instead of updating all 7B parameters in the model, LoRA freezes the original model weights and adds small "adapter" layers: new parameters that learn your specific task. These adapters typically contain about 8M parameters, less than 1% of the original model size. When you're only training 8M parameters instead of 7B, those 42 GB of training overhead shrink to under 1 GB. What required a GPU cluster now fits on a single accelerator.

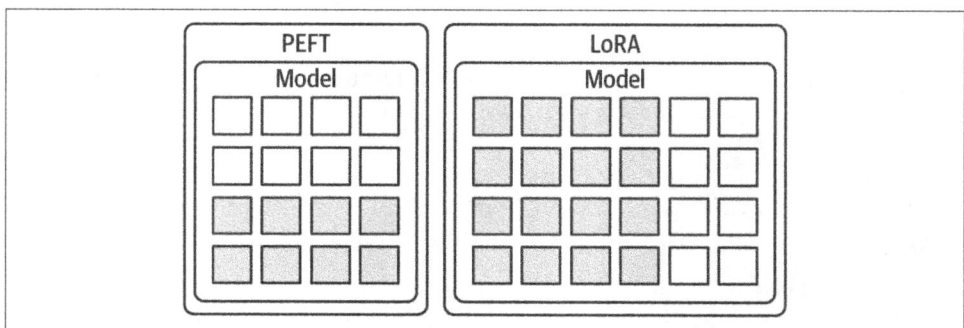

Figure 6-1. Parameter-efficient fine-tuning (PEFT) and methods like LoRA freeze the massive base model and update only a small adapter layer, drastically reducing computational costs compared to full fine-tuning

Vertex AI's supervised fine-tuning implements these parameter-efficient techniques automatically. The platform supports fine-tuning of Gemini models and popular open source models such as Llama (*https://oreil.ly/cxUF3*), Gemma (*https://oreil.ly/sZJXi*), and Qwen (*https://oreil.ly/TubFw*). The platform accepts training data as JSONL files, determines optimal adapter configurations, orchestrates training across its infrastructure, and exposes the result as a serving endpoint, illustrated in Figure 6-2. Most teams we work with take this managed path. It eliminates infrastructure concerns and accelerates time to production.

The alternative is custom training using libraries like Hugging Face's `transformers` and `trl` or higher-level frameworks like Unsloth (*https://oreil.ly/_w2IU*) and Axolotl (*https://oreil.ly/2lnlK*). This provides complete control over the training process: how the model learns, how infrastructure resources are allocated, and how the resulting model gets deployed. The trade-off is an operational burden. You become responsible for GPU cluster configuration, hyperparameter tuning, experiment tracking, checkpoint management, and deployment pipelines.

Custom frameworks make sense in specific circumstances. First, when you need training approaches the platform doesn't support. Perhaps you need different parts of your model to learn at different speeds, you need to introduce training examples in a carefully controlled order, or your domain requires specialized techniques to prevent overfitting. Second, when you're operating at a scale where infrastructure optimization justifies dedicated engineering effort. If you're training dozens of models monthly at costs that compound into hundreds of thousands of dollars, custom infrastructure optimization justifies the engineering effort. Third, when compliance requirements demand complete infrastructure control. For example, certain financial services or healthcare deployments face strict data residency rules that limit use of managed platforms.

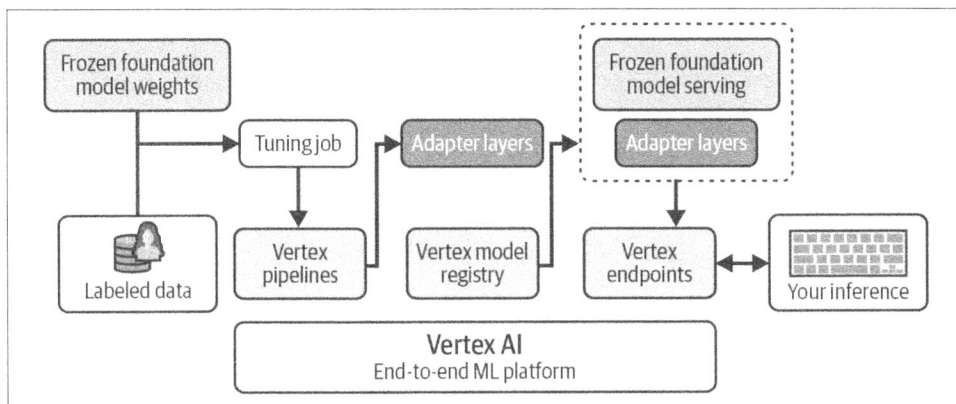

Figure 6-2. Vertex AI supervised tuning pipeline automates adapter injection and orchestrates the training workflow, eliminating the need for complex infrastructure management

For most use cases, the managed platform suffices. Teams we work with start on Vertex AI and stay there—the platform handles production workloads without requiring dedicated infrastructure expertise. Containerization and model format standards mean migration to custom frameworks involves configuration changes rather than architectural rewrites if specific requirements later justify it. The decision is economic: does the value of infrastructure control outweigh the cost of building and maintaining it? For many teams, engineering focus is better spent on data quality, evaluation frameworks, and application logic.

Distillation for Edge and Real-Time Workloads

Sometimes, even an efficiently fine-tuned model is simply too large for its target environment. If your application targets mobile devices, IoT hardware, or requires single-millisecond latency, a standard 7B+ parameter model may be unviable regardless of how you trained it.

In these scenarios, knowledge distillation (*https://oreil.ly/EFar5*) is the standard solution. Unlike LoRA, which optimizes the training process, distillation optimizes the inference outcome. The pattern involves using a large, capable "teacher" model to generate synthetic training data, reasoning traces, or labels. This high-quality output is then used to fine-tune a significantly smaller "student" model. This approach was notably validated by DeepSeek (*https://oreil.ly/4HdHU*), which successfully distilled the complex reasoning capabilities of its 670B R1 model into smaller, efficient variants.

The goal is to transfer the reasoning capabilities of the large model into a compact architecture that can run locally on-device or at extreme speeds in the cloud.

Infrastructure Questions Emerge

The implementation path—managed platform or custom framework—determines how you train. But regardless of which path you take, infrastructure questions emerge that shape both training efficiency and serving performance.

During training, you might see your job showing 40% GPU utilization despite running on expensive hardware. Or distributed training across 8 GPUs delivers only 3x speedup instead of the 8x you expected. During serving, the deployed model takes 30 seconds to load on startup, handles five requests per second when you need five hundred, or runs out of memory under real traffic patterns. The symptoms differ but the underlying cause is consistent: infrastructure constraints.

These aren't model quality problems. They're bottlenecks in how data moves through your system, how hardware resources get utilized, and how compute scales across multiple devices. Understanding which constraint you'll hit first—and why it's happening—determines everything about your infrastructure choices. The hardware you select, the storage architecture you deploy, the serving framework you configure, and the platform you run on all flow from identifying your specific bottleneck.

The Constraint You'll Hit First

You run training and it completes successfully. Or you deploy to production and inference requests return correct responses. The system functions. But performance tells a different story. Training takes twice as long as projected. Serving handles a fraction of the throughput you need. Something is limiting performance, but what?

The answer shows up in your metrics. Four characteristic patterns appear across training and serving workloads, each revealing a different fundamental constraint. Recognizing which pattern you're seeing determines everything about how you'll solve it—the hardware you need, the optimizations that matter, and the infrastructure investments that actually help.

Pattern 1: The Waiting Accelerator

Your GPU utilization sits at 50% to 70%. You optimize your code—batch sizes, data loading, model architecture. The number barely moves. You expect expensive accelerators to run near 100%, but they don't. The hardware isn't slow. It's waiting, as illustrated in Example 6-1.

Example 6-1. Processors sit idle waiting for data when the memory bus cannot keep up with the computational speed, resulting in low effective utilization

```
TPU Runtime Utilization
+---------+-----------------------------+-------------+
| Device  | HBM usage                   | Duty cycle  |
+---------+-----------------------------+-------------+
|      8  | 18.45 GiB / 31.25 GiB       | 42.50%      |
|      9  | 10.40 GiB / 31.25 GiB       | 41.20%      |
|     12  | 10.40 GiB / 31.25 GiB       | 43.10%      |
|     13  | 10.40 GiB / 31.25 GiB       | 42.80%      |
+---------+-----------------------------+-------------+
```

This is a memory bandwidth bottleneck. The problem isn't the processor's ability to compute—it's the rate at which data can move from memory to the processor. Think of it like a high-performance engine connected to a narrow fuel line. The engine could run at full throttle, but it spends most of its time idling, waiting for the next batch of fuel to arrive.

In neural network operations, the processor needs constant access to model weights. During LLM inference, generating each token requires loading attention weights from memory, performing calculations, then loading the next set of weights. If the memory bus can only deliver data at 1 TB/s but your processor can consume it at 3 TB/s, the processor spends two-thirds of its time waiting. Your utilization reads 50% not because the hardware is slow, but because it's starving for data.

This bottleneck appears most commonly in LLM serving, where generating text token-by-token creates a continuous stream of small computations, each requiring fresh data from memory. It also shows up in training when models are large relative to available memory bandwidth—the processor can multiply matrices quickly but can't get the next batch of weights fast enough to stay busy.

The symptom is distinctive: GPU or TPU utilization that stays stuck at 50% to 70% or less regardless of optimization efforts and throughput that doesn't scale proportionally when you increase batch size. The solution requires either hardware with higher memory bandwidth or techniques that reduce how much data needs to move—approaches like quantization and efficient attention mechanisms that we'll explore in the accelerator and serving sections.

Pattern 2: The Memory Wall

Your training job crashes before the first step completes. Or your serving instance starts, then immediately exits with an out-of-memory error. You're not hitting a performance limit. You're hitting a capacity limit—the model and its operational overhead simply don't fit. This is illustrated in Example 6-2.

Example 6-2. Workloads fail immediately with out-of-memory (OOM) errors when model parameters and activations exceed the accelerator's available video random access memory (VRAM)

```
TPU Runtime Utilization
+---------+--------------------------------+------------+
| Device  | HBM usage                      | Duty cycle |
+---------+--------------------------------+------------+
|      8  | 31.25 GiB / 31.25 GiB          | 10.00%     |
|      9  | 31.25 GiB / 31.25 GiB          | 10.00%     |
|     12  | 31.25 GiB / 31.25 GiB          | 10.00%     |
|     13  | 31.25 GiB / 31.25 GiB          | 10.00%     |
+---------+--------------------------------+------------+
```

The arithmetic is straightforward but unforgiving. A 70B parameter model in 16-bit precision requires 140 GB just to store the weights (70B parameters × 2 bytes per parameter). During training, you need additional memory for activations (the intermediate calculations at each layer) and gradients (the information needed to update weights). During serving, you need memory for the key-value (KV) cache (the attention mechanism's working memory that grows with each token generated). If your GPU has 80 GB of memory, the model doesn't fit. No amount of optimization changes this fundamental constraint.

This bottleneck appears across both training and serving, though for different reasons. In training, the memory wall typically appears when attempting to train large models without proper memory management techniques. Teams often discover this immediately—the first training step fails with an OOM error before any real work happens. In serving, it shows up when trying to deploy models that barely fit in memory, leaving no room for the dynamic allocations needed during inference. Under normal load, the model serves requests successfully, but when traffic increases and more requests arrive simultaneously, memory exhausts and requests start failing.

The most common occurrence is trying to run models on single GPUs when they fundamentally require multiple devices. A 70B model needs at least two 80 GB GPUs just for basic inference, more if you want reasonable batch sizes.

Solutions involve either reducing memory requirements or distributing the model across more memory. Quantization (*https://oreil.ly/veyYc*) reduces precision (16-bit weights to 8-bit or 4-bit), cutting memory usage by 50% to 75% at the cost of slight quality degradation. This addresses both capacity constraints (Pattern 2) and bandwidth bottlenecks (Pattern 1) by reducing how much data exists and needs to move. Model parallelism (*https://oreil.ly/H59i1*) splits the model across multiple GPUs, each holding a portion of the weights. Both approaches trade something— quality or hardware complexity—to fit within available memory. Without one of these interventions, you simply can't proceed.

Pattern 3: Maxed Out But Still Slow

Your GPU utilization shows 100%, sustained across the entire workload. This is illustrated in Example 6-3. Every optimization you've tried is already implemented. The hardware is processing as fast as physically possible. Yet training still takes longer than you need, or serving throughput still falls short of requirements.

Example 6-3. Sustained 100% compute utilization indicates that the hardware is processing as fast as possible, requiring faster chips or horizontal scaling to improve throughput

```
TensorCore Utilization
+---------+---------------------------+
| Chip ID | TensorCore Utilization    |
+---------+---------------------------+
|    0    | 100.00%                   |
|    1    | 100.00%                   |
|    2    | 100.00%                   |
|    3    | 100.00%                   |
+---------+---------------------------+
```

This is a compute bottleneck, and paradoxically, it's often the best kind of bottleneck to have. It often means you've optimized well—data moves efficiently, memory is utilized effectively, and the processor is doing legitimate work rather than waiting.

This pattern appears most commonly in diffusion models for image generation. Each generated image requires 50 to 100 denoising steps, each step a computationally expensive forward pass through a U-Net architecture (*https://oreil.ly/2eU3C*). The math is intensive, the processor stays busy, and every calculation is necessary. There's no waste to eliminate, no inefficiency to fix. The work itself is compute-heavy.

The solution is straightforward in concept: faster chips or more chips working in parallel. A model that takes 2 seconds per inference on a mid-tier GPU might take 0.5 seconds on a high-end accelerator. Scaling horizontally—adding more GPUs handling different requests simultaneously—also works, though with coordination overhead that limits efficiency gains.

This is most often the easiest bottleneck to diagnose and address. If your metrics show sustained high utilization and your workload is inherently compute-intensive, you have a clear path forward. The decision becomes economic: does faster hardware or more parallel capacity justify its cost for your use case? But unlike bandwidth or capacity constraints, you're not fighting inefficiency or fundamental limits. You're just constrained by the speed of computation itself.

Pattern 4: More GPUs = Worse Performance

Training on a single GPU completes in 8 hours. You add a second GPU, expecting 4 hours. Instead it takes 5 hours. You scale to 8 GPUs—the math should give you 1 hour, but you get 3 hours instead. Adding more hardware makes things slower per GPU, not faster. Something is consuming the benefit you should be getting from parallelism, illustrated in Figure 6-3.

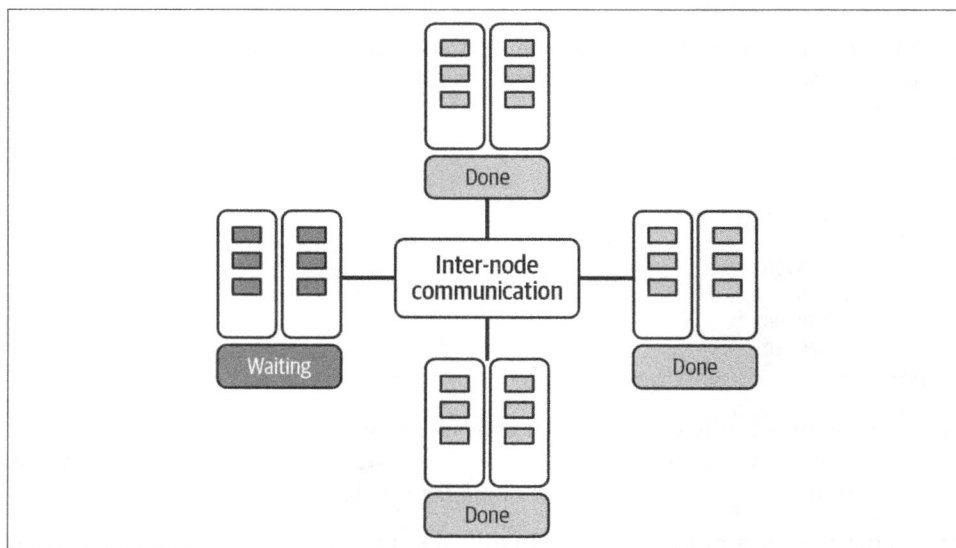

Figure 6-3. Distributed training performance degrades when compute nodes spend more time synchronizing states over the network than processing data

This is a network bottleneck, and it appears only when you distribute workloads across multiple devices. Each GPU processes its portion of the work quickly. Then comes the synchronization step: gradients must be communicated between all GPUs, averaged, and distributed back. If this communication takes longer than the computation itself, adding more GPUs just adds more coordination overhead.

The pattern is characteristic of distributed training at scale. During each training step, every GPU computes gradients for its batch of data. Before the next step begins, all GPUs must share their gradients with each other—a communication pattern called "all-reduce" where every GPU needs information from every other GPU. If you have 8 GPUs and the network between them is slow, each training step includes substantial idle time waiting for gradient synchronization to complete.

The math reveals the problem quickly. If computation takes 100 milliseconds per step and network communication takes 50 milliseconds, you're spending one-third of your time on coordination overhead. Scale to 64 GPUs and that communication time might grow to 400 milliseconds—now 80% of each step is waiting for the network. Your expensive compute sits idle while data moves between machines.

This bottleneck is invisible in development. Training on a single GPU or a few GPUs in the same machine uses fast local interconnects where communication overhead is negligible. The problem appears only when you scale to multiple servers, where GPUs must communicate over standard datacenter networks.

The solution requires fast interconnects designed specifically for this communication pattern. NVIDIA's NVLink for GPU clusters (*https://oreil.ly/QHpEK*), InfiniBand for high-performance computing (*https://oreil.ly/qxCXg*), or Google's Inter-Chip Interconnect (ICI) for TPU pods (*https://oreil.ly/iIrcA*)—these specialized networks provide the bandwidth and latency characteristics that make distributed training viable. Without them, adding more devices to your training job may make things slower, not faster.

Accelerators: Matching Hardware to Bottlenecks

Your bottleneck is diagnosed. The metrics tell you whether you're waiting for data (Pattern 1), running out of space (Pattern 2), maxing out computation (Pattern 3), or losing time to network synchronization (Pattern 4). Now comes the hardware decision: which accelerator actually addresses your specific constraint?

The choice between GPUs and TPUs isn't about which is "better" in the abstract. It's about which matches your bottleneck, scale, and operational reality. This decision is fundamentally economic. The hardware that solves your bottleneck most efficiently today might not be optimal at 10x scale.

The Decision Framework

Each bottleneck pattern has different hardware implications. Table 6-2 maps constraints to accelerator strengths.

Table 6-2. Accelerator selection by bottleneck

Pattern	Constraint	GPU best when	TPU best when	Key trade-off
Pattern 1: bandwidth	Memory-to-processor data movement	Ecosystem compatibility matters more than efficiency	Processing >1M requests/day or large training jobs where bandwidth matters	Operational simplicity vs. bandwidth efficiency at scale
Pattern 2: memory	Model doesn't fit in device memory	Single-device optimization preferred	Distributing across TPU pods with high-speed interconnect	Setup simplicity vs. pod-level scalability
Pattern 3: compute	Sustained 100% utilization	Quick iteration, familiar tools	Large-scale training where cost-per-FLOP matters	Flexibility vs. cost efficiency
Pattern 4: network	Multidevice gradient sync	Single-node clusters (e.g., 8 GPUs)	Distributed training across TPU pods (hundreds of chips)	Setup simplicity vs. scaling efficiency

TPUs excel when scale transforms architectural advantages into meaningful cost savings. GPUs excel when ecosystem compatibility, operational familiarity, or modest scale make optimization premature. Pattern 1 bandwidth bottlenecks benefit from TPU pod bandwidth and interconnect speeds (enabling efficient sharding), but this advantage amplifies primarily at large cluster scales. Pattern 3 compute bottlenecks are straightforward: you need more processing power—both platforms work, and economics determines the choice.

The Practical Decision

During initial development, GPUs typically make sense. You're iterating rapidly—trying architectures, debugging issues, testing hyperparameters. The ecosystem accelerates iteration. When you're still figuring out what works, flexibility outweighs potential cost savings.

The calculation shifts when training runs become large. A week-long job on 64 high-end GPUs (e.g., NVIDIA A100s) can cost $10,000 to $25,000 on discounted or alternative cloud pricing; on major hyperscalers it may cost significantly more depending on instance type. Run several experiments and costs can rise up to $50,000+. Public benchmarks and case studies often show several-fold (2 to 4x, sometimes higher) cost-performance advantages for large-scale training on TPUs—especially TPU v5p or newer at pod scale. In scenarios where GPUs would cost approximately $50,000 for a full training cycle, TPUs can reduce that cost into the low five-figure range depending on workload, configuration, and commitments (*https://oreil.ly/iIBg_*).

A rough heuristic: training jobs under 100 GPU-hours stay on GPUs for simplicity. Jobs exceeding 500 GPU-hours justify TPU evaluation. Between 100 to 500 GPU-hours, the decision depends on experiment volume and your team's platform comfort.

Framework support has matured significantly. Keras 3 (*https://oreil.ly/BGSXZ*) runs on TPUs through JAX, TensorFlow, or PyTorch backends. PyTorch/XLA (*https://*

*oreil.ly/Euwv_*) provides TPU execution for PyTorch models. Modern frameworks increasingly abstract hardware differences, reducing the platform lock-in that once favored GPUs.

Migration Reality

You're not locked into your initial choice. Modern serving frameworks such as vLLM (*https://oreil.ly/t0g-2*) now support both GPUs and TPUs with minimal changes to model code or serving logic. Start where you can iterate fastest—often GPUs—then optimize based on actual scale and costs.

When should you switch? Here are three general triggers:

Cost threshold
  Monthly serving costs exceeding approximately $10,000 or training costs exceeding approximately $10,000 per experiment warrant a platform benchmark comparison.

Scale stabilization
  When request patterns are predictable, optimizing for cost-per-inference justifies itself. With highly variable traffic, optimizing for operational flexibility and rapid scaling often matters more than cost efficiency.

Bottleneck diagnosis
  When you've identified Pattern 1 or Pattern 4 bottlenecks limiting performance, hardware that directly addresses these constraints becomes attractive.

The optimal choice changes as your application matures. Start with what gets you to production fastest—usually GPUs for ecosystem familiarity—then optimize based on real data once you understand your actual constraints and scale.

Storage Options

Your training job starts. GPUs initialize, the model loads, and training begins. Then progress slows. An hour passes. The progress indicator shows 2% complete. You check GPU utilization: 15%. The hardware isn't slow—it's waiting.

This storage bottleneck is often invisible during development. Training on small datasets or cached data masks the problem. But scale to production—hundreds of gigabytes of training data, millions of examples, frequent checkpoints—and storage determines whether your expensive accelerators work or wait. A training job that should take 8 hours takes 24, not because computation is slow, but because GPUs spend two-thirds of their time idle, waiting for the next batch to arrive. If you're paying $5,000 per day for accelerator capacity but storage delivers data at one-third the rate computation demands, you're getting $1,500 of actual work.

When Storage Becomes Your Bottleneck

The question isn't "What storage technology should I use?" but "When does storage become the constraint limiting my workload?"

For training, the signal is straightforward: dataset size multiplied by access frequency exceeding network storage throughput. A 2 TB computer vision dataset trained for 50 epochs means reading 100 TB of data. Standard network storage delivers 500 MB/s. That's 55+ hours just loading data before any computation happens. If your GPU cluster can process each epoch in 1 hour, you're spending 55 hours on I/O and 50 hours on computation—storage is the bottleneck.

For serving, the constraint manifests differently: cold start time multiplied by scaling frequency exceeding acceptable latency. A 70B model is 140 GB. If loading takes 10 minutes, autoscaling adds capacity 10 minutes after traffic spikes—too late to prevent user impact. If your service scales instances 20 times daily responding to traffic patterns, those 10-minute delays compound into operational problems.

The decision framework: if accelerators spend more time waiting for data than computing, or if cold starts prevent responsive scaling, storage architecture needs attention.

The Storage Pattern

Production AI workloads follow a consistent progression through three phases, each with different storage requirements.

Training phase: Managed Lustre

Training demands sustained high throughput—reading datasets repeatedly and writing large checkpoints frequently. Managed Lustre (*https://oreil.ly/q2Zz2*) delivers up to 1 TB/s by striping data across dozens of disks simultaneously, roughly 10 to 20× faster than standard network storage.

The math is direct: a 2 TB dataset on network storage at 500MB/s takes 68 minutes to load per epoch. On Lustre, even at a conservative throughput of 10 GB/s, that drops to under 4 minutes. Over 50 epochs, you save more than 50 hours of idle accelerator time. Lustre costs roughly $70 monthly for capacity that costs $2.80 in Cloud Storage (*https://oreil.ly/kxC6E*), but during active training, that premium justifies itself by eliminating wasted compute costs.

The critical requirement: collocate Lustre in the same zone as your training accelerators. A training job, for example, in us-central1-a should read from Lustre in us-central1-a. Cross-zone transfers add latency and cost that mitigates the throughput advantage.

Archival phase: Cloud Storage

When training completes, export the final model to Cloud Storage. This transitions from high-performance, high-cost storage optimized for sustained throughput to durable, cost-effective storage. A 140 GB model costs $2.80 monthly in Cloud Storage versus $70+ in Lustre. When you're maintaining multiple model versions—production model, A/B test variants, rollback versions—Cloud Storage's cost structure makes version management practical.

Serving phase: Cloud Storage FUSE + Anywhere Cache

Serving optimizes for global distribution and fast initial loads rather than sustained throughput. Cloud Storage with FUSE (*https://oreil.ly/hTV4s*) mounts buckets as local filesystems, and Anywhere Cache (*https://oreil.ly/P-MSI*) adds regional solid-state drive (SSD)-backed caches. Cold reads might take 50 to 100 milliseconds; cached reads drop to 15 to 30 milliseconds. For model loading—reading hundreds of thousands of weights sequentially—this reduces cold start times by roughly 70%.

The architecture supports multiregion serving naturally. Store your model once in a multiregion Cloud Storage bucket. Enable Anywhere Cache in each serving zone. Instances in us-west1 and europe-west1 read the same model with regional caching—no manual replication, no data transfer costs between the bucket and cache in the same multiregion location.

Serving and Deployment

Your model is trained and stored. Now you face two distinct deployment challenges: *serving the model for inference* and *deploying the agent application* that orchestrates requests. Model serving focuses on generating predictions efficiently—handling concurrent requests, managing GPU memory, returning responses quickly. Agent deployment handles everything else: request routing, conversation state, tool orchestration, and calling model endpoints. These are separate concerns with different infrastructure requirements and different deployment platforms.

Efficient serving with vLLM

To serve your model efficiently, you need a framework that maximizes GPU utilization while handling concurrent requests. vLLM achieves this by optimizing how memory is allocated during the token generation process.

The throughput problem.   Your fine-tuned model is ready. You deploy a straightforward serving setup: load the model into GPU memory, accept requests, generate responses. Initial testing works. Then production traffic reveals that the infrastructure handles a fraction of the throughput you need—a hundred requests per second when you need a thousand. The model quality is fine. The serving efficiency isn't.

The root cause is memory waste. Traditional serving approaches allocate fixed memory blocks for each request's entire potential generation, even though most requests complete early. If you allocate space for 512 tokens but the response finishes at 50 tokens, those remaining 462 token slots sit unused, unavailable to other requests. This fragmentation leaves expensive VRAM underutilized while new requests queue, unable to start because memory appears full. You're not hitting a model capacity limit—you're hitting an infrastructure efficiency limit.

vLLM (*https://oreil.ly/SdyiW*) addresses Pattern 1 (bandwidth) and Pattern 2 (memory) bottlenecks through three core innovations, each solving a specific constraint that limits throughput or increases latency.

PagedAttention.   PagedAttention (*https://oreil.ly/caR_q*) eliminates the memory waste that creates artificial capacity constraints. Instead of reserving large contiguous blocks per request, it manages memory in small, fixed-size pages—typically 16 or 32 tokens per page. These pages are allocated on demand as tokens generate and returned to the free pool immediately when requests complete.

The impact is direct: 2.5x higher throughput typically on identical hardware. A 13B parameter model that served 100 requests per second with traditional approaches now serves 250 requests per second with vLLM. You're not making the model faster or the GPU more powerful, you're eliminating the memory waste that prevented running more requests concurrently. This directly addresses Pattern 2's capacity constraint through efficiency rather than adding hardware.

Continuous batching.   Traditional batching waits for entire batches to complete before processing the next batch. If your batch size is 32 and one request generates 500 tokens while others complete in 50 tokens, the next 31 requests wait for that single slow request to finish.

Continuous batching eliminates this wait. Requests join and leave batches dynamically during generation. As soon as a request completes, a new request from the queue takes its slot. The batch composition changes with every token generated. The utilization impact is substantial: 85% to 90% GPU utilization versus 40% to 50% with naive batching. This optimization matters most during traffic spikes, exactly when you need it.

Disaggregated serving.   LLM inference has two distinct phases with different computational characteristics. The prefill phase is compute-intensive, processing the initial prompt through a forward pass that generates KV cache for all prompt tokens. The decode phase is memory bandwidth—intensive, generating output tokens one at a time by constantly loading attention weights.

Disaggregated serving splits these phases across different accelerators matched to their bottlenecks. Dedicated prefill instances use high-compute hardware optimized for intensive matrix operations. Dedicated decode instances use memory-optimized hardware optimized for bandwidth-intensive attention operations. The result is faster response times and lower costs simultaneously—you're matching accelerator characteristics to workload bottlenecks rather than compromising with one hardware type that's mediocre at both phases.

Configuration That Matters

vLLM exposes several parameters that balance throughput, latency, and resource utilization, illustrated in Example 6-4. Understanding what they control and how they map to bottleneck patterns helps configure serving for your specific workload.

Example 6-4. vLLM production configuration mapped to bottleneck pattern

```
from vllm import LLM, SamplingParams

prompts = [
    "Explain why storage throughput can bottleneck GPUs.",
    "Give me a short summary of TPU benefits.",
]

# Initialize with production-optimized settings
llm = LLM(
    model="google/gemma-2-27b-it",
    # Pattern 2: Split across 2 GPUs if model doesn't fit one
    tensor_parallel_size=2,
    # Pattern 2: Use 90% of GPU memory for KV cache
    gpu_memory_utilization=0.9,
    # Pattern 1: Maximum concurrent sequences
    max_num_seqs=256,
    # Pattern 1: Cache common prefixes to reduce bandwidth
    enable_prefix_caching=True,
)

# Sampling configuration
sampling_params = SamplingParams(
    temperature=0.1,
    top_p=0.9,
    max_tokens=512,
)

outputs = llm.generate(prompts, sampling_params)
```

Tuning to your bottleneck

If you're hitting Pattern 2 (memory capacity) with OOM errors, reduce `gpu_memory_utilization` from 0.9 to 0.85 or 0.8, leaving headroom for memory spikes. Alternatively, decrease `max_num_seqs` to limit concurrent requests and their memory footprint.

If you're hitting Pattern 1 (bandwidth) with low GPU utilization, ensure you're maximizing memory use (`gpu_memory_utilization=0.9`) and `enable_prefix_caching=True` for conversational workloads where system prompts repeat across requests. Prefix caching computes these once and reuses results, dramatically reducing the attention weights that must be loaded from memory.

If you're hitting Pattern 3 (compute-bound) with sustained 100% utilization, your configuration is already optimized. Improved throughput requires faster hardware or more parallel capacity.

The `tensor_parallel_size` parameter determines how many accelerators the model splits across. Set this based on Pattern 2 constraints: if your model fits on 1 GPU, use 1. If it requires 140 GB but you have 80 GB GPUs, use 2. More parallelism means more communication overhead, so use the minimum number of devices that fit your model comfortably.

Multiplatform support

vLLM supports both GPU and TPU serving with the same API and configuration patterns. This enables practical optimization paths: develop on GPUs for rapid iteration and familiar tooling, then benchmark TPU deployment when traffic patterns stabilize and request volume grows.

The serving framework abstracts hardware differences, so the evaluation becomes purely economic, and the configuration becomes about matching serving parameters to the specific constraint limiting your workload.

Connecting Models to Agents

vLLM handles model serving: efficiently generating predictions from your fine-tuned models. But agents built with frameworks like ADK need to connect to these model endpoints to access their reasoning capabilities. The model serves as the agent's cognitive engine or brain, while the agent framework handles orchestration, tool integration, and conversation management.

This separation creates architectural flexibility. Your agent code can remain stable while you swap model endpoints (upgrading from a 7B to a 70B model, switching between different providers, or A/B testing fine-tuned variants). Tools such as LiteLLM (*https://oreil.ly/WmhAJ*) provide standardized interfaces, allowing agent frameworks to communicate with any model endpoint using a consistent API format, as shown in Example 6-5.

Example 6-5. Connecting an ADK agent to a vLLM endpoint with LiteLLM

```
from google.adk.agents import Agent
from google.adk.models.lite_llm import LiteLlm


# Configure LiteLLM to connect to your model endpoint
model_client = LiteLlm(
    model="openai/google/gemma-2-27b-it",  # Model served by framework
    api_base="https://your-vllm-service/v1",   # Your model endpoint
    api_key="not-needed"
)

# Agent uses this client for all reasoning
agent = LlmAgent(
    model=model_client,
    name="customer_service_agent",
    instruction="You are a helpful customer service agent..."
)
```

When deploying to production, you're managing two distinct infrastructure concerns: model-serving endpoints configured with vLLM and the optimizations discussed previously, plus agent application logic deployed on platforms designed for orchestration workloads. The agent calls your model endpoint, receives predictions, and uses those predictions to determine next actions.

Agent Deployment Platforms

Your serving framework determines how efficiently your model generates predictions. The deployment platform determines how your agent application scales and how it's monitored. The right choice depends less on which platform is "better" and more on your team's capabilities, scaling requirements, and how much infrastructure management you're willing to own. Platform deployment options for ADK agents are illustrated in Figure 6-4.

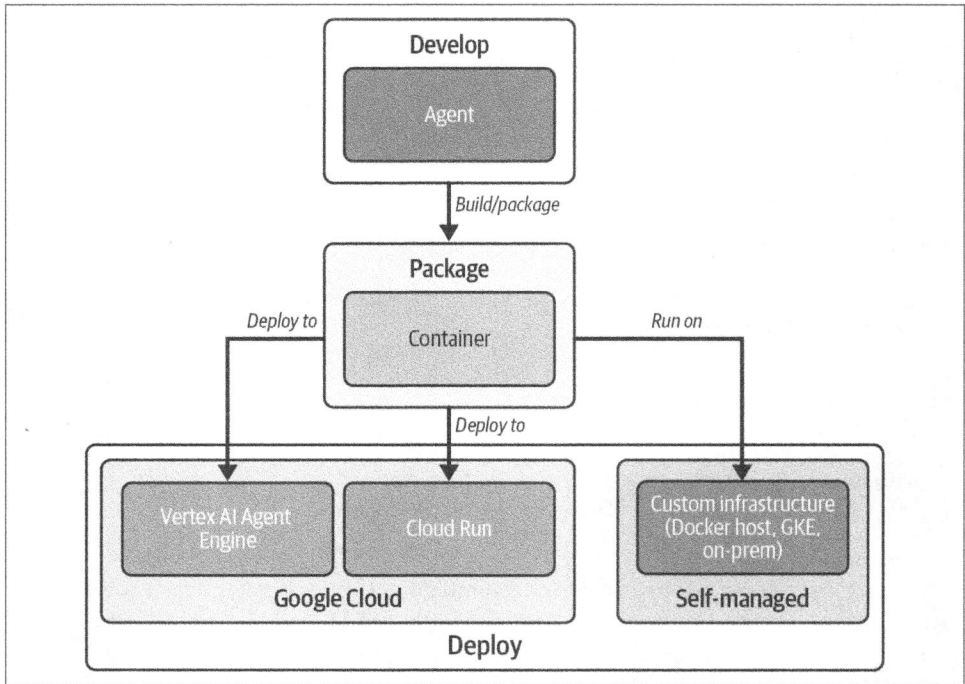

Figure 6-4. ADK deployment options

Agent Engine

Agent Engine provides the fastest path from agent code to production. The platform is purpose-built for AI agents, handling conversation state, session persistence, and scaling automatically. You provide the agent code, configure basic parameters, and the platform manages infrastructure, load balancing, and monitoring.

The value extends beyond simple deployment. As requirements evolve, Agent Engine accommodates growth without platform migration. You start with an agent endpoint. As your application becomes more advanced, you can add tools through MCP or scale from a single agent to a complex multiagent system. This evolution happens within the same platform. Example 6-6 shows how to deploy an ADK agent to Agent Engine.

Example 6-6. Deploying an agent to Agent Engine

```
# Using ADK CLI
adk deploy agent_engine \
    --project=my-project \
    --region=us-central1 \
    --staging_bucket=gs://my-staging-bucket \
```

```
    --display_name="Production Agent" \
    /path/to/agent

# Using Python SDK
import vertexai
from vertexai import agent_engines
from agent import root_agent

vertexai.init(
    project="my-project",
    location="us-central1",
    staging_bucket="gs://my-staging-bucket"
)

app = agent_engines.AdkApp(
    agent=root_agent,
    enable_tracing=True,
)

remote_app = agent_engines.create(
    agent=app,
    config={
        "requirements": ["google-cloud-aiplatform[adk,agent_engines]"]
    }
)


print(f"Deployed: {remote_app.resource_name}")
```

Teams appreciate the managed operational model. Scaling adjusts automatically. Security and access controls integrate with Google Cloud's IAM. Model versioning and session management work through the platform. You focus on whether the agent solves user problems, not whether infrastructure scales correctly.

The trade-off is reduced control over infrastructure details. You work within the platform's abstractions. For many applications—particularly those iterating on agent logic—this constraint is liberating rather than limiting.

Cloud Run

Cloud Run occupies the middle ground: containerized deployment with automatic scaling, but without managing clusters. You package your agent with its dependencies in a container, deploy it, and the platform handles load balancing, SSL termination, and autoscaling based on request volume.

The promise is "scale-to-zero" cost optimization, but for agent workloads, this requires careful consideration. Cold starts include not just container startup but loading any local resources your agent needs. Production deployments typically use min-instances=1 or higher to maintain consistent latency—you sacrifice scale-to-zero benefits but ensure that users always hit a warm instance. Example 6-7 shows how to deploy an ADK agent to Cloud Run.

Example 6-7. Deploying an agent to Cloud Run

```
# Using ADK CLI (Python)
adk deploy cloud_run \
    --project=my-project \
    --region=us-central1 \
    --service_name=my-agent \
    --with_ui \
    /path/to/agent

# Using gcloud (any language with Dockerfile)
gcloud run deploy my-agent \
    --source . \
    --region us-central1 \
    --min-instances=1 \
```

Cloud Run fits teams wanting containerized flexibility with variable traffic patterns. If your application sees 10x traffic variance between peak and off-peak, Cloud Run's autoscaling handles it without manual capacity planning. The containerization provides flexibility—you can add MCP tools, implement external state management with Redis or Firestore, or transform the agent into a multiagent system without changing platforms.

GKE

GKE provides complete infrastructure control through Kubernetes orchestration. For agent deployment, this means flexibility in routing patterns, sophisticated resource management, and fine-grained control over how your agents run. GKE Autopilot reduces operational overhead by managing nodes automatically, while Standard mode gives complete control for advanced scenarios. Example 6-8 shows how to deploy an ADK agent to GKE.

Example 6-8. Deploying an agent to GKE

```
# Using ADK CLI (Python)
adk deploy gke \
    --project=my-project \
    --cluster_name=agent-cluster \
    --region=us-central1 \
    --with_ui \
    /path/to/agent

# Using gcloud with Kubernetes manifests
# Manual deployment (after building container and creating manifest)
kubectl apply -f deployment.yaml
```

For complete GKE deployment instructions including cluster setup, Kubernetes manifests, and service configurations, see the GKE deployment documentation (*https:// oreil.ly/8vU1z*).

GKE offers AI-specific capabilities: node pool separation lets you run orchestration logic on standard nodes while reserving specialized hardware for specific workloads. The Horizontal Pod Autoscaler scales based on custom metrics—request latency, queue depth, or application-specific signals. Advanced routing through service meshes enables sophisticated traffic management.

Keep in mind that GKE for agent deployment is separate from GKE for model serving. The GKE Inference Gateway (*https://oreil.ly/fhWBJ*) and GPU node pools (*https://oreil.ly/WDmma*) are powerful tools for serving models, but agent deployment on GKE in context of the ADK focuses on orchestrating your agent application code, not serving model inference.

GKE makes sense in specific circumstances: when you need routing logic that managed platforms don't support, when you're orchestrating multiple agents with different resource requirements, or when you've hit platform constraints blocking critical features. It requires Kubernetes expertise and active operational management.

Google Distributed Cloud

Google Distributed Cloud (*https://oreil.ly/R7L-i*) (GDC) extends GKE to on-premises and edge environments for organizations facing data sovereignty, air-gap, or extreme latency requirements that make cloud deployment impossible. The platform uses the same Kubernetes foundation as cloud GKE, meaning containerized agents deploy with identical manifests and configurations.

The deployment process follows the GKE patterns documented previously. The primary differences are infrastructure endpoints—your local instances instead of cloud APIs, your private registry instead of Google Artifact Registry—and operational responsibility. You own hardware procurement, capacity planning, and full stack management.

Platform comparison

Table 6-3 maps platform capabilities to common requirements.

Table 6-3. Agent deployment platform comparison

Aspect	Agent Engine	Cloud Run	GKE	GDC
Best for	Production agents, minimal ops	Variable traffic, cost-sensitive	Complex requirements, max control	Sovereignty, air-gap, edge deployments
Operational complexity	Low (fully managed)	Medium (serverless config)	High (full K8s management)	Very high (full stack + hardware)

Aspect	Agent Engine	Cloud Run	GKE	GDC
Time to production	Fastest	Fast	Variable	Variable
Cold start latency	100–500 ms	100–2000 ms	5–30 seconds	Variable
Data residency	Google Cloud regions	Google Cloud regions	Google Cloud regions	On-prem/edge, your jurisdiction
Infrastructure control	Managed	Managed compute	Managed K8s control plane	Complete (you own hardware)
Scaling	Managed auto-scaling	Managed auto-scaling	Unlimited, custom metrics	Limited by on-prem capacity

The pattern across successful deployments is to start where you can iterate fastest, then migrate based on actual constraints rather than anticipated ones. Agent Engine prioritizes speed to production and operational simplicity. Cloud Run balances flexibility with managed infrastructure. GKE provides control at the cost of increased operational complexity.

Platform decisions shape your operational reality for months, but modern containerization means they're not permanent. A well-configured Cloud Run deployment serving thousands of requests per second might never need migration. But when you hit specific limitations such as routing logic the platform doesn't support or resource management needs requiring Kubernetes control, you have clear migration paths without starting from scratch.

Looking Ahead

You've navigated from fine-tuning decision through infrastructure constraints to production deployment. The fine-tuning framework helped determine when prompt engineering reaches its limits. The bottleneck patterns revealed which constraints would limit performance. Accelerator choices matched hardware to specific bottlenecks. Storage architecture ensured that data moved efficiently through training and serving phases. The serving framework optimized memory usage and throughput. The deployment platform handles scaling and operational concerns. Technical capability is in place.

But production systems require ongoing attention that initial deployment doesn't address. The questions shift from "How do we build this?" to "How do we keep it working?" Models drift as data distributions evolve and user patterns change. A model fine-tuned on January conversations might perform differently on June conversations as language patterns, product offerings, or user expectations shift. Infrastructure that addressed initial bottlenecks might face new constraints as traffic scales. The serving configuration optimized for 1,000 requests per day might not be optimal at 100,000 requests per day. Pattern 1's bandwidth constraint might give way to Pattern 2's capacity limit as batch sizes grow.

Costs compound in ways that aren't obvious during initial deployment. Serving expenses that seemed reasonable at launch—$5,000 monthly for handling modest traffic—might reach $50,000 monthly as adoption grows. Which optimizations actually reduce costs at this scale versus just adding operational complexity? Should you invest in infrastructure changes, or would better caching solve 80% of the problem? When fine-tuned model accuracy drops 5% over three months, the diagnosis isn't obvious. Is that data drift where the real-world distribution has shifted? A subtle training bug that only manifests over time? Changing user expectations where what counted as "helpful" in March differs from what users expect in June? The symptoms are clear, but the causes require investigation.

Chapter 7 tackles these operational realities head-on. How do you track model versions and their complete lineage—which training data, hyperparameters, and infrastructure configuration? How do you monitor not just that latency increased, but why it increased and what infrastructure change would actually help? When does model drift justify the engineering effort and computational expense of retraining versus refining prompts or adjusting serving configuration? How do you build the processes and tooling that transform one-time deployment into continuous operation? Technical capability gets you to production. Operational maturity separates demonstrations from deployments that deliver value for months and years.

Learning Labs

To reinforce the concepts covered in this chapter and gain experience with model fine-tuning and inference infrastructure, we recommend exploring the learning resources available in the Chapter 6 folder of the book's GitHub repository (*https://oreil.ly/CvfC_*). Key resources you will find linked there include:

- **Hands-On Code Examples**
  - Fine-tune Gemma with Keras and LoRA (*https://oreil.ly/wJgvk*): A tutorial on using Keras and Low Rank Adaptation (LoRA) to fine-tune Gemma
  - Train an LLM using JAX, Ray Train, and TPU Trillium on GKE (*https://oreil.ly/jKRJ9*): Train Llama 3 8B LLM on GKE using MaxText (*https://oreil.ly/RdKcF*), Ray Train (*https://oreil.ly/B84Hn*), and TPUs
  - Vertex AI Model Garden Community Notebooks (*https://oreil.ly/AIBu6*): A comprehensive collection of production-ready notebooks for fine-tuning and deploying open models like Llama 3, Gemma, and Mistral on Vertex AI
  - Distributed Tuning of Gemma on TPU v5e (*https://oreil.ly/TzFw_*): A guide to fine-tuning Gemma using JAX and LoRA on TPU v5e slices and deploying the model with vLLM on GPUs

— Serving Gemma with vLLM on Cloud Run (*https://oreil.ly/V9STx*): A step-by-step codelab demonstrating how to containerize and serve the Gemma 3 model using vLLM on Cloud Run

— Serve Gemma open models using GPUs on GKE with vLLM (*https://oreil.ly/3_UVj*): A comprehensive guide to deploying Gemma 3 on GKE using vLLM and NVIDIA L4 GPUs

— Implementing High-Performance LLM Serving on GKE (*https://oreil.ly/4QP6v*): A developer guide that walks through step-by-step the implementation of the advanced, AI-aware GKE Inference Gateway

• **Video Tutorials**

— Optimize model serving GKE Inference Gateway (*https://oreil.ly/7h74_*): A deep dive into configuring the GKE Inference Gateway for model-aware load balancing and efficient GPU utilization

— Scaling AI with Google Cloud's TPUs (*https://oreil.ly/qz-7o*): An architectural overview of TPUs, covering Matrix Multiply Units (MXUs), High Bandwidth Memory (HBM), and the decision framework for choosing TPUs over GPUs

— Deploying scalable and reliable AI inference on Google Cloud (*https://oreil.ly/O6bCZ*): A guide to high-level architectural patterns for production AI, covering multi-region availability, the "cattle, not pets" approach to infrastructure, and observability strategies

— AI workload orchestration options (*https://oreil.ly/KJetV*): A guide comparing different orchestration options like GKE and Cloud Run to help you choose the right platform for scaling your AI agent workloads

## CHAPTER 7

MLOps for Production-Ready AI and Agentic Systems

Over the past six chapters, you've built a comprehensive foundation: preparing data for GenAI applications (Chapter 2), constructing multimodal agents (Chapter 3), orchestrating agent teams (Chapter 4), establishing evaluation frameworks (Chapter 5), and optimizing models and infrastructure (Chapter 6). Each of these capabilities represents a critical pillar of what we call agent operations (AgentOps)—the systematic practices that transform working prototypes into production-ready systems.

Figure 7-1 maps these pillars across nine key dimensions. This chapter extends the pillars you've learned with production-specific practices while introducing three pillars essential for sustainable operations: observability, security and safety, and cost and capacity.

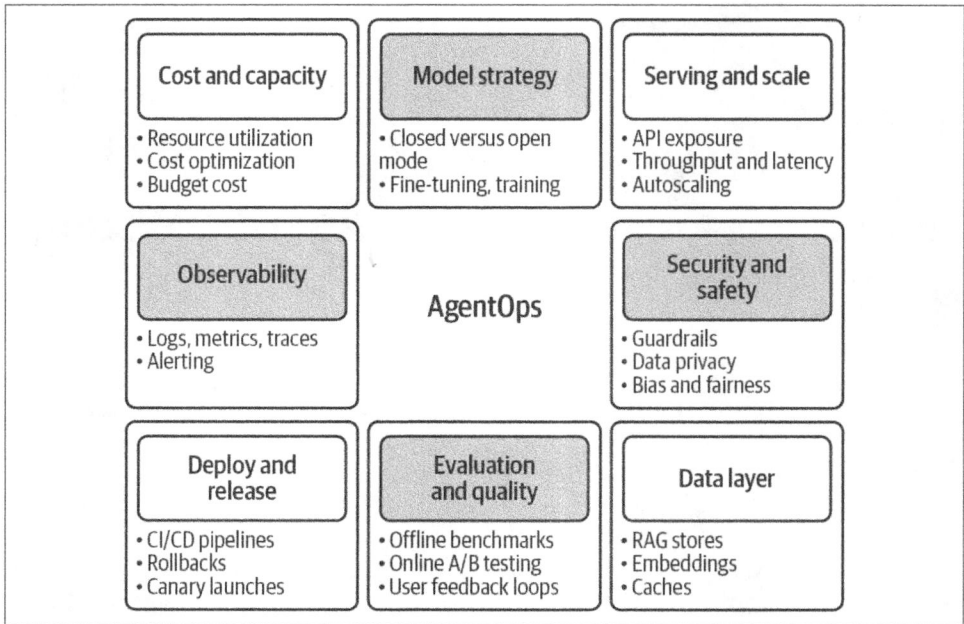

Figure 7-1. The nine pillars of AgentOps

The gap between "the model works" and "the model works in production" is wider for GenAI models than traditional ML. Identical prompts produce different outputs. Language evolves constantly. Agents maintain state across sessions. No single metric captures quality. Costs can explode through hidden operational overhead.

These challenges compound over time. Models that perform well at deployment gradually degrade as language patterns shift. Without proper versioning, teams can't identify which model version is running or what data trained it. Without comprehensive monitoring, degradation goes unnoticed until users complain. Without automated rollback mechanisms, recovery becomes a manual, error-prone process.

The unique characteristics of GenAI systems require adapted MLOps practices that account for their generative, stateful, and evolving nature. The inherent unpredictability of AI models—their non-deterministic behavior and potential for emergent properties—makes it essential to build security and governance considerations into operational workflows from the start.

At the core of any ML system lie three interconnected components: models, data, and code. Traditional MLOps manages these through established pipelines—data preparation, model training, and CI/CD deployment. But the shift to agent-based systems fundamentally changes this landscape, as illustrated in Figure 7-2. Instead of local data, you manage distributed knowledge bases and context stores. Instead of model training alone, you orchestrate prompt engineering and agent configuration.

Instead of simple deployment, you coordinate multiple agents, tools, and memory systems.

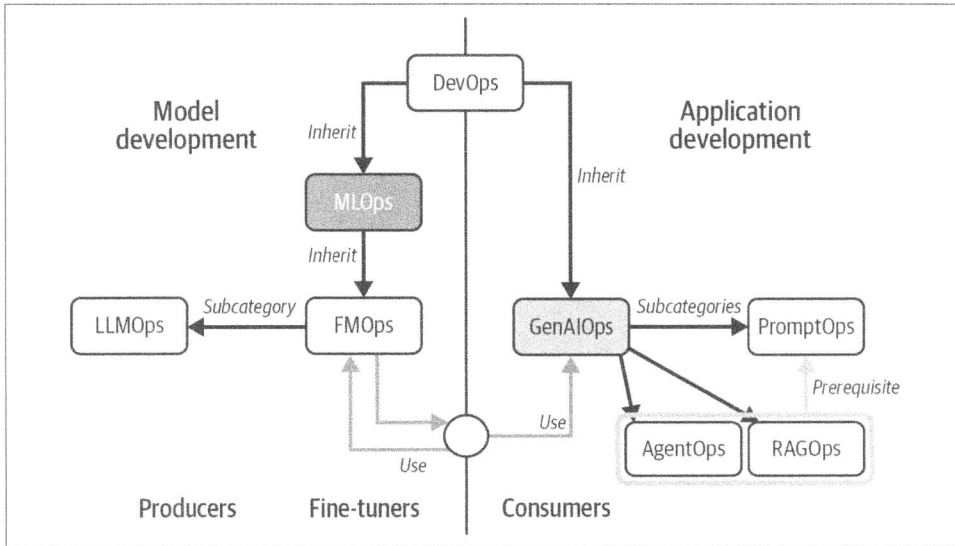

Figure 7-2. In modern AI systems, DevOps provides foundational CI/CD practices, MLOps adds model training and data pipelines, foundation model operations (FMOps) performs model fine-tuning and training, and AgentOps provides prompt orchestration and multiagent coordination

From Ad Hoc to Systematic: The Current State of Teams

Many teams today operate in what we call "FMOps" mode—manually curating examples, rewriting production code for each model update, and dealing with unsupported dependencies. The workflow is fragmented, as shown in Figure 7-3: exploratory analysis happens in notebooks, data preparation is manual, model training lacks reproducibility, and deployment requires extensive reconfiguration each time.

The transition to agent-based systems adds new complexities. Teams now manually sample from prompt libraries, configure tool and memory systems by hand, and rewrite agent orchestration logic for each change. Agent response evaluation happens sporadically. Production issues trigger reactive firefighting rather than systematic improvement.

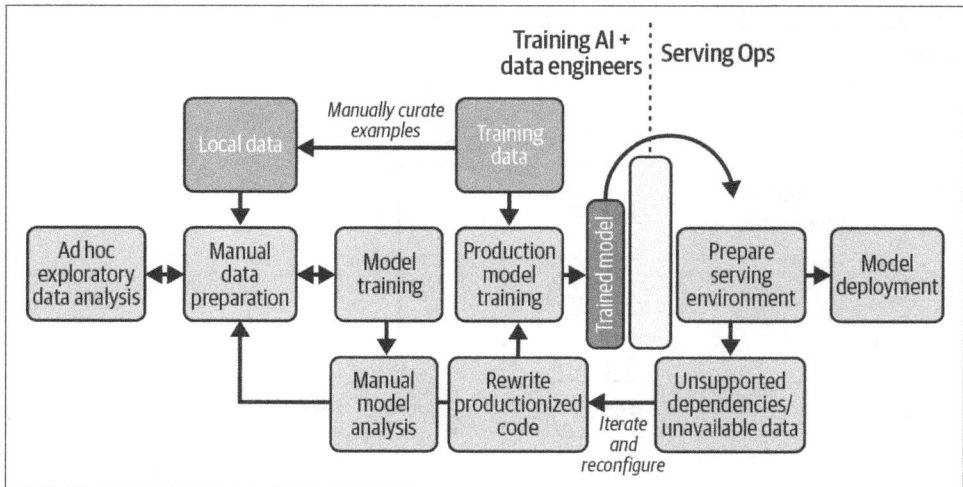

Figure 7-3. The fragmented FMOps workflow showing disconnected stages from exploration to deployment

The Evolution of MLOps

The journey from traditional MLOps to operations for modern agent systems represents a fundamental shift in how we think about AI in production. Understanding this evolution helps contextualize why traditional approaches fall short.

Between 2018 and 2022, the industry adapted DevOps practices (*https://oreil.ly/ l5Tqh*) for machine learning, establishing what we now call MLOps. This specialization addressed ML-specific challenges DevOps wasn't designed for: managing predictive models that transformed inputs to outputs, maintaining accuracy metrics, catching data drift, and ensuring reproducible training pipelines. MLOps represented a transition from general software operations to operations specialized for statistical models.

The emergence of LLMs in 2023 required further specialization. Suddenly, we weren't just tracking F1 scores—we were managing prompt libraries, monitoring token costs, and implementing safety filters. The operational question evolved from "Is the model accurate?" to "Is the output safe, relevant, and cost-effective?"

Today's agent systems demand yet another specialization. They maintain a persistent state, make autonomous decisions with real-world consequences, and exhibit emergent behaviors when working together. The operational focus has shifted to an entirely new question: "Did the agent complete its multistep task efficiently, safely, and in alignment with business goals?" This evolution is summarized in Table 7-1.

Table 7-1. Evolution of MLOps

Era	Primary focus	Core challenge	Key metrics	Operational question
MLOps (2018-2022)	Predictive models	Model drift, data quality	Accuracy, F1-score, AUC	Is the model's predictive accuracy degrading?
GenAI Ops (2023)	Generative models	Prompt engineering, safety	Token usage, latency, cost	Is the output safe, relevant, and cost-effective?
Agent Ops (2024+)	Autonomous systems	Decision making, tool reliability	Task completion, reasoning quality	Did the agent complete its task efficiently and safely?

This evolution marks a shift to fundamentally different operational paradigms, going beyond a simple increase in complexity. Each era builds upon the last, introducing new dimensions that demand specialized approaches.

Building Reproducible Training Pipelines

The journey from experimental notebooks to production pipelines requires systematic approaches to versioning, tracking, and automation. These systems form the foundation that enables teams to understand not just what went wrong, but when, why, and how to fix it.

Data Versioning and Lineage

Building on the data-readiness foundations from Chapter 2, production MLOps requires additional layers of control that go beyond initial preparation. While Chapter 2 established the importance of data quality, governance, and accessibility for GenAI systems, production environments face the ongoing challenge of maintaining reproducibility as data continuously evolves. This means not just having high-quality data, but being able to re-create exact conditions months after deployment—tracking every input that influenced model behavior.

The versioning challenge manifests most painfully when models begin producing incorrect outputs weeks or months after deployment. Consider a scenario in which clinical note summarization systems suddenly begin omitting critical medication dosages. The investigation reveals that a seemingly minor update to the data pipeline changed how structured fields were extracted, causing dosages to be stripped from the training data. Without comprehensive versioning, teams spend weeks in forensic analysis, unable to identify when the change occurred or which models were affected by the corrupted data.

Production data versioning requires managing three distinct types of data, each presenting unique challenges. Let's examine each type and the specific versioning strategies it demands.

Training data

Training data—the datasets used for fine-tuning or few-shot learning—requires immutable snapshots with cryptographic hashes or checksums to ensure integrity. The challenge emerges when training data stored in live databases gets modified after model deployment. For example, a customer service model suddenly starts mishandling refund requests. Investigation requires retraining with the original data to isolate whether the issue stems from data changes, model drift, or code updates. But if someone has since "cleaned" the training database—correcting labels, removing outliers, or updating categories—teams can't re-create the exact conditions that produced the production model. Without this ability to reproduce the training environment, debugging becomes guesswork.

The solution involves creating timestamped, immutable copies that preserve the exact state of data at training time—achievable through Vertex AI datasets (*https://oreil.ly/x5X-f*), leveraging BigQuery's built-in snapshot (*https://oreil.ly/fy_QH*) and time-travel capabilities for structured data, or implementing Object Versioning in Cloud Storage (*https://oreil.ly/6ZpWk*) buckets with retention policies for unstructured content.

> Versioning preserves what data was used, but as traditional ML has long shown, it can't fix training data that never represented real-world variability—a challenge that extends to LLM fine-tuning (which narrows foundation model distributions) and RAG systems (which ground responses in whatever reality their knowledge bases capture, including systematic gaps and biases).

Context data

Context data for RAG systems presents different versioning challenges. Knowledge bases that provide context require their own versioning strategy because incremental updates can introduce contradictions—whether accidental or malicious. For instance, when a contract analysis system begins hallucinating clause interpretations, investigation often traces back to incremental knowledge base updates that introduced contradictory precedents.

Beyond accidental corruption, RAG systems face deliberate poisoning attacks where adversaries inject malicious content into knowledge bases. Research demonstrates that just five (*https://oreil.ly/Q243q*) strategically crafted documents in a knowledge database can achieve a 90% attack success rate, causing the system to generate attacker-chosen responses to specific queries. This "memory poisoning" can occur gradually over time, making it difficult to detect without comprehensive versioning and integrity checks.

Effective versioning maintains complete snapshots of the knowledge base, with the ability to pin specific agent deployments to specific knowledge base versions, while also enabling detection of unauthorized modifications through cryptographic verification.

Prompt templates

Often overlooked, prompt templates represent data that directly impacts model behavior. What appears to be a minor adjustment to improve clarity can fundamentally shift model behavior—customer service interactions might shift from helpful to overly formal, product descriptions from engaging to generic. Prompt templates require the same versioning rigor as model weights, including A/B testing for changes and gradual rollout procedures.

Solutions for prompt versioning range from Vertex AI prompt management (*https:// oreil.ly/dpygR*) for centralized governance, to storing prompts as versioned records in BigQuery, maintaining them in Git repositories for code-like version control, or leveraging specialized open source tools such as Promptfoo (*https://oreil.ly/20D34*) and Pezzo (*https://oreil.ly/2ldYL*).

Data lineage

Data lineage for GenAI systems extends far beyond traditional tracking of which data trained which model. Modern systems need to capture the complete transformation pipeline, as shown in Figure 7-4. Tracking preprocessing steps captures how raw data becomes training-ready, including tokenization choices, cleaning steps, and augmentation techniques. When models exhibit unexpected biases, teams need to trace back through these transformations to identify where bias was introduced or amplified.

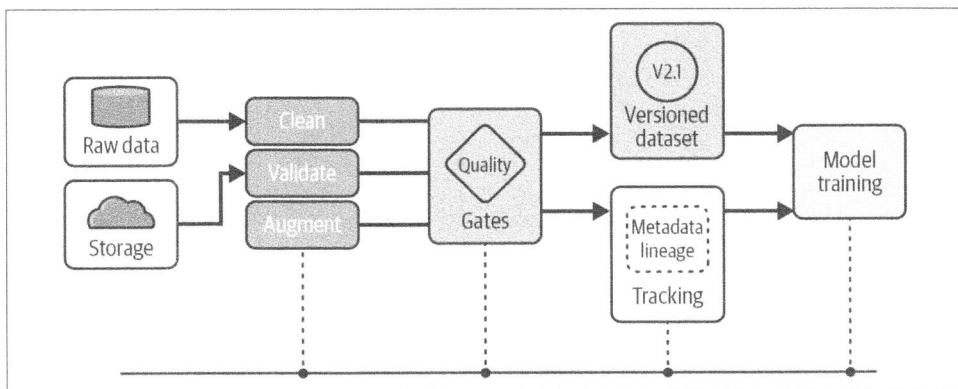

Figure 7-4. Data lineage tracking system showing the flow from raw data through transformations to model training

Tracking how datasets are combined is especially important when mixing proprietary and public data. The interaction between different data sources can create emergent behaviors that neither source exhibits independently. The lineage system records which data passed or failed quality checks and the criteria used, enabling teams to identify systematic issues in data quality that correlate with model failures.

Temporal lineage maintains timestamps not just for when data was created, but when it was validated, when it entered the training pipeline, and when models using it were deployed. This temporal tracking becomes essential when investigating gradual performance degradation—teams can correlate model behavior changes with specific data events. Vertex ML Metadata (*https://oreil.ly/LOcnR*) provides a managed solution for capturing this complete lineage graph, automatically tracking artifacts, executions, and their relationships—from raw datasets through preprocessing steps to model training and deployment—enabling teams to answer critical questions such as which dataset version produced a specific model or which hyperparameters led to performance degradation. Example 7-1 demonstrates how teams can trace problematic models back to their training data.

Example 7-1. Using Vertex ML Metadata to trace model lineage and identify problematic training data

```
from google.cloud import aiplatform

# Initialize Vertex AI
aiplatform.init(project=PROJECT_ID, location=LOCATION)

# Find models with poor performance metrics
problematic_models = aiplatform.Artifact.list(
    filter='schema_title="system.Model" AND metadata.accuracy.number_value<0.85'
)

for model in problematic_models:
    # Trace back through the execution that created this model
    executions = model.get_executions()

    for execution in executions:
        # Find input datasets used during training
        input_artifacts = execution.get_input_artifacts()

        for artifact in input_artifacts:
            if artifact.schema_title == "system.Dataset":
                print(f"Model {model.display_name} "
                        f"(accuracy: {model.metadata.get('accuracy')})")
                print(f"  → Trained with dataset: {artifact.uri}")
                print(f"  → Dataset version: {artifact.display_name}")
                print(f"  → Created: {artifact.create_time}")

                # Check for known data quality issues
```

```
if artifact.metadata.get("validation_status") == "failed":
    print(f"  ⚠ WARNING: Dataset failed validation checks")
```

Experiment Tracking

Every training run generates dozens of artifacts—model weights, evaluation metrics, hyperparameters, training curves—but for agentic systems powered by LLMs, traditional experiment tracking falls short in critical ways. The fundamental shift is that lower loss doesn't necessarily mean better agent behavior.

Consider a real scenario: a customer service agent fine-tuned on support transcripts achieves excellent perplexity (*https://oreil.ly/Zhw7K*) scores (a measure of how well the model predicts text), suggesting that it's learned the language patterns well. In production, however, it generates frustratingly repetitive responses—constantly asking "I understand your frustration, can you tell me more?" without progressing toward solutions. The model learned to predict support agent language patterns perfectly (hence good perplexity), but optimizing for prediction made it favor common, safe phrases over task completion.

Similarly, a model with 95% accuracy on benchmark question-answering tasks might seem superior to one scoring 92%. But the higher-scoring model achieves those numbers by being more confident in its predictions—including on edge cases where it should express uncertainty. In production, this manifests as confident hallucinations on unusual queries, while the "worse" model's lower confidence actually makes it safer by triggering human review more appropriately.

This disconnect between traditional metrics and agent behavior quality fundamentally changes what you track. Beyond individual metrics, modern experiment tracking for agent systems requires capturing the lineage and dependencies across experiments, not just the results of individual runs. Figure 7-5 illustrates how lineage chains track not just parent models but entire sequences of prompt templates, context data versions, and fine-tuning iterations. An agent model fine-tuned first on customer service data, then further fine-tuned on technical support, behaves differently (*https://oreil.ly/RbodU*) than one trained on the combined dataset. Similarly, a model using v1.0 prompts with a knowledge base from March produces different behavior than the same model with v2.0 prompts and an updated knowledge base from June. These behavioral differences—stemming from any combination of the three data types—often only emerge in production, making comprehensive lineage tracking essential.

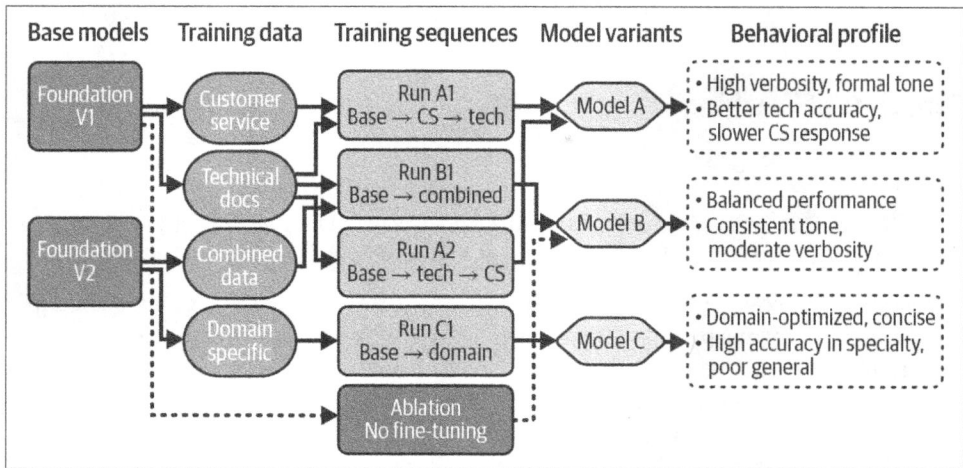

Figure 7-5. Experiment lineage tracking showing how different training sequences and data combinations influence final model behavior

Ablation studies (*https://oreil.ly/uy0LE*) systematically track what happens when different components are removed. Teams might discover that their model's improved performance comes entirely from prompt engineering rather than expensive fine-tuning, fundamentally changing their optimization strategy. Ensemble relationships become important when using multiple models or routing between them—tracking how different combinations perform reveals that ensemble disagreement rate often serves as the best predictor of when human review is needed.

Model Registry and Governance

Your model registry (*https://oreil.ly/CqvBs*) becomes the source of truth for what's deployed where. Each model needs comprehensive documentation that goes beyond version numbers and accuracy metrics, tracking the complete lifecycle from development through retirement, as illustrated in Figure 7-6.

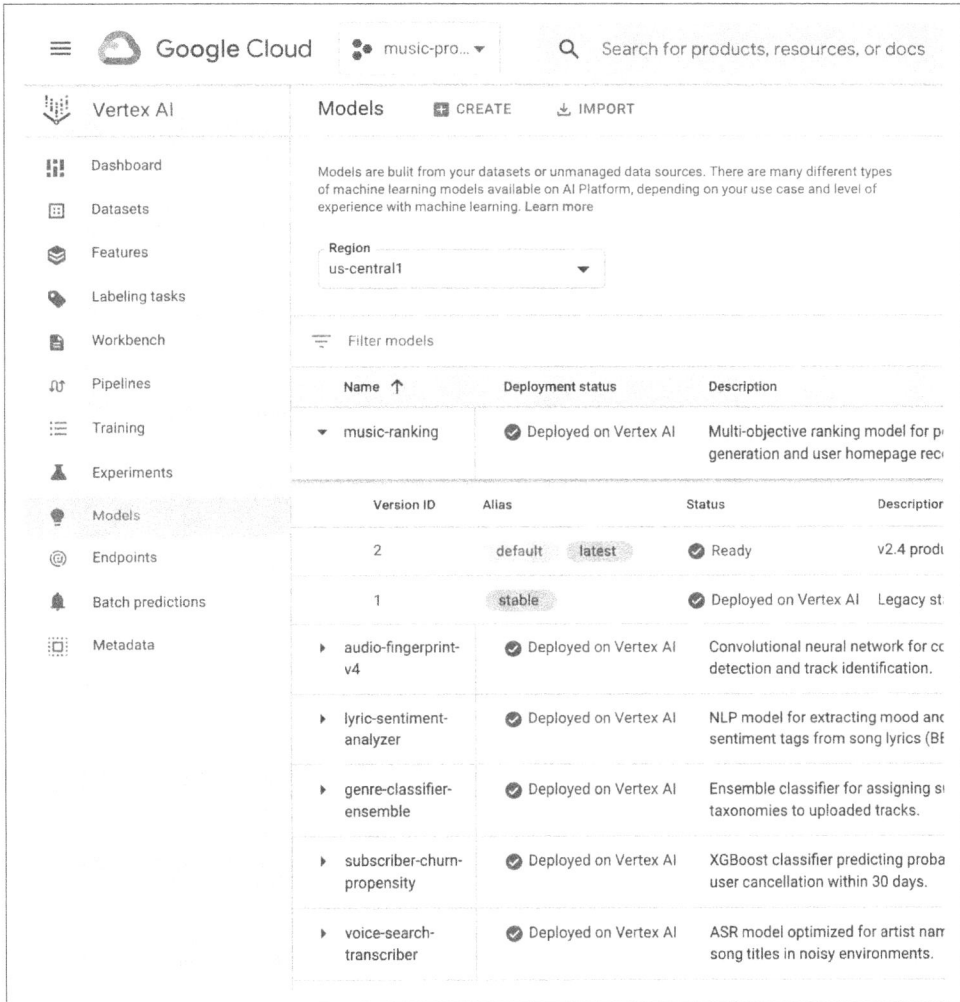

Figure 7-6. Model registry lifecycle management showing review, refresh, and retirement stages

Capability boundaries must be explicitly documented—not just what the model can do, but what it cannot or should not be used for. Figure 7-7 shows an example model card for an object detection model that documents limitations and performance boundaries.

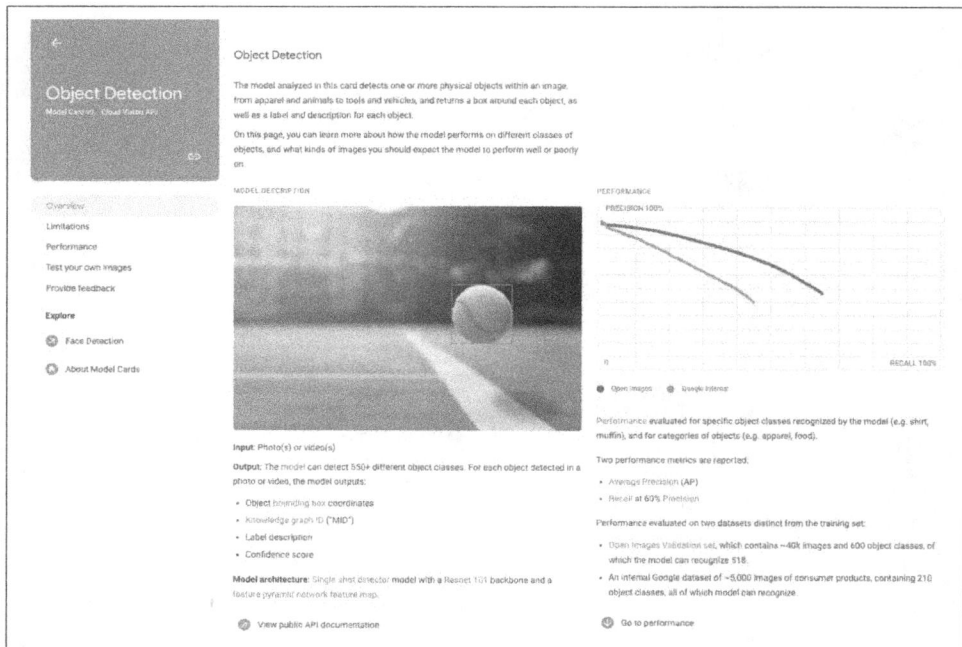

Figure 7-7. Object detection model card

For agentic systems, behavioral characteristics require careful documentation of known quirks, biases, and tendencies. Customer service systems might document that certain model versions tend to be more verbose at specific times, allowing downstream systems to adjust accordingly. These behavioral notes become critical when debugging production issues that manifest under only specific conditions. For examples of comprehensive model documentation, see Google's model cards (*https:// oreil.ly/gynuj*) for the Gemini and Gemma model families, which detail capabilities, limitations, biases, and operational considerations across dozens of pages.

Operational requirements specify not just compute needs but the complete operational context. Some models require specific prompt formats, particular token limits, or companion models for safety filtering. Often teams discover that their models produce compliant outputs only when paired with specific safety settings (*https:// oreil.ly/JwDp1*) or classifiers—information that must be captured in the registry to prevent non-compliant deployments.

This comprehensive documentation becomes particularly important when exposing models as agents through standardized protocols like A2A (Agent-to-Agent) (*https:// oreil.ly/JVou5*), where the Agent Card must accurately represent the model's capabilities to enable proper interagent collaboration.

Unlike traditional ML models that might run indefinitely, LLM models often have planned obsolescence due to evolving capabilities (*https://oreil.ly/TQ9Yt*), changing regulations, or linguistic drift (*https://oreil.ly/5JcEq*). The registry should track not just when a model was deployed, but when it should be reviewed, refreshed, or retired. This proactive lifecycle management prevents the gradual degradation that occurs when models outlive their intended operational window.

Model governance for production LLMs requires multistakeholder approval that goes beyond technical validation. Technical approval validates performance metrics, resource requirements, and integration compatibility, including verification that the model meets latency SLAs, stays within cost budgets, and properly integrates with existing monitoring. Business approval confirms that the model serves its intended purpose and aligns with business objectives—product descriptions must align with brand voice, financial advice must match company strategy.

Compliance approval ensures that regulatory requirements are met, which in healthcare includes HIPAA compliance verification and in finance might include fair lending law compliance. These approvals often require evidence from specific test suites designed to probe compliance boundaries. Ethical review examines potential biases, fairness issues, and societal impact.

Automated Retraining

Models shouldn't wait for manual intervention to improve, but automated retraining for LLMs presents unique challenges that go beyond traditional ML systems.

Semantic drift detection recognizes that language evolves continuously. Social media applications, for example, track semantic drift by measuring how user queries diverge from training data vocabulary. New slang and emerging topics cause gradual degradation even when traditional metrics remain stable. Retraining triggers when semantic similarity between user inputs and training data drops below carefully calibrated thresholds.

Performance degradation in LLMs rarely follows smooth curves. Travel booking systems, for example, discover that model performance degrades in step functions correlating with seasonal changes—summer vacation queries differ fundamentally from business travel patterns in training data. Pattern-based triggers that recognize these shifts prove more effective than simple threshold monitoring.

Regulatory triggers represent a unique aspect of LLMOps. New regulations or policy changes may necessitate immediate retraining. Organizations achieve this through automated monitoring pipelines that scrape regulatory websites, parse updates through Pub/Sub or Kafka, and trigger retraining workflows when relevant changes are detected—ensuring continuous compliance without manual intervention.

Handling Catastrophic Shifts and Phase Transitions

The retraining strategies discussed assume gradual or predictable change. But what happens when the world fundamentally changes overnight? The COVID-19 pandemic demonstrated this for healthcare systems—models predicting patient care needs suddenly failed because their core assumptions about "normal" utilization patterns had collapsed. This wasn't drift; it was a phase transition where retraining couldn't help fast enough.

Catastrophic shifts require different responses than automated retraining:

Detection signals
 Prediction confidence collapses across the board (not just edge cases), multiple independent metrics degrade simultaneously, and ensemble models suddenly disagree on predictions they previously aligned on.

Fallback strategies
 Gracefully degrade to simpler rule-based systems, increase HITL intervention thresholds, and implement confidence-based circuit breakers that pause automation when uncertainty exceeds safe bounds.

Architectural preparation
 Maintain diverse model ensembles trained on different time periods, regularly test "crisis mode" workflows like disaster recovery drills, and document model assumptions explicitly in your registry so you know when to disable them.

The goal isn't preventing model failure during catastrophic shifts—that's impossible. The goal is ensuring that systems degrade gracefully and signal clearly when human judgment should supersede automation.

However, automated retraining for LLMs carries unique risks that require careful mitigation. Model collapse (*https://oreil.ly/DTMFQ*) occurs when retraining on model-generated outputs leads to progressive degradation. You can maintain "genetic diversity" by always including original human-generated content in retraining sets to mitigate this degradation.

Feedback loop amplification presents another risk. Customer service systems that retrain on highly rated interactions might gradually become excessively apologetic and verbose, as users tend to rate longer, more apologetic responses higher. Balance user feedback with objective quality metrics to prevent these unintended behavioral shifts.

For RAG systems, automated knowledge base updates can introduce context pollution or poisoning. For example, technical documentation systems experience poisoning when automated crawlers add outdated information to their knowledge base.

Two strategies help maintain quality: *temporal weighting* applies decay factors based on document age (e.g, recent = weight 1.0, one-year-old = 0.5, three-year-old = 0.2), ensuring that newer information dominates without discarding historical context. *Source authority scoring* assigns provenance-based weights (e.g., official docs = 1.0, community forums = 0.5), prioritizing reliable sources during retrieval. Combine both approaches for robust protection: a recent blog post (high temporal weight, low authority) won't outrank slightly older official documentation (medium temporal weight, high authority), maintaining reliability in your knowledge base.

Comprehensive Monitoring

Building on the evaluation metrics from Chapter 5, production monitoring transforms one-time assessments into continuous observation. While evaluation tells you if a model or agent is good enough to deploy, monitoring tells you if it stays good enough in production. The challenge is that degradation often happens gradually and invisibly—by the time users complain, significant damage may have already occurred.

> The observability landscape for agent systems is evolving rapidly. While this chapter focuses on Google Cloud's native capabilities (Cloud Trace, Cloud Monitoring, Vertex AI tooling), many enterprise customers build their monitoring stack using specialized partner solutions that integrate with GCP infrastructure such as AgentOps.ai (*https://oreil.ly/yQ3NJ*) and Arize (*https://oreil.ly/fKogq*). Google Cloud's partner ecosystem enables you to leverage best-in-class observability tools while benefiting from GCP's infrastructure and AI services. The monitoring principles we discuss apply regardless of which tools you choose—native, partner, or hybrid approaches.

Agent Monitoring

Multiagent systems introduce observability challenges beyond traditional LLM metrics. When agents coordinate tasks through tool calls, loops, and interagent communication, understanding system behavior requires visibility into execution flows and resource consumption patterns.

Cloud Trace for agent execution

The ADK provides automatic tracing through the `trace-to-cloud` flag, which instruments your agent to send detailed execution data to Cloud Trace (*https://oreil.ly/aJo57*) using OpenTelemetry (*https://oreil.ly/wpPti*). As shown in Figure 7-8, every agent invocation, tool call, and LLM interaction is captured as structured spans that show the complete request journey.

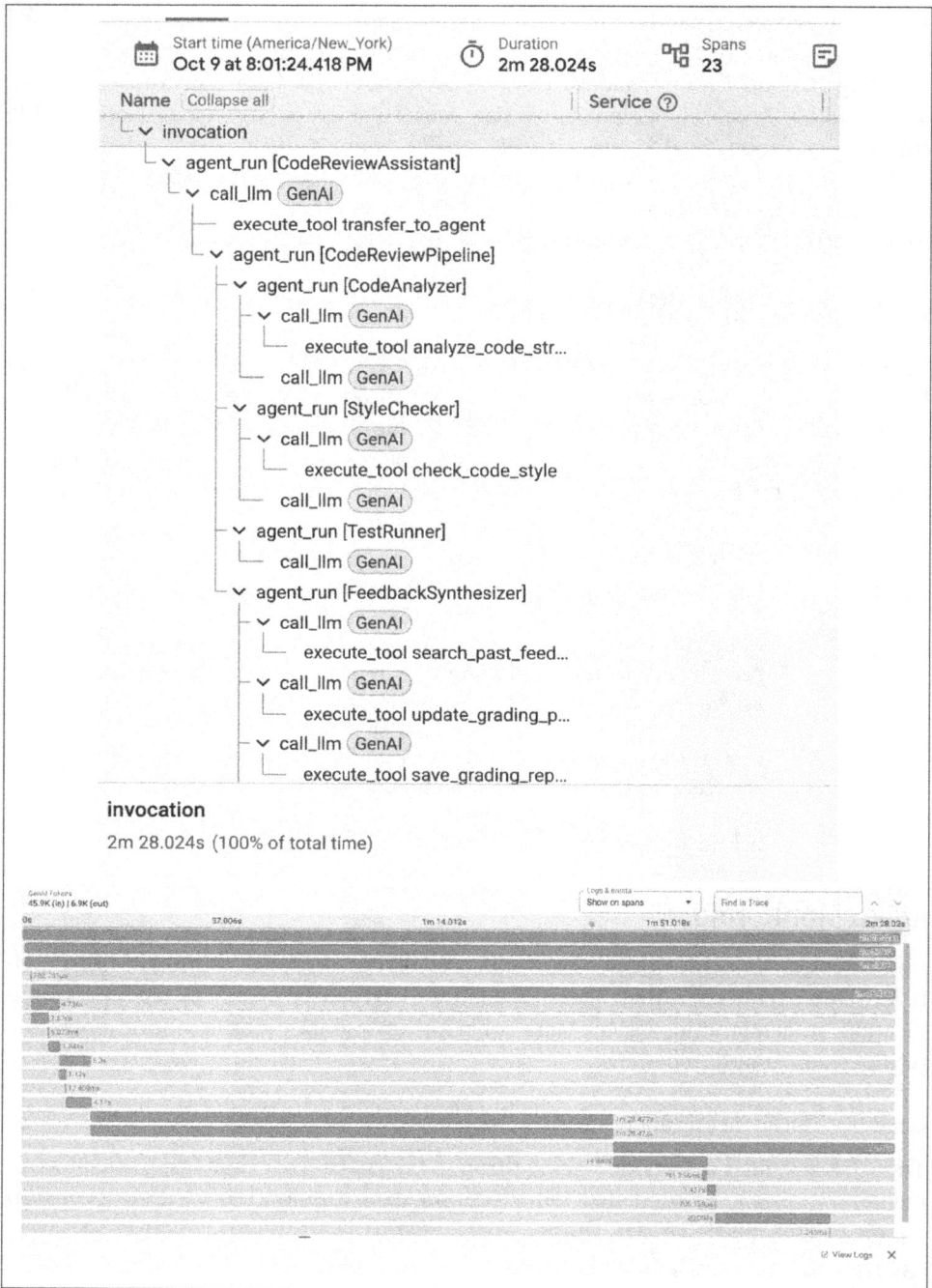

Figure 7-8. Cloud Trace waterfall for a code review agent showing execution spans and timing

In this example, the root span represents the complete user request lasting 2 minutes and 28 seconds. Nested within are spans for each operation: the Code Analyzer completed in 4.7 seconds, while the Test Runner—requiring actual code execution—consumed 1 minute and 28 seconds. Each LLM call displays token counts for precise cost attribution, tool invocations reveal latency to external dependencies, and loop iterations show nested cycles demonstrating convergence patterns.

This visibility transforms debugging from guesswork into forensic analysis. When users report slow responses, traces reveal whether delays stem from LLM inference, tool execution, or orchestration overhead. In Figure 7-8, test execution accounts for 59% of total time—an obvious optimization target.

Token usage and cost attribution

Each LLM call in the trace captures input and output token counts, enabling precise cost tracking at the operation level. Figure 7-9 shows token usage detail extracted from a trace, revealing that the Code Analyzer consumed 1123 input tokens and generated 490 output tokens for a single analysis operation.

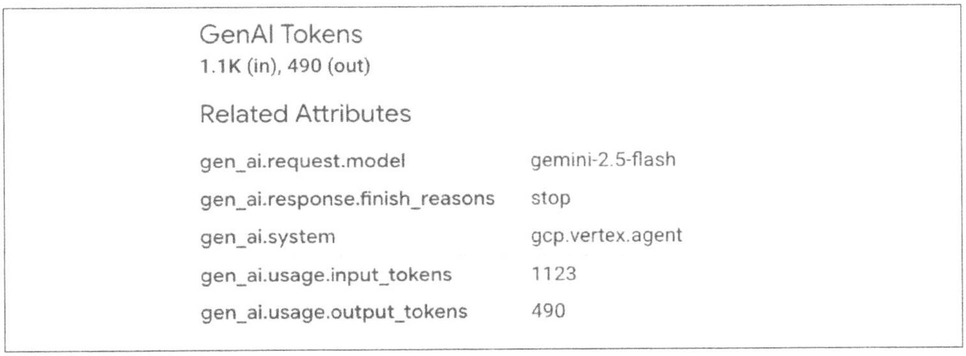

GenAI Tokens
1.1K (in), 490 (out)

Related Attributes

gen_ai.request.model	gemini-2.5-flash
gen_ai.response.finish_reasons	stop
gen_ai.system	gcp.vertex.agent
gen_ai.usage.input_tokens	1123
gen_ai.usage.output_tokens	490

Figure 7-9. Token usage detail from trace showing input/output token counts

This granularity reveals which agents or operations consume the most resources, informing architectural decisions about model selection, caching strategies, or prompt optimization. Teams can calculate exact costs per operation by multiplying token counts by model pricing, enabling precise attribution when multiple agents with different model configurations collaborate on tasks.

Loop and iteration visibility

For agents that use iterative refinement, traces show complete loop execution with each iteration nested hierarchically. Figure 7-10 demonstrates a fix pipeline (*https://oreil.ly/2VDOT*) that attempted two iterations before successfully passing all validation checks. Each iteration contains the complete sequence of subagent executions—

Code Fixer, Fix Test Runner, and Fix Validator—with individual timings and token usage.

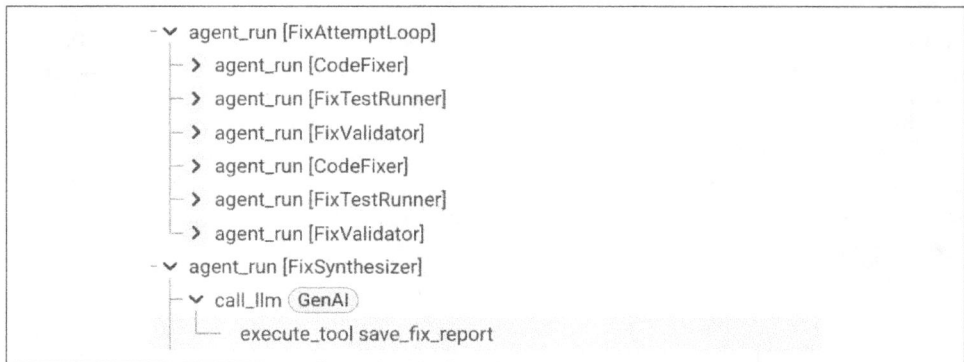

```
- ∨ agent_run [FixAttemptLoop]
    |- > agent_run [CodeFixer]
    |- > agent_run [FixTestRunner]
    |- > agent_run [FixValidator]
    |- > agent_run [CodeFixer]
    |- > agent_run [FixTestRunner]
    |- > agent_run [FixValidator]
  - ∨ agent_run [FixSynthesizer]
    |- ∨ call_llm (GenAI)
        |___ execute_tool save_fix_report
```

Figure 7-10. Loop iterations nested in trace showing convergence

This hierarchical view makes it easy to understand how agents converge to solutions. If a fix loop ran three times before succeeding, you see three complete cycles with their respective metrics, revealing whether the agent is converging efficiently or struggling with a particular class of problems. When loops hit their maximum iteration count without success, the trace provides a complete record of what was attempted and why it failed.

Custom monitoring with Prometheus

Beyond ADK's built-in tracing, production systems often require domain-specific metrics that standard observability doesn't capture. The Prometheus sidecar pattern (*https://oreil.ly/GLBj4*) addresses this by deploying a lightweight monitoring container alongside your agent service. The sidecar collects custom metrics, such as model-specific performance counters, custom business logic timings, or specialized resource utilization measurements, and exports them to Cloud Monitoring, where they integrate with your existing dashboards.

For example, when serving models via vLLM, a Prometheus sidecar can expose detailed LLM performance metrics like token generation throughput and GPU memory utilization that aren't available through standard Cloud Run metrics. This pattern proves particularly valuable when agents interact with specialized infrastructure or when you need metrics aligned with specific SLAs or business key performance indicators (KPIs).

Technical Monitoring

Technical metrics for GenAI systems go far beyond traditional latency and throughput measurements. Each metric tells a story about system health and UX, but the relationships between metrics often matter more than individual values, as shown in Figure 7-11.

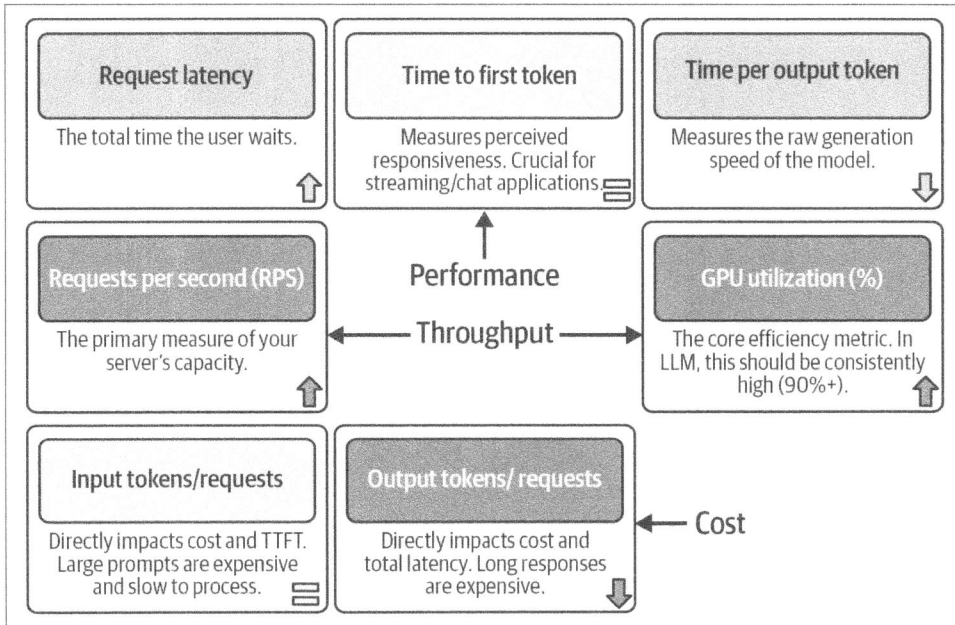

Request latency	Time to first token	Time per output token
The total time the user waits. ⬆	Measures perceived responsiveness. Crucial for streaming/chat applications.	Measures the raw generation speed of the model. ⬇

Performance

Requests per second (RPS)	↕ Throughput ↕	GPU utilization (%)
The primary measure of your server's capacity. ⬆		The core efficiency metric. In LLM, this should be consistently high (90%+). ⬆

Input tokens/requests	Output tokens/ requests	← Cost
Directly impacts cost and TTFT. Large prompts are expensive and slow to process.	Directly impacts cost and total latency. Long responses are expensive. ⬇	

Figure 7-11. Key performance metrics for LLM infrastructure showing the interplay between latency, throughput, and resource utilization

Time to First Token (TTFT) determines perceived responsiveness in ways that total latency doesn't capture. In our experience, users often abandon sessions if TTFT exceeds 10 seconds, even if the total response time remains acceptable. This leads to architectural decisions that prioritize initial token generation—implementing speculative decoding, using smaller "starter" models that hand off to larger models for complete responses, or streaming partial results while complex reasoning continues in the background.

Breaking down latency into components reveals bottlenecks that averages hide. Queue time spikes indicate capacity issues—either under-provisioning or poor load balancing. Model load time drives cold start delays, making the difference between 3-second and 30-second initialization. Context assembly often dominates RAG system latency, especially for knowledge-intensive queries. Token generation scales unpredictably with complexity—while simple responses scale linearly with length, complex reasoning can cause exponential slowdowns. Chapter 6 covered infrastructure optimizations—including model baking, quantization, and serving framework choices—that address these cold start bottlenecks.

Hallucination Detection

Beyond the evaluation metrics covered in Chapter 5, production systems require specific techniques for detecting when models generate factually incorrect content.

Claim extraction and verification identifies factual assertions in generated text, then verifies them against source documents. Summarization use cases track three critical metrics: unsupported claim rate (percentage of claims not found in source material), contradicted claim rate (percentage of claims that contradict the source), and claim coverage (percentage of source facts included in the summary).

The common finding is that hallucinations often occur in transitional phrases rather than core claims. Models correctly state facts but hallucinate connections between them, creating seemingly logical narratives that don't exist in the source material. This "connective tissue hallucination" proves particularly dangerous because it seems plausible and is harder to detect than outright factual errors.

For factually grounded applications—RAG systems, document summarization, and knowledge retrieval—Google's grounding API (*https://oreil.ly/IWZj-*) provides an approach to automated verification, as shown in Example 7-2.

Example 7-2. Using Google's grounding API for automated hallucination detection

```
from google.cloud import discoveryengine_v1 as discoveryengine

client = discoveryengine.GroundedGenerationServiceClient()

# Configure grounding check
grounding_config = client.grounding_config_path(
    project=project_id,
    location="global",
    grounding_config="default_grounding_config"
)

# Check if response is grounded in facts
request = discoveryengine.CheckGroundingRequest(
    grounding_config=grounding_config,
    answer_candidate=("Titanic was directed by James Cameron and "
                      "released in 1997."),
    facts=[
        discoveryengine.GroundingFact(
            fact_text=("Titanic is a 1997 American romantic disaster film "
                       "directed by James Cameron."),
            attributes={"source": "movie_database"}
        )
    ],
    grounding_spec=discoveryengine.CheckGroundingSpec(
        citation_threshold=0.6
    )
```

```
)
response = client.check_grounding(request=request)
# Returns: support_score: 0.99, indicating high factual grounding
```

Beyond the overall support score, the API performs detailed claim-level analysis in which each sentence receives an individual grounding assessment with citations linking it to supporting facts. Teams can enable anti-citations to detect contradictions where generated content directly conflicts with source material, or configure the API to check grounding against entire Vertex AI Search (*https://oreil.ly/LwSZ9*) data stores rather than inline facts for scalable verification across large knowledge bases.

CI/CD for AI Systems

The evaluation strategies from Chapter 5 and infrastructure patterns from Chapter 6 converge in your CI/CD pipeline. This isn't just about deploying code—it's about orchestrating the entire lifecycle of models, data, and configurations in a way that maintains consistency, enables rollback, and ensures reproducibility.

Cloud Build

Cloud Build (*https://oreil.ly/kApsf*) provides the foundation for continuous integration of AI systems, automating the building, testing, and packaging of models alongside their supporting infrastructure, as shown in Figure 7-12. Cloud Build triggers can automatically initiate pipelines when new training data arrives, model weights are updated, or configuration changes are committed, ensuring that every change goes through proper validation before reaching production. Built artifacts—container images and model packages—are stored in Artifact Registry (*https://oreil.ly/wVrs5*), providing versioned, secure storage for all deployment artifacts.

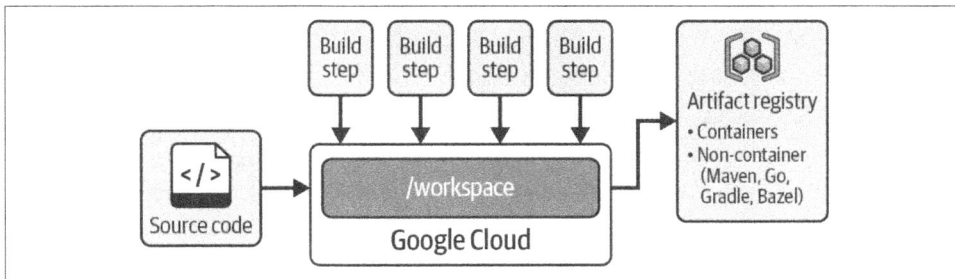

Figure 7-12. Cloud Build CI/CD pipeline showing automated build steps from source code to artifact storage

RAG applications require additional CI/CD considerations beyond standard model deployments, including knowledge base versioning, vector store synchronization, and retrieval quality testing. For detailed RAG-specific patterns, see Google Cloud's architecture documentation (*https://oreil.ly/Wwzly*).

Cloud Deploy

Production deployments for GenAI systems require strategies that handle state, maintain consistency, and enable safe rollbacks. Cloud Deploy (*https://oreil.ly/DUpB3*) orchestrates these deployments, providing declarative deployment pipelines that manage the progression from development through staging to production environments, as shown in Figure 7-13. Binary Authorization (*https://oreil.ly/ddQ-o*) adds a critical security layer to these deployments, ensuring that only verified and approved model bundles can be deployed to production.

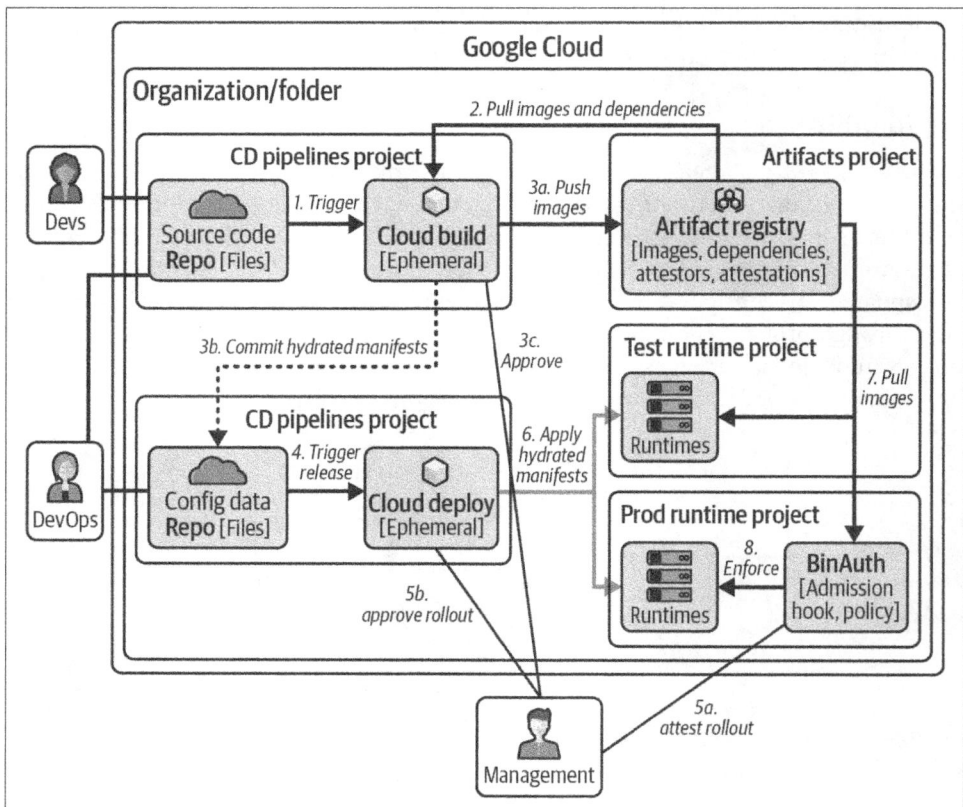

Figure 7-13. Cloud Deploy orchestrating progressive deployments from development through test to production environments with approval gates and Binary Authorization

Security and Governance as Foundation

Security and governance aren't add-ons but fundamental platform capabilities that enable everything else. The unique characteristics of GenAI systems—their ability to generate arbitrary text, learn from interactions, and make autonomous decisions—create novel security challenges that traditional approaches don't address.

Security Framework for AI Agents

Google's security framework for AI agents provides a structured approach to these challenges through three core principles. First, "human controllers" ensures accountability and user control by preventing agents from acting autonomously in critical situations without clear human oversight. Second, "limited powers" enforces appropriately scoped privileges, ensuring that agents have only the capabilities necessary for their intended purpose. Third, "observable actions" requires transparency through robust logging of inputs, reasoning, actions, and outputs, enabling both security decisions and user understanding. These principles, illustrated in Table 7-2, form the foundation of secure agent deployments.

Table 7-2. Google's three principles for secure AI agents, showing control focus and infrastructure needs

Principle	Summary	Key control focus	Infrastructure needs
Human controllers	Ensures accountability and user control, and prevents agents from acting autonomously in critical situations without clear human oversight or attribution.	Agent user controls	Distinct agent identities, user consent mechanisms, secure inputs
Limited powers	Enforces appropriate, dynamically limited privileges, ensuring that agents have only the capabilities and permissions necessary for their intended purpose and can't escalate privileges inappropriately.	Agent permissions	Robust authentication, authorization, and accounting (AAA) for agents, scoped credential management, sandboxing
Observable actions	Requires transparency and auditability through robust logging of inputs, reasoning, actions, and outputs, enabling security decisions and user understanding.	Agent observability	Secure/centralized logging, characterized action APIs, transparent UX

Model Armor: A Key Security Component

These three core principles require comprehensive architectural decisions across identity management, authorization, and observability systems. Model Armor provides critical runtime protection for the "limited powers" principle by preventing models from generating harmful or sensitive content. As shown in Figure 7-14, Model Armor (*https://oreil.ly/6tyBK*) operates as a security filter in the inference pipeline, screening both inputs and outputs to enforce content policies.

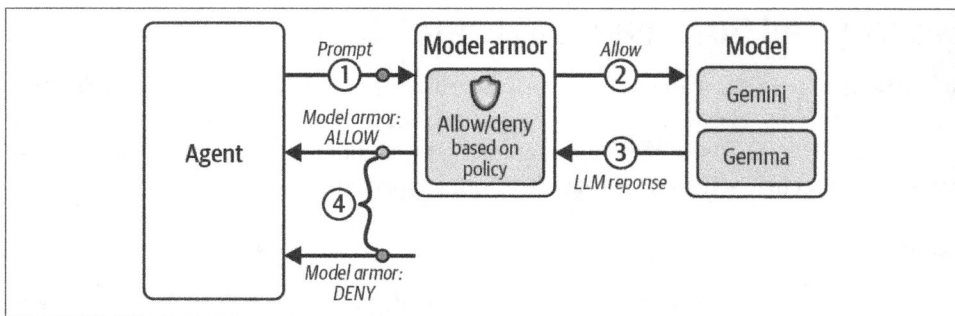

Figure 7-14. Model Armor integration showing input screening, processing, and output filtering stages

The service addresses the primary security risks in LLM deployments through multiple detection layers. Prompt injection attacks—where users attempt to override system instructions—are blocked through pattern recognition and behavioral analysis. Sensitive data protection prevents PII and confidential information from leaking through model responses. Safety filters enforce organizational policies on harmful content, while malicious URL detection prevents distribution of compromised links through generated text.

Configuration requires balancing security with usability. During initial deployment, teams typically use "Inspect Only" mode to understand baseline behavior and false positive rates. This mode logs potential violations without blocking, providing visibility into what production traffic would trigger. Once teams understand their traffic patterns, they transition to "Inspect and Block" mode with appropriately tuned thresholds. Financial services might require high confidence thresholds for all safety categories to minimize false positives on legitimate financial discussions, while educational platforms might use "medium and above" thresholds to catch more potential issues. For Sensitive Data Protection, organizations configure specific infoTypes to detect, such as credit card numbers and SSNs for ecommerce or medical record numbers and diagnosis codes for healthcare applications.

Model Armor baseline settings establish organizational baselines that individual applications can't override, ensuring minimum security standards across all deployments. These hierarchical controls enable security teams to enforce compliance requirements while giving application teams flexibility within those boundaries.

Cost Management

GenAI applications can generate surprising costs that spiral quickly without proper controls. A customer service chatbot that costs $50 per day during testing can balloon to $5,000 per day in production when traffic scales. An agent system that

---

makes innocent-seeming tool calls can trigger cascading API requests that multiply costs exponentially. Understanding and managing these costs requires systematic approaches that go beyond simple monitoring to intelligent optimization and strategic control.

The True Cost Model

The total cost of an LLM interaction includes multiple components that are often overlooked or poorly understood, as shown in Figure 7-15. Direct model costs from input and output tokens represent only part of the picture. Input tokens include not just user queries but entire prompts and context, which for RAG systems can be substantial—a single query might include thousands of tokens of retrieved context before the actual question even appears.

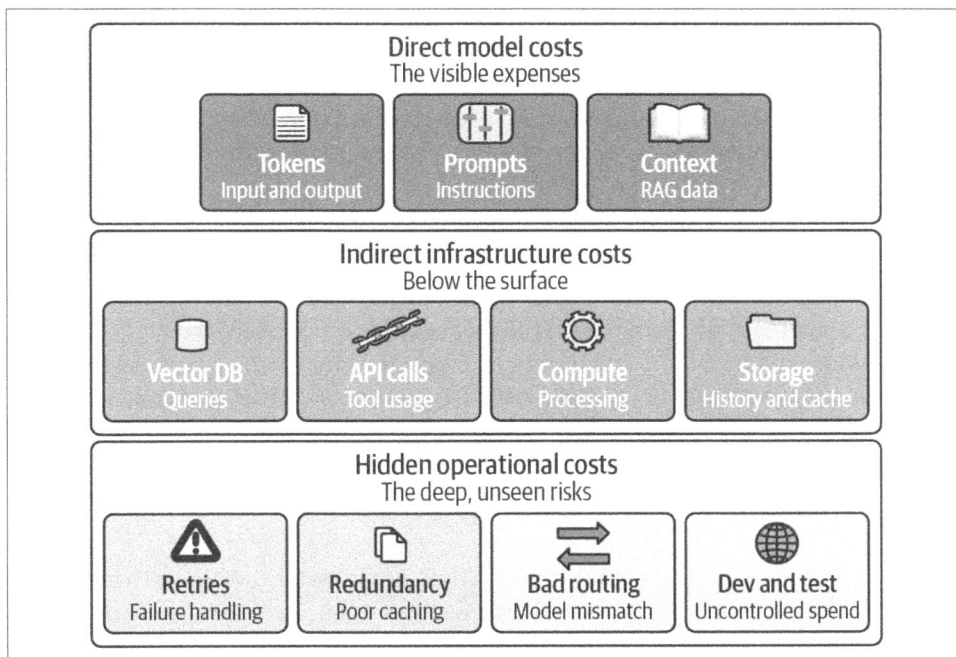

Figure 7-15. Cost breakdown showing direct model costs, indirect infrastructure costs, and hidden operational costs

Indirect costs often exceed direct model costs. Vector database queries for RAG systems add up quickly, with complex retrieval strategies executing multiple similarity searches per request. API calls for tool usage accumulate, especially when tools make multiple subcalls—an agent that checks weather, searches calendars, and queries databases for a single user request might trigger a dozen API calls. Storage for conversation history grows continuously, particularly for multiagent systems that maintain state across sessions. Compute for preprocessing and postprocessing adds overhead to every request, from tokenization to response formatting.

Hidden costs surprise teams when they appear on bills. Retry costs from failures can explode when systems don't implement exponential backoff—a service outage can trigger thousands of retry attempts in minutes. Redundant calls from poor caching waste resources on repeated computations, where the same context gets processed multiple times per day. Inefficient routing sending simple queries to expensive models multiplies costs unnecessarily. Development and testing in production environments generates enormous unexpected bills. One startup discovered they were spending thousands monthly on development testing in production because they hadn't set up proper staging environments with cost controls, only realizing this when their monthly bill arrived.

Cost Attribution Strategies

Cost attribution must track multiple dimensions to be actionable. Without clear attribution, optimization becomes guesswork—you can't improve what you can't measure. Organizations should implement attribution across several key dimensions:

User segment
Understanding whether costs align with value creation helps identify where to optimize versus where to invest. Enterprise users generating higher costs but proportionally higher revenue indicates healthy unit economics—spending $10 to serve a customer who generates $100 makes sense. Conversely, if certain user segments consume resources without corresponding value—free tier users making expensive agent calls, or trial accounts triggering costly tool invocations—usage limits or tier adjustments become necessary. A SaaS company might discover that their "pro" tier users account for 80% of costs but only 40% of revenue, suggesting that either pricing adjustments or feature restrictions are needed.

Feature
Identifying which capabilities drive costs helps prioritize optimization and informs product decisions. Simple chat features might have acceptable per-query costs of a few cents, while complex report generation features with multiagent coordination might cost several dollars per request. This granular tracking enables informed decisions about feature development and pricing. One analytics platform discovered its "AI insights" feature cost $1 to $3 per generation but was included free in their $29/month plan—clearly unsustainable. Either the feature needed optimization, users needed limits, or pricing required adjustment.

Time
Temporal patterns reveal optimization opportunities that static analysis misses. Peak hours from 9 A.M. to 5 P.M. might show 10 times higher costs than overnight periods, suggesting opportunities for batching non-urgent tasks. Seasonal

patterns help forecast capacity needs—an ecommerce agent system might see costs spike during holiday shopping seasons. Weekly patterns expose usage anomalies—if Tuesday consistently costs twice as much as other weekdays, investigation might reveal a scheduled report that could be optimized or moved off-peak. Understanding these patterns enables strategic resource allocation and budget forecasting that aligns with actual usage.

Agent

For multiagent systems, tools such as Cloud Trace (*https://oreil.ly/A7yIP*) support granular cost attribution at the token level, enabling you to track costs separately for orchestrator agents versus specialist agents versus tool-calling agents. This granularity reveals whether your orchestration overhead exceeds the value it provides or whether certain specialist agents are underutilized and could be consolidated.

Intelligent Cost Operations

Modern cost management for AI systems goes beyond spreadsheets and manual analysis. Google Cloud provides AI-powered tools that continuously analyze spending patterns, identify waste, and generate actionable recommendations. These intelligent systems learn from usage patterns across the entire platform, applying machine learning to detect anomalies and surface optimization opportunities that human analysis would miss.

FinOps hub with Gemini Cloud Assist

Google Cloud provides AI-powered cost intelligence through two complementary interfaces: Cloud Billing reports (*https://oreil.ly/yujPw*) for understanding spending patterns and FinOps hub (*https://oreil.ly/vrMlm*) for identifying optimization opportunities. Gemini Cloud Assist (*https://oreil.ly/T2oct*) integrates with both, providing natural language insights and recommendations that make cost management accessible without requiring deep financial analysis expertise.

Cloud Billing reports with AI assistance

Cloud Billing reports with Gemini Cloud Assist transforms how you analyze spending. Rather than manually configuring filters and aggregations to understand your costs, you can describe what you want to see in natural language. Ask "Show me daily Compute Engine costs by SKU for the last 5 days" or "Help me understand my Vertex AI spending by project for the last 30 days," and Gemini Cloud Assist automatically configures the report settings and filters to create the visualization you need.

More importantly, Gemini Cloud Assist analyzes each report and provides insights that summarize what matters most. Using FinOps-trained models developed in partnership with Google's research teams, the system identifies:

Overall costs
> Total spending for the time period with trend direction (increasing or decreasing)

Cost drivers
> Which projects or services are responsible for the biggest changes, both in absolute dollars and percentage, with direct links to the Anomalies page when unusual patterns are detected

Savings opportunities
> How much you've saved through existing optimizations, with links to FinOps hub for additional recommendations

Budgeting suggestions
> Recommendations to create budgets for tracking and controlling spending

These insights appear automatically as you view reports, eliminating the need to manually analyze charts and tables to extract meaning. The AI does the heavy lifting of pattern recognition and prioritization, surfacing what's most important for your attention.

FinOps hub for optimization intelligence

While Cloud Billing reports help you understand *what* you're spending, FinOps hub helps you identify *where* you're wasting resources and *how* to optimize. Gemini Cloud Assist in FinOps hub analyzes your infrastructure and provides key optimization and utilization insights.

The Utilization insights dashboard reveals resource efficiency issues with concrete savings potential. Figure 7-16 shows an example of these AI-generated insights, where Gemini Cloud Assist has identified $401.68 in potentially wasted Compute Engine usage, highlighted a high-cost project with $233.95 in monthly optimization potential, and pinpointed a specific region where resource optimization could save $179.13 per month. Each insight includes direct links to take action, such as view detailed utilization data, apply recommendations, or investigate anomalies.

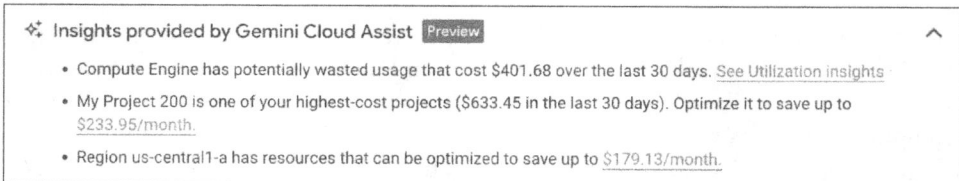

✧ Insights provided by Gemini Cloud Assist `Preview`   ∧

- Compute Engine has potentially wasted usage that cost $401.68 over the last 30 days. See Utilization insights
- My Project 200 is one of your highest-cost projects ($633.45 in the last 30 days). Optimize it to save up to $233.95/month.
- Region us-central1-a has resources that can be optimized to save up to $179.13/month.

Figure 7-16. Gemini Cloud Assist providing actionable cost insights in the FinOps hub interface

These insights go beyond generic recommendations. The system understands context—a Vertex AI endpoint running 24/7 with zero traffic in the last 72 hours suggests a forgotten development resource. A project consuming 10 times its normal resources over 3 days might indicate a legitimate load test or a runaway process. Gemini Cloud Assist surfaces these patterns with enough detail to make informed decisions. Beyond generating insights, the system can draft email reports (*https://oreil.ly/3zE_0*) summarizing recommendations, streamlining communication with engineering teams and stakeholders.

Beyond console insights

For teams needing custom analysis or integration with existing BI tools, Cloud Billing supports data exports to BigQuery (*https://oreil.ly/KjzXf*). This enables building custom dashboards in Looker, integrating cost data with business metrics, or creating specialized alerts. However, for most teams, the AI-powered insights in FinOps hub and Cloud Billing reports provide sufficient visibility without requiring SQL expertise.

Spending Controls

Cost optimization reduces baseline spending, but spending controls prevent unexpected overages. These controls act as guardrails that catch runaway costs before they become budget crises. Think of optimization as improving your car's fuel efficiency, while controls are the governor that prevents the engine from over-revving.

User-level controls

User-level controls implement progressive restrictions based on usage patterns, balancing service availability with cost protection. A well-designed control system provides clear communication and graceful degradation rather than abrupt service cutoffs.

Consider a three-tier approach: first, implement *proactive notifications* when users approach predefined thresholds—perhaps at 70%, 85%, and 95% of their quota. These notifications should be actionable, explaining current usage, projected costs, and options to adjust behavior, such as "You've used 850 of 1,000 agent requests this month. At your current pace, you'll exceed your limit in 3 days. Consider upgrading to Pro for unlimited requests." This transparency helps users understand their consumption and make informed decisions.

Second, implement *graceful degradation* when limits are reached. Rather than completely cutting off service, route users to smaller, cheaper models, return cached responses for repeated queries, or limit access to expensive features while maintaining core functionality. A customer service agent might switch from multiagent orchestration to single-agent mode after quota exhaustion, providing degraded but still useful service. Or complex tool calling might be disabled while basic question-answering continues. The key is maintaining some level of service rather than a hard failure.

Third, reserve *hard stops* for only extreme overages or suspected abuse. If a user exceeds their quota by 10 times in an hour, that's likely a bug or attack rather than legitimate usage. Hard stops prevent a misbehaving application from generating thousands of dollars in unexpected charges. But for normal overages—a user who exceeds monthly limits by 10% because of legitimate increased usage—graceful degradation preserves the customer relationship while protecting costs.

Make these transitions transparent through clear UI messages and API responses. When a user hits a limit, the response should explain what happened, why, and what they can do about it. This transparency builds trust and reduces support burden—users understand their situation rather than being confused by cryptic errors.

Technical circuit breakers

Technical circuit breakers act as automatic safety valves when costs spike unexpectedly, preventing small issues from becoming large bills. These controls monitor several dimensions and trigger automated responses when thresholds are breached:

Rate of spend monitoring
Track cost per minute or cost per hour rather than just daily totals. A service that normally costs $2/hour suddenly costing $50/hour indicates a serious problem—perhaps a retry loop, a distributed denial-of-service (DDoS) attack, or a configuration error. Circuit breakers should trigger when spending rate exceeds normal patterns by a defined multiple (perhaps 5 to 10 times). The response might be to pause non-critical workloads, disable expensive features, or switch to degraded modes while operations teams investigate.

Individual request cost thresholds
Monitor costs per request, not just aggregate spending. A single agent request that costs $10 suggests something is wrong—perhaps an infinite tool call loop, an absurdly large context, or a bug that's spawning dozens of subagents. Set per-request cost limits appropriate to your application. A complex research agent might legitimately cost $1 per request, but a simple chatbot costing that much likely has a bug. When individual requests exceed thresholds, log detailed diagnostics, reject the request, and alert operations.

Error pattern detection
High retry rates or error rates often precede cost spikes. If your agent system suddenly shows 50% error rates with automatic retries, there is increased likelihood you'll get an expensive bill as retries multiply. Circuit breakers should trigger on

error patterns—if error rate exceeds 20% for 5 minutes, pause processing and alert. This prevents cascading failures from becoming cascading costs.

Adaptive throttling

Implement throttling that adapts to spending rate. When costs approach limits, progressively slow down request processing. Instead of handling 100 requests per second, drop to 50, then 25, as costs increase. This buys time for investigation while preventing complete service outage. Users experience degraded performance rather than failure, and costs stabilize rather than spiking.

When circuit breakers trigger, they should pause processing, log detailed diagnostics, and alert operations teams rather than silently continuing to generate costs. The goal is rapid detection and intervention before small issues become large bills.

The implementation of these controls requires careful calibration. Too restrictive, and you frustrate users and limit legitimate usage. Too permissive, and you risk unexpected costs that can damage both budgets and customer relationships. Start with monitoring and alerting to understand normal patterns, then gradually implement controls based on actual usage data rather than assumptions. Review and adjust controls quarterly as usage patterns evolve—what was appropriate for 100 users might need adjustment at 10,000 users.

Looking Ahead

This chapter equipped you with the operational practices to maintain and evolve AI systems in production. We've explored the complete lifecycle from reproducible training pipelines through comprehensive monitoring to deployment strategies. The depth we've covered—from the nuances of semantic drift detection to the complexities of multiagent failure modes—reflects the real challenges teams face when moving beyond prototypes.

The practices we've discussed form the foundation for reliable production AI. Operational excellence is just one piece of the puzzle, however. How do you measure your organization's overall readiness for AI? How do you progress from isolated successful projects to enterprise-wide AI transformation?

Chapter 8 introduces the AI and agentic maturity framework, helping you assess where your organization stands across multiple dimensions—from technical capabilities to cultural readiness. We'll move from tactical operations to strategic transformation, showing you how to build not just reliable AI systems, but an AI-ready organization.

Learning Labs

To reinforce the concepts covered in this chapter and gain experience with operationalizing AI systems, we recommend exploring the learning resources available in the Chapter 7 folder of the book's GitHub repository (*https://oreil.ly/3H0r9*). Key resources you will find linked there include:

- **Courses**
  - 5-Day Gen AI Intensive Course with Google (*https://oreil.ly/M4t00*): A comprehensive overview of Generative AI technologies. We specifically recommend Day 5: MLOps for Generative AI, which covers adapting MLOps practices for GenAI and provides a code walkthrough of the Agent Starter Pack.
  - 5-Day AI Agents Intensive Course with Google (*https://oreil.ly/1pkxu*): A hands-on program for building autonomous systems. Focus on Day 5: Prototype to Production, which provides a technical guide to the operational lifecycle, deployment, and scaling of AI agents using the Agent2Agent (A2A) protocol.
- **Video Tutorials**
  - Agentic Security Fundamentals (*https://oreil.ly/gnid0*): A technical workshop covering the OWASP Top 10 for LLMs, implementing input/output filtering with Model Armor, and managing agent identity and authentication
  - Operationalize AI Agents (*https://oreil.ly/cxOKk*): A deep dive on the end-to-end architecture for building, deploying, and evaluating agents, covering the transition from MLOps to GenAIOps and the importance of tool registries

The AI and Agentic Maturity Framework

The journey through the first seven chapters has equipped you with a technical blueprint for building and deploying AI and agentic systems. We've navigated the complexities of data readiness, orchestrated intelligent agent teams, and mastered the art of evaluation and tuning AI applications with robust operational processes for continuous integration, deployment, and retraining. The lessons learned by practitioners in these chapters—moving from a prototype to a production-ready system—form the essential foundation.

With the technical expertise you've gained, we can now shift our focus to the strategic evolution of AI within an enterprise, an endeavor that must be framed within local and global governance standards. This is the central purpose of this chapter: translating the hands-on knowledge you've gained thus far into a comprehensive AI and agentic maturity framework. This framework moves beyond purely technical and operational readiness to integrate the essential principles of trustworthy and compliant deployment, grounding them in the standards set by landmark legislation like the European Union's AI Act (*https://oreil.ly/-1_Ko*).

The goal of this final chapter is to help you develop a forward-looking strategy that cultivates and maintains long-term AI fluency across your entire organization. This evolution will include critical behavioral and cultural shifts around AI integration into daily activities for productivity and efficiency, as well as shifts in risk management, operating transparency, and accountability of AI-assisted processes. Next, we'll provide you with a working framework to assess your organization's capabilities and chart a course for continuous growth and value delivery. This framework will help you assess your organization's *holistic* maturity, ensuring that your technical and behavioral efforts drive real, strategic transformation.

What Is the AI and Agentic Maturity Framework?

The AI and agentic maturity framework is a conceptual tool that aims to help you and your organization assess current capabilities and readiness for AI adoption and make informed strategic decisions about where and how to invest and grow based on alignment of AI capabilities with key business outcomes. We hope the framework will help leaders like you define a common purpose for AI investment and ensure that projects deliver tangible value and ROI, such as increased efficiency, improved customer experience, or new business models and opportunities for monetization of products or services.

The Maturity Dimensions and Phases

To conduct a comprehensive assessment of AI and agent maturity, an organization must evaluate criteria across three key dimensions of readiness, illustrated in Figure 8-1: (1) Vision and Leadership, (2) Talent and Culture, and (3) Operational and Technical Practice.

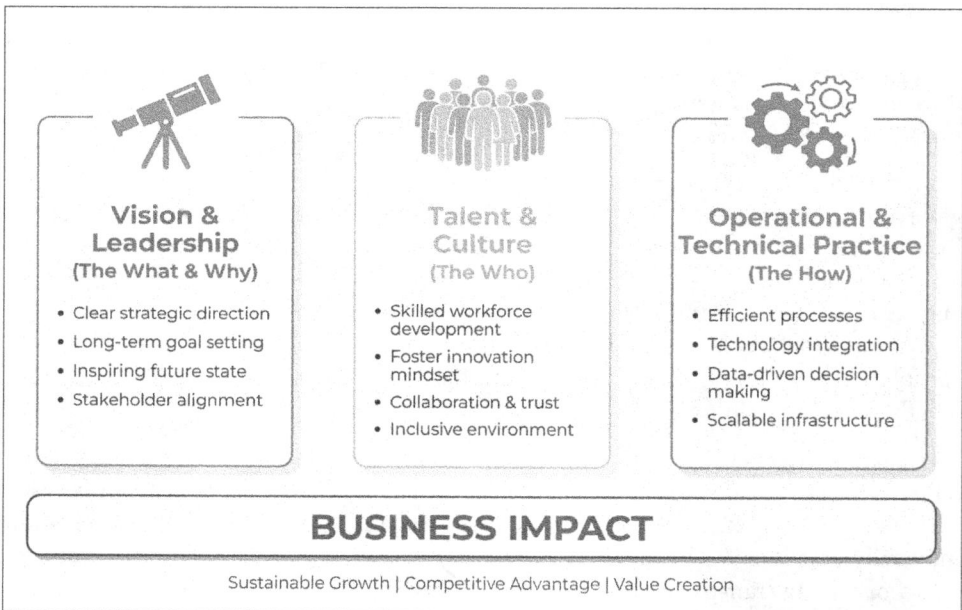

Figure 8-1. The AI and Agentic Maturity framework includes 3 key dimensions: Vision and Leadership, Talent and Culture, and Operational and Technical Practice. Maturity across all dimensions is necessary to drive business impact.

Organizational maturity evolves from a state of awareness and experimentation (Tactical phase) to one of fully integrated enterprise-scale adoption, execution, and support (Transformational phase), as shown in Figure 8-2. Between these two phases is a Strategic phase, where organizations are connected, agile, standardized, and technically skilled with AI and agentic approaches. Notably, the business value unlocked by moving from one phase to the next is exponential, rather than linear, with ROI for leadership, technical specialists, and the entire organization becoming deeper and more visible across all areas and levels of the enterprise. In fact, democratization of innovation within and across business units of an organization is a hallmark of moving from the Strategic to the Transformational phase of the AI and agentic maturity framework.

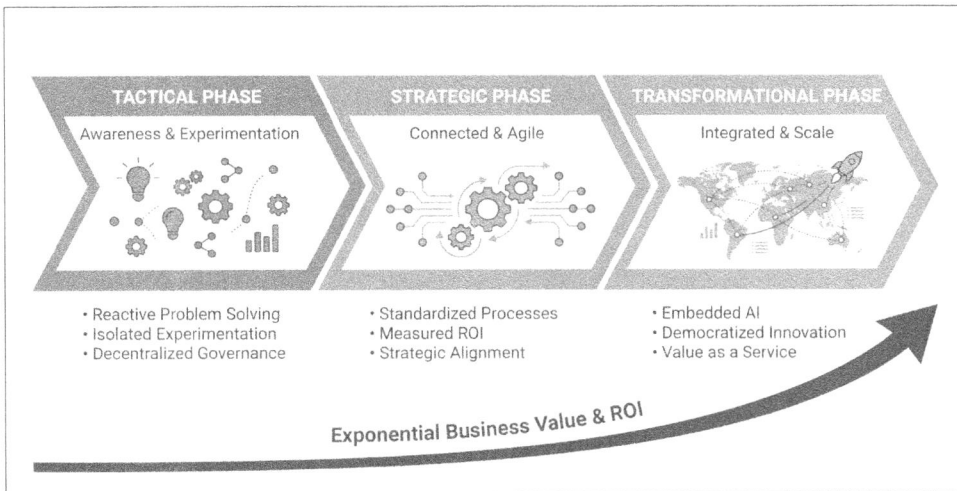

Figure 8-2. The AI and Agentic Maturity framework proceeds across three phases: Tactical, Strategic, and Transformational. Value delivered is exponential, rather than linear, as organizations progress from one phase to the next.

There are excellent frameworks that have been proposed for AI adoption and MLOps maturity, including the 2020 AI Adoption Framework (*https://oreil.ly/TvQVG*) white paper, published by Google Cloud (this was truly a source of inspiration for Steph when she was working as a manager of a data science and MLOps team). We also recommend reading this 2024 blog post (*https://oreil.ly/qsTnq*) describing an approach to scaling an agentic maturity model, as well as the ROI of AI 2025 (*https://oreil.ly/Aftb-*) report, published in November 2025 by Google Cloud. Here, our objective is to coalesce and extend on themes articulated in previous frameworks to prepare you and your organization to move beyond traditional machine learning into a secure, diversified, and highly governed enterprise ecosystem of both generative and non-generative solutions with an increasing degree of automation human-AI collaboration.

> For the careful reader, if you're familiar with the 2020 AI Adoption Framework white paper (*https://oreil.ly/jYMXy*), published by Google Cloud, you will notice that we adhere to the same three phases of organizational maturity: *Tactical*, *Strategic*, and *Transformational*. Here, we focus on the progression through these maturity levels for each dimension of our AI and agentic maturity framework: *Vision and Leadership*, *Talent and Culture*, and *Operational and Technical Practice* (Figure 8-3). To illustrate the application of our framework, we provide representative examples for each phase of maturity, taken from our collective field experiences. Finally, we provide a few points of advice and educational resources for practitioners and teams who want to understand how to develop into the next phase of maturity. This is the world we (Ayo, Sarita, Lavi, and Steph) live and work in on a day-to-day basis and we're excited to share our insights from years of working with customers with you!

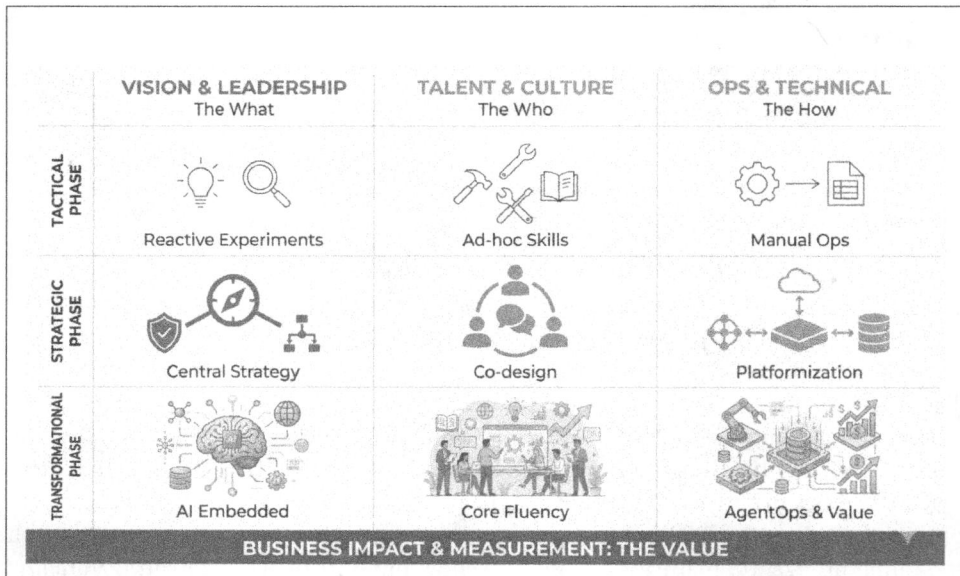

Figure 8-3. The progression of AI and Agentic Maturity from the Tactical to the Transformational phase for all three dimensions. As organizations progress from one phase to the next, they become more agile and automate away manual tasks, which frees up time and resources for greater innovation.

Vision and Leadership (The "What" and the "Why" Dimension)

This first dimension of our maturity framework, Vision and Leadership, includes:

- Short- to long-term vision and roadmap for AI and agents
- The level of executive and resource alignment and investment
- Organizational intent and integration with business operations and objectives and key results (OKRs)

An organization's journey to AI and agent maturity begins with the evolution of its core strategy and leadership commitment. Getting started begins with awareness and acknowledgment that AI can or should be adopted for business. But this is phase 0; the transition to a Tactical, Strategic, and Transformational phase of maturity is marked by a shift from ad hoc, isolated AI and agentic pilots to centrally governed, strategically integrated business capabilities assisted and automated by AI. Ultimately, a mature organization views AI not as a tactical cost center, but as an embedded, competitive driver that fundamentally redefines its market position and operational standards, ensuring proactive compliance and measurable value. A mature organization has a proactive vision that is tightly coupled to the overarching purpose and aims for AI in the enterprise. A mature organization also has awareness and proactive preparedness for global governance and compliance standards and is prepared to meet and exceed standards with impact assessments, documentation on risk-mitigation approaches, and clear and comprehensive oversight of high-risk decisions.

Tactical phase

In the initial Tactical phase of maturity, the vision and intent for AI in the enterprise may be unclear, is not centrally defined, and is very commonly ad hoc. AI and agentic approaches arise out of isolated problem solving or individual interest among teams, departments, or business units. Even the most successful AI projects may remain siloed. With little or no explicit executive sponsorship, the value of AI is unrecognized and unmeasured, and there is a high probability of redundancy and wasted time and resources rebuilding or reinventing solutions for small immediate problems. Leaders in management may govern and drive an isolated vision for AI-related projects, but the C-suite may not be directly engaged or aligned, which weakens the link between AI efforts and realized business KPIs and organizational intent.

Funding for AI is project-specific, opaque, and may be drawn from innovation or IT department budgets that fluctuate in year-to-year availability. Each project owner, team, or department determines the technical approach/tools, governance, and ethics policies for their AI solution or product they're responsible for, and this may exclude key stakeholders and SMEs who could improve quality, relevance, and thorough evaluation of the AI solution for risk level. The focus in the Tactical phase of maturity is quick wins and proofs of concept. AI may be viewed as a technology cost, not a business driver, resulting in "pilot purgatory," where projects succeed locally but fail to scale across an organization.

In cases where a larger business unit is united in pursuing multiple AI pilots, leadership may reactively become aware of value and opportunistically carve out resources to support scaling and visibility of projects. Leadership may become aware that resources simply do not exist within the organization to advance or scale successful AI or agentic projects or that key limitations related to people, processes, or technology exist. This realization of enterprise versus ad hoc business value can propel organizations from the Tactical to the Strategic phase of AI and agentic maturity. Without investment, this fragile state may result in abandonment of AI projects, a regression to completely manual processes, or complete reliance on third-party AI tools that could be comparatively more opaque or inflexible in application to specific or nuanced business use cases.

Strategic phase

In the next, Strategic phase of maturity for the Vision and Leadership domain, AI is recognized as a key competitive lever and a strategic enabler. A dedicated multiyear budget (for people, processes, and technology), executive sponsorship and oversight, and a well-articulated link between holistic AI investment and key business outcomes is a hallmark of the transition into the Strategic phase. The roadmap for prioritizing and expanding AI initiatives is often guided by a centralized AI governance team or center of excellence, which evangelizes AI and brings together key SMEs and relevant stakeholders on each initiative to identify and classify risks and benefits.

Importantly, at the Strategic phase of maturity, an organization's leadership can articulate and has documented an established set of responsible AI principles and mechanisms to continuously vet and monitor projects for bias, compliance, safety, and security. Successful organizations at this phase also invest in formal change management, recognizing that AI adoption is as much a people transformation as a technology deployment. This transforms the position of the organization from reactive to proactive; the organization has performed risk assessments before deploying AI and agentic solutions, has risk-mitigation strategies in place, and has a routine process for human oversight in place. Standardization, repeatability/reusability, and transparency are required and enforced across enterprise AI initiatives. The organization is moving from experiments to enterprise-wide products or programs. The focus is on a clear path to scaling validated use cases across the business for fast wins and measurable return on investment.

Transformational phase

In the Transformational phase of maturity, AI and agentic capabilities are embedded into the business model itself, fundamentally redefining value creation, market position, and corporate identity. For example, all or most personas or job roles within the organization actively leverage AI for day-to-day operational efficiency and productivity and can speak to its value. AI is seamlessly integrated into go-to-market products or used to track and predict go-to-market performance. In this phase, the CEO is a visible champion for AI, articulating its role in the company's future and actively creating a culture around AI. Funding for AI, including upskilling opportunities for employees, is viewed as an investment in market advantage with rapid reallocation of resources to high-potential opportunities. Long-term R&D in AI is the standard in this phase, and the vision and roadmap for AI is forward-looking, highly innovative, and deeply integrated into the latest research and state-of-the-art technologies. Both technical and business teams are proficient with understanding and anticipating how AI and agents fit specific use cases, how to measure business outcomes, and how to safely scale or expand the reach and impact of AI initiatives. Beyond the CEO, a coalition of C-suite leaders—including the CFO, CIO, CHRO, and Chief Strategy Officer—must align on AI investment priorities.

In the Transformational phase of Vision and Leadership maturity, there is a key shift in the organization as AI and agents are the default way to operate, driving sustained competitive advantage and shaping industry standards. Moreover, the mature organization is fully aware of the high stakes for non-compliance in places such as the European Union (i.e., fines up to 35 million euros or 7% of global turnover, whichever is higher (*https://oreil.ly/CizYN*)) and is prepared for such standards around AI governance, even if they do not immediately apply. Such preparation is not viewed by the mature organization as a trade-off; a 2025 Axis Intelligence report (*https://oreil.ly/yzU-X*) found that organizations with mature AI governance frameworks outperformed competitors by $8.4 billion annually in combined operational efficiency, risk mitigation, and revenue acceleration.

Vision and Leadership Questions to Ask: Moving From Tactical to Transformational

Use these questions to assess your organization's current maturity phase and identify gaps to address.

- Tactical Phase Indicators
  - What are the top three business KPIs our AI systems are expected to impact this quarter? How will we measure that impact?
  - Who decides when an AI pilot is successful enough to scale—and what criteria do they use?
  - What is our "error budget" for AI initiatives? How much experimentation failure is acceptable before we pause investment?
- Strategic Phase Indicators
  - Is AI funding from a dedicated, multiyear budget—or annual, fluctuating allocations that create start-stop cycles?
  - Who centralizes governance for AI solutions across business units to prevent duplication and ensure reusability?
  - Is our hiring and upskilling plan explicitly aligned with the AI roadmap?
  - What measurable mechanism ensures our Responsible AI principles are enforced and audited before deployment of new AI products?
- Transformational Phase Indicators
  - How many job roles actively use AI or agentic tools today? What is our plan to make AI the default operating method for all employees?
  - Can our CEO clearly articulate AI's role in our company's future market identity—and does leadership model AI-first behavior?
  - How does our AI strategy create measurable competitive advantage in the next 24 months?
  - What proactive steps are we taking to meet global AI compliance standards (e.g., EU AI Act) before they become mandatory in our markets?

Example: breaking out of the Tactical phase

"Vision and Leadership Questions to Ask: Moving From Tactical to Transformational" on page 243 shows questions that will help organizations move from the Tactical to the Transformational phase of Vision and Leadership. Let's look at an example of how an organization might transition out of the Tactical phase. A new chief innovation officer (CIO) is hired at Cymbal Health, a fictional health payer system. She recognizes the potential of AI, and after interviewing the heads of departments, realizes that there are pockets of exciting but largely invisible AI work being done across the enterprise. The CIO establishes a temporary AI task force that consists of data scientists, MLOps engineers, and analysts across three departments and together they identify high-impact use cases and key business outcomes. The team will undertake an initiative to build a clinical note summarizer using one of three foundational LLMs, which will be evaluated against each other. The team receives dedicated but temporary funding from the CIO and begins the project with immediate success, including interest from the clinical teams who depend on the notes to process claims and prior authorizations. The CIO thinks that this pilot might convince the CEO that AI will improve accuracy and efficiency of billing and coding departments at Cymbal Health. The project is still a pilot, but it now has a clear objective and a connection to a potential business outcome (faster claims processing and reduced errors). So far, the AI task force is the only group executing on AI strategy, but after the success of this project, the CIO would like to hire at least five more individual contributors and create a more permanent task force to oversee and guide AI projects across Cymbal Health.

Advice from the authors

This is a great example of a company in the Tactical phase of AI and agentic maturity with respect to Vision and Leadership. Leadership has recognized the promise and potential of AI, but there is a great deal of fragmentation in vision and lack of purposeful use of AI to drive horizontal enterprise outcomes. Cymbal Health may move into the Strategic phase, contingent on a few key actions. Here are some points of advice and resources to support the transition into the next phase of maturity:

Strengthen the business and strategic case

The team must deliver the pilot within the context of measurable business outcomes and value. Focus the project not just on showing a technical capability, but on demonstrating a direct impact on KPIs for the billing and coding departments at Cymbal Health. For example, show a quantifiable increase in accuracy or a reduction in the time it takes to process claims, leading to cost savings. This will be the evidence needed to convince the CEO that AI can be a pivotal business accelerator, not just a proof of concept.

Formalize resource readiness

The current project uses dedicated funding from the CIO, but true scalability requires a robust, company-wide foundation. Use this pilot project as a forcing function to establish standards and governance over the way that data is sourced, cleaned, and protected to ensure that it is high-quality, secure, auditable, and ready for use in a regulated environment. This will ensure that the solution is not a one-off script but a reliable, scalable system that can be expanded later, ideally with oversight from a central team or center of excellence.

Cultivate executive buy-in and AI literacy

While the CIO is an important strategic advocate for AI, moving to the Strategic phase of maturity requires broader sponsorship. The exploration team should actively evangelize their work, sharing progress and results with other senior leaders and potential stakeholders across the organization. By demonstrating the benefits of the pilot, they can begin to build a coalition of support and foster a culture of AI literacy.

For those seeking a more profound understanding of the strategic imperative of AI leadership, we direct your attention to the curated selection of thought leadership from sources such as *Harvard Business Review*, McKinsey, and Google Cloud, meticulously compiled within the "Further Reading" appendix.

Talent and Culture (The "Who" Dimension)

An organization's ability to capitalize on AI and agents ultimately hinges on its people and their collective mindset. The journey from low to high maturity in this dimension is marked by a transformation from siloed expertise and general skepticism to widespread AI literacy and a culture of psychological safety. A truly mature organization moves beyond hiring a few data scientists or AI engineers to embedding AI roles, fostering continuous upskilling, and embracing innovation as a core cultural value across the entire enterprise.

Maturity with respect to Talent and Culture is defined by an organization's cultural openness to innovation and the availability of a skilled workforce. Growing and maturing depends on the presence of AI technical and subject matter expertise as well as the overall AI literacy of the workforce and even the psychological safety built around surfacing new and transformative ideas and concepts related to AI and agentic use cases. This dimension of the AI and agentic maturity framework intersects with the Vision and Leadership domain because it depends on leadership's commitment to and sponsorship of expanded AI roles and education in the enterprise as well as the types of products and services built and delivered externally by the organization.

Tactical phase

At this initial phase of AI and agentic maturity, the majority of the organization's Talent and Culture are largely unprepared and may even be resistant to pervasive changes brought by AI and agents. Technical knowledge is siloed and there is a lack of cohesive strategy for adaptation to AI tools or assistants in the workplace and across various personas/users. Enterprise access to materials for AI upskilling may be limited to individuals, teams, or departments and is not integrated into broader skill development programs. A small number of individuals or individual teams drive AI projects in isolation, and even when these teams successfully launch AI projects or products, there is limited visibility and means to evangelize such work. The culture of hiring is more reactive than proactive, based largely on ad hoc AI project needs.

At the Tactical phase, most AI work happens in technical silos or might even be contracted out of the organization, and there may be little to no structured collaboration between AI specialists, business units, and executive leadership, leading to friction and missed opportunities. Failure of AI experiments may be seen negatively, stifling innovation, and eroding confidence of individuals moving into the field for the first time. There is no formal mechanism for cross-functional collaboration, when and where support for experimentation and scaling could be beneficial. At this phase, it is not uncommon for a majority of employees to view AI as a niche tool rather than a way to accelerate productivity, efficiency, or innovation within and outside of the enterprise. Talent and Culture is in early phases of development at the tactical stage, but does exist, perhaps independently of or outside of a larger strategic mission to cultivate it.

Strategic phase

At this next phase of maturity, an organization has a conscious strategy to develop its workforce and foster a culture that supports AI and agent adoption. There is a growing understanding, acceptance, and education. Full integration of skilled workforce talent across the organization may still be a work in progress. However, the organization now has a defined strategy to recruit and retain AI expertise, and there are defined and distinct career paths for AI professionals. Upskilling through AI literacy programs and incentivized certifications is available to a wider range of employees, including those who may evolve into a new role due to automation of manual or routine tasks. There is a structured change management program to address concerns, communicate AI's benefits, and integrate AI into day-to-day workflows. Training focuses on human-AI collaboration and codesign. At this phase, leadership promotes and encourages a safe-to-fail environment for AI experimentation and ideation.

Employees now view AI as an augmentative force, improving their work rather than replacing it. Efforts are made by the C-suite and management to explain AI's role and build confidence in its application. It is clear that AI is not replacing the workforce but augmenting it in helpful and positive ways. A key component of the Strategic phase of AI and agentic maturity across the Talent and Culture dimension is organizational investment in its people to meet the demands of a rapidly evolving field. Leadership is actively shaping the culture through training, communication, and structured collaboration, leading to a positive feedback loop where increased adoption leads to a workforce that is ready and willing to engage and get the most benefit out of AI and agents.

Transformational phase

At this level of AI and agentic maturity with respect to Talent and Culture, an organization has fully embraced an AI-first model of operating, where AI fluency is a core competency. The culture is one of continuous coevolution with AI, which is now viewed as a way to drive innovation. Employees are trained to work alongside and augment AI systems and are given the training resources to continue to upskill and refine understanding and actions. A mature talent management strategy is integrated and anticipatory; AI and agentic expertise is a core competency across many roles, not just specialists. Adaptation to AI-driven change becomes an inherent part of the organization's cultural DNA. Employees might even proactively identify new AI opportunities to shape their own roles. In this phase, unlike others, AI and agents have become essential partners to the workforce, are deeply rooted into the mission of the enterprise, and there is a strong understanding of ethical, safe, secure, and compliant use of AI. Human oversight of AI systems is embedded in the foundation of the enterprise.

Talent and Culture Questions to Ask: Moving from Tactical to Transformational

Use these questions to assess your organization's current maturity phase and identify gaps to address:

- Tactical Phase Indicators

  — How will we mandate and fund structured collaboration between AI specialists and business unit SMEs to ensure viable and relevant solutions?

  — What is the explicit governance for reviewing failed AI experiments? Will they be treated as learning investments or budget losses, and who communicates this?

- Strategic Phase Indicators

  — If AI automates 30% of a non-technical role, what incentivized upskilling pathway is available to that employee for higher-value, AI-augmented tasks? Is this training universally accessible?

  — When hiring VPs or HR leads, is AI fluency a core, non-negotiable competency? If not, what is the timeline for making AI expertise a basic qualification across all leadership?

- Transformational Phase Indicators
  - Instead of hiring for current AI needs, what is our strategy for cultivating skills for emerging agentic paradigms anticipated in 18 months? Is there a dedicated R&D budget for upskilling?
  - How do we define our unique human-AI collaboration model? Can every employee articulate how AI augments their job, and how do we measure the cultural impact (e.g., job satisfaction, innovation output) beyond technical metrics?

Example: moving beyond the Strategic phase

Cymbal Retail, a fictional multichannel apparel and home goods retailer, has successfully moved beyond isolated AI pilots (like a single chatbot or basic inventory forecasting). Its leadership, having defined a strategic AI roadmap, now faces the challenge of scaling AI across core functions—from personalized marketing to supply chain optimization. The Talent and Culture efforts become focused on closing organizational gaps to support this scale. Cymbal's HR and technology departments collaborate on a "Future of Retail" upskilling plan. Targeted AI literacy training paths are launched for 500+ managers, focusing on using AI-generated insights for merchandising and logistics. New roles, such as AI Translation Specialist (to bridge data scientists and buyers), are actively recruited. The CEO hosts quarterly AI town halls, actively addressing the fear of replacement by showcasing new human-AI teaming roles.

Cymbal Retail launches a central Applied AI Center of Excellence (CoE), composed of data scientists and AI engineers, business process owners, and legal experts. The CoE's mandate is to build reusable AI frameworks (e.g., a personalized product recommendation model) and deploy them as a service for the marketing, ecommerce, and supply chain teams. Finally, Cymbal allocates a small, dedicated budget for a "fast-fail sandbox" where cross-functional teams can test new agent ideas.

Advice from the authors

Cymbal Retail is clearly in the Strategic phase of AI and agentic maturity with respect to the Talent and Culture dimension. This is a pivotal phase because successful ramping of education and human-AI partnership can lead this organization to the Transformational phase, over time. Here are our points of advice for maturing within and beyond the Strategic phase:

Embed human-agent teaming as the default operating model
Facilitate coevolution with specialized agents, such as partnering product managers with both forecasting models and a dedicated Marketing Discovery Agent that proactively identifies gaps and drafts new product requirements. This AI

assistance changes the human's role to curate the agent output and execute the creative vision.

Establish a self-service agent creation and sharing platform
Instead of relying on the central AI CoE for all AI and agentic ideas and products, leverage no-code tools for store managers and merchandisers. Empower the entire workforce to build, customize, and share lightweight agents or agent prototypes to automate their own daily tasks. This democratizes AI and fosters a culture of continuous innovation.

Integrate AI ethics and responsible AI into the core skillsets and incentives for employees
Move beyond formal and siloed governance principles by expanding training to annual human-agent teaming ethics training. Ensure that the workplace is supported in ethical use of advanced agents and has a path for reporting concerns. Create playbooks for best practices that can be shared and discussed across the organization horizontally and within verticals.

For a deeper exploration of AI upskilling and cultural transformation, we direct your attention to the curated selection of thought leadership from sources such as IBM and Boston Consulting Group, meticulously compiled within the "Further Reading" appendix.

Operational and Technical Practice (The "How" Dimension)

The third dimension of AI maturity is the execution engine that turns strategy and talent into reliable, scalable value. The progression from low to high maturity here is characterized by a fundamental shift from manual, fragile development pipelines to an automated, self-sustaining system of MLOps/AgentOps. A truly mature organization achieves seamless integration across its expansive technical subdomains, making its AI capabilities a source of competitive efficiency, robust security, and continuous business value.

This dimension of our maturity framework is the most expansive. At a mature phase of Operational and Technical Practice, the theoretical and the applied world of AI and agents comes together seamlessly, with state-of-the-art tools competitively driving business value and the organization operating as a constantly evolving and almost self-sustaining entity through automated ML/AIOps. Here, we'll dive into the AI and maturity phases related to "how" AI is built, maintained, and managed for maximum business value and ROI. We acknowledge that these subdimensions are intertwined and interdependent on one another. We propose at least six subdomains that fuel operational and technical aspects of AI and agentic maturity:

- Data quality, accessibility, and interoperability (also discussed in Chapter 2)
- Engineering processes and best practices

- Evaluation, monitoring, explainability, and product lifecycle management
- Safety, security, governance, and management of risk
- Technical tools, frameworks, and flexibility
- FinOps practices

As we did previously, we will review the Operational and Technical Practice domain and each of the six subdomains with respect to the three phases of the AI and agentic maturity framework, with an example and resources to follow.

Tactical phase

The initial tactical phase of maturity is characterized by fragmentation, manual effort, and high friction across the AI and agentic lifecycle (Figure 8-4). The focus remains on isolated functions rather than enterprise-wide operational reliability. Because of this, AI projects are technical islands, disconnected from upstream data teams and downstream deployment teams, and built largely by hand by single developers. Lack of standardization results in reactive product management and makes the organization at this phase slow, brittle, and largely incapable of scaling successful AI pilots. Limited codesign, collaboration, and united standards for governance make it unlikely that AI will sustainably drive business goals or objectives.

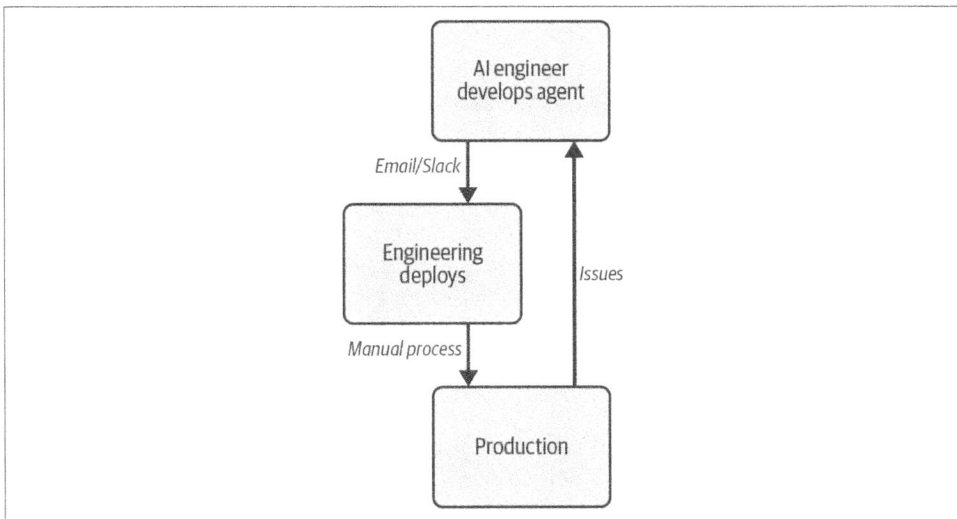

Figure 8-4. An example of a disconnected workflow, characteristic of the Tactical phase of Operational and Technical Practice within the AI and agentic maturity framework

Let's look at each of the subdomains:

Data quality, accessibility, and interoperability

At the Tactical phase, the data used to develop AI and agentic applications is siloed, unversioned, and fragmented. Key features or attributes needed for tasks may live across local servers and legacy databases on-prem and in the cloud. Data quality may be inconsistent and unvalidated and different business departments may have their own business logic for defining features and outcomes. Data pipelines for AI projects must be built manually and as one-off approaches for each use case and business stakeholder. The data itself may not have a consistent ETL process, and mismatches in standards applied to data ingestion processes (e.g., delays in availability) may compromise the production data pipeline (e.g., a need for real-time inference). Data transformations are performed manually by individual data-users, resulting in non-versioned feature sets. AI or agentic projects or products are often delayed until data quality, accessibility, and interoperability are fully addressed. It can be difficult or impossible to reproduce training datasets.

Engineering processes and best practices

At the Tactical phase, MLOps/AgentOps is generally non-existent, manual, or non-reproducible. AI and agentic application progression from experimentation and development to deployment might be manual code-to-deploy from notebooks or a single Python script, for example, to production. No standardized continuous integration, continuous deployment, continuous testing (CI/CD/CT) for pipelines exists, making updates slow, rollbacks risky, and pipelines error-prone. In the Tactical phase, there may be varying levels of engineering expertise on the team, and deployment might be handled by individual developers or a single senior DevOps engineer on the same or a different team. Engineers may be tasked with taking agents to production through manual steps. Engineers may have varying levels of confidence, skill, and adherence to best practice such as code annotation and version control. Standard practices in the enterprise, such as containerizing code using Docker or Kubernetes, may be employed ad hoc.

Evaluation, monitoring, explainability, and product lifecycle management

At the Tactical phase, evaluation, explanation, and monitoring of deployed solutions is also reactive and ad hoc. Solutions are not evaluated for explainability before they are deployed. Model performance monitoring is minimal and might focus on only accuracy or latency. There is little production telemetry (logging input and output data). Monitoring for model drift or data/feature quality degradation in production may not exist and is certainly not automated at this phase, leading to unexpected failures and unplanned or unpredictable resource allocations to emergencies that compromise business continuity. Building new tools or products is slowed by the need to react to unexpected production issues.

The team lacks technical capabilities to explain, trace, or debug model or agent reasoning once in production.

Safety, security, governance, and risk management

AI security at the Tactical phase is passive, relying on general IT security policies like perimeter network protection. There are no specific technical controls embedded at the inference layer to mitigate prompt injection, data leakage via model output, or adversarial attacks. Identity and access management is absent or ad hoc for expensive resources, leading to uncontrolled access to production models and sensitive training data. In general, teams become aware of security concerns or issues as they arise from their users. Responses are reactive and may be overwhelming when teams do not explicitly codesign or consult with security teams during the process of building AI and agentic products.

Technical tools, frameworks, and flexibility

This phase is characterized by unmanaged tooling sprawl. The technical ecosystem consists of disparate unmanaged open source tools and environments that lack a consistent operational footprint. Deployments suffer from dependency issues such as conflicting library versions. The absence of a unified platform means no standardization in how models are packaged, served, or secured, limiting horizontal scaling. Teams building AI applications and agents focus on use of model APIs and model tuning is rare, with more focus on prompt optimization as the mechanism to modify model output and performance of applications. There may or may not be clear separation of staging, development, and production environments.

FinOps practices

At this phase, costs are largely unallocated and resources run the risk of being overprovisioned. Bills may arrive as one large, generalized expense. Project teams do not consistently tag resources, making it impossible or at least difficult to attribute costs to specific AI models, agents, or business outcomes. Teams might over-provision GPU and compute resources for AI tasks "just in case." There is no effort to stop idle training environments or optimize LLM model serving sizes. Cost is viewed as an engineering or IT problem and teams are not incentivized or trained to be cost-aware. The finance team may be involved only during budgeting or when the bill is unexpectedly high. There are no thresholds put into place for individuals or teams to avoid overspending.

Strategic phase

At this next phase of maturity, the organization is leveraging centralized platforms (discussed at the end of this chapter). Technical teams adhere to defined, repeatable processes to efficiently develop, deploy, govern, and trace AI and agentic systems at scale with common packages and libraries. There is team and organizational consensus about best practices for code optimization, review, and packaging (Figure 8-5). Considerations such as built-in safety filters for harmful content and explainability tools are present and can be leveraged as part of the platform, rather than relying on custom development. The organization is shifting from custom-built, one-off solutions to an industrialized "AI factory" capable of handling a portfolio of strategic projects by creating reusable assets. Standardized processes, MLOps automation, and governance frameworks in alignment with the security team enable the organization to scale AI reliably and with speed. Developer teams are more agile and adaptable to planned and unplanned changes, and there is collaboration across all teams involved from data ingestion to model maintenance, issue handling, and product management post-production.

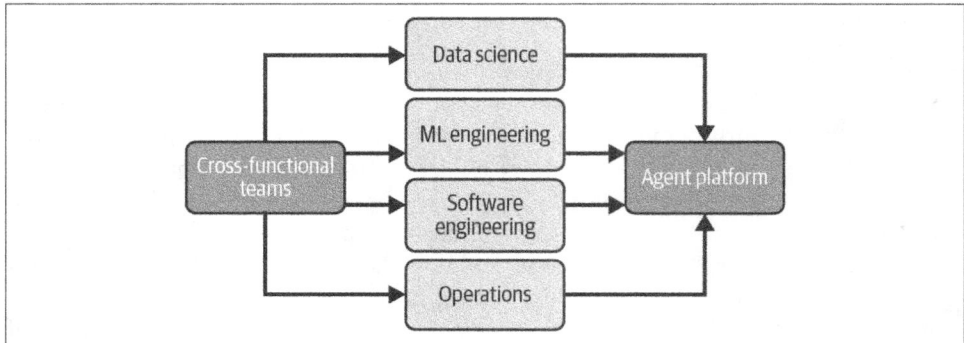

Figure 8-5. An example of a cross-functional team structure, where siloes are replaced by a team working seamlessly together to build integrated, reusable, secure, and auditable assets on a shared agent platform. This centralization is characteristic of the Strategic phase of Operational and Technical Practice within the AI and agentic maturity framework.

Here's the status of the subdomains:

Data quality, accessibility, and interoperability
> A central data lake or mesh exists, often in the cloud, and data quality standards are enforced for AI initiatives and underlaid by business collaboration. Data pipelines for ingestion, processing, and transformation are automated and reusable for common use cases (e.g., feature stores are used). At this phase of maturity, data is centralized and governed, making AI and agentic projects relatively quick to begin. Data, analytics, and AI/ML teams are agile and can deliver higher reliability AI and agentic products with faster time to market.

Engineering processes and best practices
> At this phase, operational processes are standardized and automated. A common MLOps platform such as Vertex AI is adopted to seamlessly train, test, validate, explain, and deploy AI and agentic solutions. The full lifecycle is defined and

versioned, and metadata are centrally tracked in a registry. Processes are reproducible and modular. Technical best practices are shared across the team, making collaboration and codesign seamless. Automated CI/CD/CT is mandatory, integrating A/B testing and canary testing for low-risk, gradual production rollouts. The focus is on low-friction, repeatable deployments at volume. Transparency and auditability are high at this phase, making it possible for technical and non-technical teams to review decision points and steps taken along the entire pipeline of AI and agentic development.

Evaluation, monitoring, explainability, and product lifecycle management

At this phase, monitoring is proactive and rollbacks are easily integrated. Production solutions are continuously monitored for performance decay and drift against pre-defined thresholds and alerting is in place to let the central engineering team know when performance is approaching thresholds where actions are needed. Proxy business indicators are also measured continuously to ensure that solutions are delivering ROI in production. A central product management function governs the entire portfolio of models and agents with explainability guiding decisions and improvements in model development and tracking. Automated rollback capability is integrated into the CI/CD pipeline, guaranteeing recovery to the last stable version with minimal human intervention. Logging analytics are used to understand root causes of anomalies or drift detected in production.

Safety, security, governance, and risk management

Technical guardrails and mandatory gating for security are embedded into the AI process and technical approach at this phase. Red teaming—a specialized, proactive testing methodology used to secure AI systems, especially LLMs, by simulating real-world adversarial attacks before they happen—may be employed to focus on vulnerabilities unique to AI, such as prompt injection, data leakage, and bypassing safety guardrails (jailbreaks). Data deidentification via tokenization or masking for PII and PHI is applied in lower development and staging environments. A dedicated review board vets models and agents and signs off on them before production deployment. The security team and chief information security officer (CISO) are closely aligned with and considered part of the team(s) who build and deploy AI and agents for the enterprise. Safety, security, and privacy are defined and enforced.

Technical tools, frameworks, and flexibility

The organization has chosen a standardized, scalable, and unified platform to host most AI and agentic workloads, reducing security and deployment friction. Core frameworks and software development kits (SDKs) such as ADK are used across teams and integrate naturally with MCP and A2A, allowing seamless multiagent development and orchestration. Teams and collaborating business units share ownership of AI and agentic products and solutions. The team agrees on a common language for most AI and agentic application builds but is adept at moving between languages for the most appropriate approach. Containerized environments and standardized APIs are used to build efficiency into the processes and practices of the team. Speed of delivery is short and accuracy is high, with code review occurring by automated and HITL methods. The team's flexibility, adaptability, and agility start to skyrocket at this phase.

FinOps practices

In this Strategic phase, enhancements include greater cost accountability and proactive rightsizing. Mandatory resource tagging is enforced to allocate costs to business units, projects, or agents. Central tools provide showback reports to project owners and managers. Clear policies exist for resource optimization such as automated shutdown schedules for non-active environments and rules for model sizing for specific types of tasks. Engineers, finance, and business owners meet regularly to review cost reports.

Transformational phase

At this phase of AI and agentic maturity within the Operational and Technical Practice domain, an organization's use of AI and agents is somewhat self-governing (e.g., through human alerts), adaptive, and fully integrated with core business systems. The organization achieves a self-optimizing operational loop where the platform itself uses AI to intelligently recommend, manage, secure, and improve on its own performance (Figure 8-6). The technical team maximizes speed, efficiency, resilience, and quality of products by synergizing with AI throughout development, deployment, and lifecycle management.

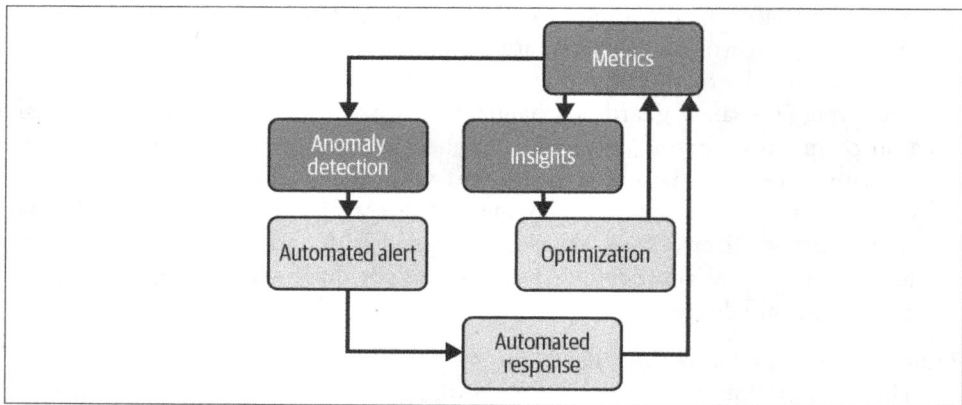

Figure 8-6. An example of automated feedback and optimization loops at the Transformational phase of Operational and Technical Practice within the AI and agentic maturity framework

Let's look at what's occurring in the subdomains:

Data quality, accessibility, and interoperability

At the Transformational phase, data quality is autonomously managed by agents that detect, flag (for human review), and remediate (with user approval) issues. Data is universally accessible and instantly available across the organization, contingent with robust identity and access control and automated controls for removing or obscuring PII and PHI in lower environments. Systems have been designed for interoperability, so that upstream processes of data ingesting, processing, and transformation are hidden from data consumers. In this phase, users quickly get to business insights from raw data that is prepared, governed, and accessible in line with common and agreed-upon rules applied through a semantic layer.

Engineering processes and best practices

In the Transformational phase, MLOps can now really be thought of as AIOps in practice; agents autonomously retrain and redeploy models in production in response to live data triggers and/or human-defined thresholds and rules. Agent orchestration is managed seamlessly with frameworks such as ADK, and agents are monitored using platform tools for evaluation. AI and agentic applications are continuously monitored with the newest tools integrated into the standard developer platform.

Evaluation, monitoring, explainability, and product lifecycle management

In the Transformational stage, monitoring is not only for performance metrics, but also for business value and ROI in real time. Agents proactively predict future performance decay based on trends and flag potential failures before they occur. A common characteristic at this stage is the development of HITL integration or protocol. A2H protocols solve the problem of smart escalation and HITL workflows. Rather than a failure simply stopping the process, A2H provides a structured, contextual, and secure way for the agent to determine the need for human intervention, escalate with full context, choose the right channel (e.g., Slack, email), and receive instruction or approval. A2H can be used as a "smart hand-off" mechanism, which ensures that your automated AI agent workflows are safe and effective by seamlessly integrating human judgment when it's needed.

Safety, security, governance, and risk management

Security and governance agents are embedded within the pipeline, automatically enforcing privacy and security before code execution. Dynamic consent and provenance tracking are the default for all data and model usage. In the Transformational phase, there may be specialized teams dedicated to testing potential vulnerabilities of AI and agentic solutions and running simulations of responses to malicious attacks. When applied to AI and agentic products, the red team/blue team/purple team framework shifts its focus from traditional network infrastructure (firewalls, servers) to the unique algorithmic and content-based vulnerabilities of the AI system itself. AI red teaming is the proactive testing of an AI system to find safety, security, and ethical risks. It goes beyond finding traditional software bugs to find flaws specific to machine learning behavior. The blue team's role is to build and maintain the security and safety mechanisms that detect and mitigate the attacks found by the red team. In the AI context, purple teaming ensures that the discoveries made by the red team are quickly and effectively turned into better defenses by the blue team. Purple teaming is essential because AI threats change constantly.

Technical tools, frameworks, and flexibility

In the Transformational phase, it's possible that all or most of the organization's agent capabilities are exposed as APIs for seamless integration with external partners and systems via A2A protocol. The platform itself adapts to new technological advancements automatically. Teams know when it's best to build versus buy and seamlessly integrate with other first-party as well as third-party systems. Orchestration is seamless and the team is not only using the latest technologies but developing and innovating new tools and technologies for others in the field to leverage for common business challenges. Technical teams are experts not only within the organization, but in the greater AI and agentic community. Often, these teams are also key contributors to and publishers among open source community resources, understanding industry and cross-industry trends and gaps.

FinOps practices

In the Transformational phase of AI and agentic maturity for Operational and Technical Practice, AI and agentic spend is forecast based on AI usage and business demand. Allocation is dynamic, automatically adjusting project budgets based on instant revenue impact or strategic priority. Dedicated FinOps agents autonomously trigger model retraining, scaling, and deployment changes to maintain a target cost-per-value metric. Financial optimization is continuous and fully automated. The organization operates under a "value-as-a-service" financial model where funding for R&D is as important as the costs of maintaining production solutions for business. Cost is relevant when the cost-to-value ratio is outside of an acceptable predetermined range. Budget decisions are driven by automated ROI analysis with human oversight and review.

Operational Questions to Ask: Moving from Tactical to Transformational

Use these questions to assess your organization's current maturity phase and identify gaps to address:

- Tactical Phase Indicators
  - Would a mid-level engineer be able to replicate a top AI engineer's production environment, training data, and model artifacts in under four hours if the AI engineer left tomorrow? If not, what is the cost of that technical debt in deployment delays and risks?
  - Currently, security is a reactive final check. What budget and process will be dedicated to red teaming LLM-powered agents pre-launch, and who is the CISO-aligned contact responsible for mandatory inference-layer security control sign-off?

- Strategic Phase Indicators
  - What is our roadmap for implementing a semantic layer or universal governance, making all governed, cleaned data instantly available to any agent or developer, eliminating manual custom feature pipeline creation for new use cases?
  - What is the weekly dollar loss from unaddressed model drift that goes unnoticed until user reports?
  - What is the timeline for integrating automated monitoring and alerting for business value proxies, not just technical accuracy?

- Transformational Phase Indicators
  - We can now allocate costs. What is the target cost-per-value metric (e.g., cost per successful claims processed by an agent) we need to achieve, and what automated FinOps agents will we deploy to dynamically scale, compute, and change model sizes to autonomously maintain that metric in real-time?
  - Beyond problem alerting, what is our first agent-driven automation to autonomously manage and redeploy its own model in production (AIOps), in response to a pre-approved data quality trigger? Who owns the A2H protocol for smart-human escalation if automation fails?

Example: an organization operating in the Transformational phase

Cymbal Media, a fictional global content and advertising platform, operates its entire publishing and ad-serving ecosystem as a self-optimizing intelligence network. Its focus is not on managing models, but on setting high-level business goals and intervening only when an agent flags an *ethical* or *unforeseen* risk. Data is organized into a hyper-connected mesh where Data Quality Agents are embedded at every ingestion point. These agents autonomously detect, isolate, and remediate corrupt or biased data streams in real time. All data is API-accessible and tagged with automatic provenance/lineage metadata, ensuring universal and auditable availability for all agents and users. Model training, deployment, and pipeline maintenance are fully AIOps-driven. Deployment Agents automatically trigger model retirement or update rollouts based on predictive monitoring alarms. The core Agent Orchestration Layer is self-aware, constantly optimizing the routing and chaining of specialized agents (e.g., Content Creation Agent → Ad Targeting Agent → Compliance Agent) to meet editorial and revenue goals. Monitoring extends far beyond model drift—it's predictive. Drift Forecasting Agents flag models likely to fail in the following 48 hours due to external factors (e.g., a major world event impacting news consumption patterns). The product lifecycle is managed in a "Value Dashboard" that displays real-time Net Revenue Generated per Agent, providing instant ROI for every automated workflow.

Governance is no longer an afterthought; it's code. Security Guardrail Agents are embedded at the inference layer of every agent, automatically enforcing PII redaction, token limits, and ethical guardrails before agent code is allowed to execute. Audit trails are immutable and automatically generated for every agent decision, creating a fully transparent compliance record that adapts instantly to new regulations (e.g., a new advertising law automatically updates the constraint agent).

All internal and third-party systems are connected via an API-first architecture utilizing A2A protocols. This allows Cymbal's agents to seamlessly exchange data and hand off tasks to external partner agents (e.g., requesting a financial transaction from a partner bank's agent), making the company's technical boundary fluid and highly interoperable. FinOps is managed by a Cost-Optimization Agent that operates in a closed loop with the MLOps platform. This agent dynamically rightsizes AI inference compute, optimizes API calls, and automatically scales down training clusters based on real-time usage and a pre-defined cost-per-value (CPV) threshold. Budget is treated as a dynamic resource, automatically reallocated across high-performing agent portfolios based on real-time revenue impact.

Advice from the authors

Cymbal Media is in the Transformational phases of Operational and Technical maturity. Maintaining this state, however, requires constant intentional focus and investment from practitioners and leadership. Cymbal Media is a model for other organizations and is operating at a state that is rarely achieved. Here is some advice for maintaining this position in the industry and in the AI and agentic maturity framework:

Embrace the perpetual reinvention

At the Transformational phase, the biggest threat might be complacency. Leadership should continue strategic scanning including challenging the stability of the current operational model, monetizing the operational platform, and understanding how future societal and geopolitical factors, not just technical ones, might affect the way that AI and agentic systems are built and regulated.

Elevate human roles and creativity

Since the technical "How" is now truly automated in this phase, the human "operator" role must shift entirely to strategic creativity, boundary-setting, and ethical oversight. One suggestion would be to shift performance incentives away from simply deploying agents and toward innovating *within* ethical and FinOps constraints. Reward the team that achieved the highest revenue gain while maintaining the lowest CPV ratio and the highest compliance score.

Guarantee elasticity and trust

Focus on making the self-optimizing platform more resilient, verifiable, and open to the next generation of technology. One way to develop a truly elastic and resilient AI and agent maturity is by avoiding vendor lock-in and diversifying the ecosystem of tools and technologies applied for business. Technical specialists should become accustomed to and comfortable with change, creating an adaptable living system for thinking out the current and future state of AI.

We recommend the included "Further Reading" appendix for additional reports from Gartner and Google on real-world use cases and the future of workforce AI.

How the Three Dimensions of AI and Agentic Maturity Can Work Together

We often talk about prioritizing AI and agentic use cases. Effectively doing so involves bringing together the three dimensions of maturity that we've discussed previously. Vision and Leadership are needed to define core business challenges, while Talent and Culture support the execution of the product or solution to address the challenge within the context of Operational and Technical Practice capabilities and processes to turn an idea into reality. In Figure 8-7, we illustrate the process of use case mapping, which should be performed with all relevant user personas involved (such as business stakeholders, SMEs, analysts, data scientists, and engineers). Along this process, we define two axes against which GenAI use cases can be measured. On the x-axis, *ease of execution* ranges across a high to low scale. Ease of execution depends on key input from technical teams as well as the operational and technical tools available. As we learned in Chapters 5, 6, and 7, execution of these use cases is inclusive of more than testing and experimentation. We must factor in evaluation, tuning, optimization, and AI/AgentOps needs before we generate business value. Along the y-axis, the potential *business value* delivered ranges from low to high. There may be trade-offs between ease of execution and value delivered. However, a visualization of these trade-offs can be illuminating, and the exercise of mapping use cases against these axes has been something that we, the authors, have often used as starting points in our conversations with customers.

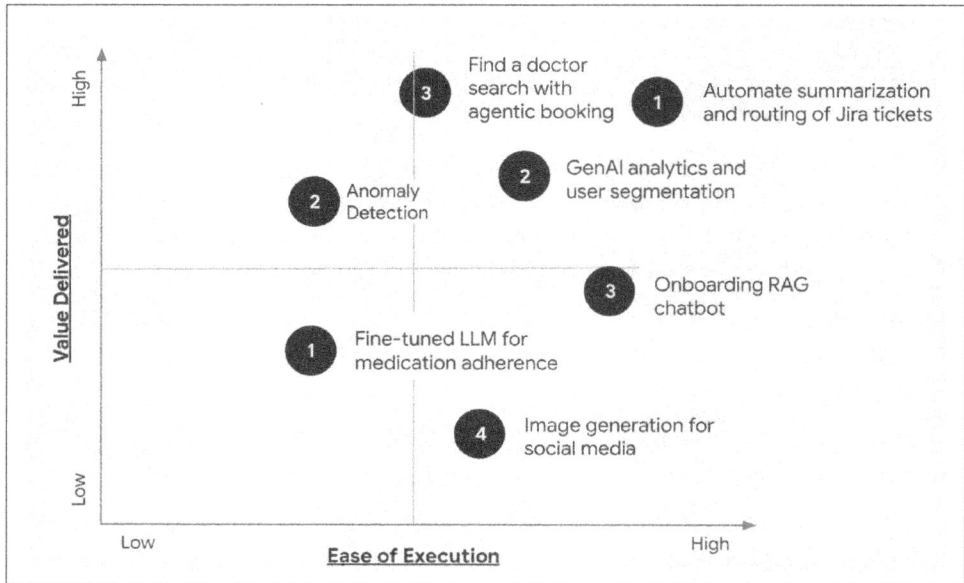

Figure 8-7. An example of a hypothetical use case prioritization mapping exercise for business impact while considering ease of execution

We sometimes refer to an easy-to-execute GenAI use case as "low-hanging fruit." By that, we mean a project that is easily achievable, requires minimal initial effort or technical complexity, and can deliver fast, clear, and measurable business value. Low-hanging fruit use cases are often prioritized early in an organization's GenAI journey because they help build internal capability, generate quick wins, and secure executive buy-in for more ambitious and more technically or operationally complex projects (often called "moonshots"). In our experience, use cases that bring value and are (relatively) easy to achieve in short time frames involve search and summarization use cases. *Finding* and *understanding* information with the help of GenAI enhances productivity and efficiency across almost every business area of an organization!

Use case mapping is crucial for assessing an organization's readiness for enterprise-scale AI. When performed with cross-functional teams, this process systematically documents and quantifies potential projects against axes like value and complexity/feasibility. This exercise not only surfaces high-potential use cases but also reveals hidden data gaps and internal capability requirements that would otherwise go unnoticed. This mapping provides the initial blueprint for an AI maturity timeline, which is then refined by integrating two key human-centric approaches: Design Thinking and Critical User Journeys (CUJs). Both of these frameworks ensure that technical, leadership, and end-user perspectives are consistently integrated throughout the planning and development of LLM-powered solutions.

Design Thinking is the essential human-centered, iterative process that prevents "AI for AI's sake." Its primary function is to ensure that any proposed AI or agentic solution aligns with genuine human needs and strategic organizational goals, rather than becoming merely a technological showcase. This approach mandates deep user empathy, often involving observational interviews and repeated testing with intended end users. Complementing this, CUJs define the single, most important sequence of steps a user takes to achieve a primary goal. CUJs drive ruthless prioritization by forcing builder teams to focus resources on delivering maximum business impact and superior UX, specifically targeting well-understood pain points, existing workflows, and user-defined success criteria.

From Framework to Reality: What Are Teams Actually Building, and How?

We've said a lot about the framework and the key dimensions of the framework, and we've given you some examples and resources. But what's the bottom line? *What do we actually see and hear in the field? What types of technical systems are industry-leading teams actually building? How is leadership and vision evolving? What are the changes we've seen with respect to Talent and Culture?* Below, we'll share how our technical conversations have evolved and provide some insights into what we've seen with respect to shifts in leadership and culture over the past two years.

Technical Conversations

In the past one to two years, our conversations with customers have evolved from a focus on choice of models (and ever-changing leaderboard scores for LLMs) and prompting strategies to methods for grounding models in structured and unstructured data (RAG) and choosing the right vector database and embeddings model for the use case. We've gone from discussing fully managed or DIY RAG with tools added to support actions and reasoning loops integrated for more explainability and deeper insights. Today, we're talking a lot more often about agents—from single agents to multiagent orchestration. While use cases are still driving conversations in this area, organizations are bringing bigger and more systemic challenges that require deep thought about what steps could be safely automated to remove manual toil, reduce errors, and increase efficiency. Now we're not only discussing task-specific

LLM performance, but talking about the greater connective tissue that surrounds and supports truly scalable and secure use of agentic AI. This connective tissue includes the frameworks for experimenting, optimizing, evaluating, deploying, and tracing complex systems that rely on various LLMs and considerations around agent memory and true automation. At the same time, such complexity of agentic systems must be obscured from end users for an exceptional and differentiated UX. To easily scale this complexity and centralize AI and agentic practices across the organization, many business leaders and practitioners are choosing a platform approach. We'll dive into some platforms next and describe their benefits.

> LLM leaderboard scores are essentially report cards for LLMs, ranking them based on how well they perform on standardized tests called benchmarks. These benchmarks measure an AI's specific capabilities, such as its ability to answer complex questions (knowledge), solve math and logic problems (reasoning), or generate correct computer code (coding). These scores matter because they introduce competition that drives companies to build smarter, faster, and more reliable AI, and they act as a tool for businesses to objectively choose the best available model to power their applications, directly influencing the quality of the AI tools you interact with every day. LMArena.ai is one of the most popular and influential LLM leaderboards in the world.

Leadership, Talent, and Culture Conversations

Developing and executing an AI and agentic strategy across an enterprise involves more than your technical teams, it requires an honest assessment of the Talent and Culture of an entire organization. Leaders who have taken their organizations through the Tactical, Strategic, and even the Transformational phases of AI and agentic maturity understand when and why no-code and low-code AI tools and software as a service (SaaS) make sense, and when a code-first approach, where you have complete control over everything from infrastructure to agentic framework to home-grown evaluation and validation tools, is more appropriate. One of the most exciting and inspiring things about working with customers every day is hearing how leadership is embracing change management, during a time of unprecedented change. Innovative ideas such as hackathons, incentivized technical certifications, peer-to-peer training, and creation of new career tracks and mobility to roles that involve use of AI in the enterprise are just a few of our favorites. Other leaders are choosing to democratize AI for every user across the organization (and reduce the risk of shadow AI) by giving access to a broad set of tools on a safe, secure, and private enterprise platform—from no-code agents (developed with natural language as code) to access to model gardens, where developers can choose from hundreds of models and tools and leverage both open source and proprietary code. Leaders operating at the Strategic and Transformational phases are not relying only on developers (in the traditional sense) to ideate and build, they're opening up new opportunities for every user and every role to contribute to the culture and strategy around AI and agents in the enterprise. Indeed, crowdsourcing ideas and solutions for business challenges is a unique way to get past our own blind spots and identify when a simpler solution such as a traditional machine learning classification model is more appropriate than a highly complex multiagent solution.

Why and How a Platform Approach Can Accelerate an Organization's AI and Agentic Maturity

Throughout this book, we've consistently underscored the need for an integrated AI and agentic platform because the leap from isolated experimentation to sustained enterprise production—the journey from Tactical to Strategic to Transformational maturity—is fundamentally an exercise in overcoming operational friction.

Practitioners face a dizzying array of decision points: model and framework selection, the need to establish and maintain stringent quality standards, requirements for ensuring sustainable and interoperable connections to critical enterprise knowledge and systems, managing rapidly shifting cost considerations, and navigating an evolving regulatory and compliance landscape. These challenges are further compounded by the constant, aggressive need for skill ramp-up and model maintenance. A cohesive platform eliminates operational friction by providing the centralized engine required for velocity, governance, and close proximity of data, AI, and reporting tools.

How Platforms Support Critical Requirements for Enterprise AI

Platforms are explicitly designed to support three core imperatives that accelerate individual productivity and organizational maturity by turning manual toil into managed, repeatable processes.

Imperative	Platform role	Maturity shift enabled
Enterprise governance	Centralizes control, standardization, and transparency across the entire lifecycle	Tactical → Strategic: shifts the organization from individual ethics to auditable, enterprise-wide compliance and responsible AI standards
Seamless integration	Serves as the interoperable middleware connecting AI assets to core business systems	Tactical → Strategic: moves AI from an isolated pilot to a deeply embedded transformative business capability
Production velocity	Abstracts infrastructure complexity and automates the MLOps/AgentOps pipeline	Strategic → Transformational: enables the team to move from repeatable deployments to continuous, self-optimizing AIOps and competitive time-to-market

We've chosen to highlight two key AI and agentic platform categories designed to address these challenges: foundational AI/ML platforms and specialized agentic platforms. For organizations leveraging the Google Cloud ecosystem, these are best exemplified by Vertex AI Platform and Gemini Enterprise Platform, respectively. You may remember back in Chapter 1, where we first introduced you to Vertex AI Platform. We hope that it now makes sense why we've chosen to close this book with this important part of the Google Cloud AI portfolio.

Vertex AI Platform

Vertex AI Platform serves as a technical engine that translates the principles of the AI and agentic maturity model into production reality. It's a comprehensive, managed platform where the technical MLOps principles that you mastered in Chapter 7 become the foundation for enterprise scaling and efficiency to drive value for an organization.

Enterprise governance: from isolated code to auditable lineage

A core characteristic of the strategic organization is rigorous, measurable, and comprehensive governance. Vertex AI provides the technical framework to enforce standards at scale:

Auditability via Model Registry, Artifact Registry, and ML Metadata
> Establishing the single source of truth for model lineage is essential for repeatability, audibility, and transparency. Model Registry, Artifact Registry, and ML Metadata features in Vertex AI Platform provide a strong technical foundation for strategic maturity, ensuring that every deployed model's data, code, and parameters are recorded and traceable for mandatory regulatory audits or easy debugging. For example, in Chapter 7, we saw exactly how to implement ML Metadata to track model lineage (Example 7-1). Becoming proficient with these features within Vertex AI Platform accelerates developer teams, ensuring that they can take on more complex tasks at high velocity and with meticulous traceability and auditability.

Responsible decision making with XAI
> Deploying a high-stakes model is a risk mitigation exercise. Vertex Explainable AI (XAI) provides the feature attributions that allow human reviewers to peer inside models and validate reasoning before deployment. This shifts the organization from trusting a model blindly to enforcing human oversight, a key element of strategic governance. Chapter 5 took us through some of the other tools for understanding and explaining how AI systems are working and can be evaluated with quantitative approaches. Chapter 6 showed us how to tune models to make sure that behavior and performance of AI and agentic systems are appropriate for enterprise deployment.

Trust and data isolation

As we saw in Chapter 2, for regulated industries such as healthcare and financial services, the data isolation and security controls on Vertex AI are fundamental. The platform provides a secure environment where customer data and proprietary prompts are not used to train Google's foundation LLMs, directly supporting the compliance needs that are required to move past the Tactical phase of AI and agentic maturity.

Seamless integration: embedding AI as a business asset

Vertex AI Platform ensures that models and agents are not isolated technical islands but are deeply interoperable with the systems that run the business—a hallmark of the Strategic phase of maturity:

Secure data access

Native integration with Google BigQuery is critical, as we saw in Chapter 2. This integration allows models to access petabytes of high-quality, fresh enterprise data for training and serving without time-consuming and insecure data movement. This seamless data layer is a prerequisite for reliable production integration.

Actionable agents

For agentic systems, Vertex AI Extensions (function calling) moves the solution from informational to actionable. As you saw in Chapters 3 and 4, this capability allows models to securely connect to an execute code or actions against external business APIs (e.g., retrieving inventory, updating a customer record, and more). This enables the agent to become an active operational entity, a capability often seen only at the Transformational phase of AI and agentic maturity.

Grounding for trust

To make output of AI systems reliable for enterprise use, it must be trustworthy. As we saw in Chapter 2 and throughout this book, Vertex AI provides managed and DIY methods for RAG, to "ground" model responses in proprietary data, drastically reducing hallucinations and making outputs trustworthy and relevant for internal business use and expanding the use cases available at strategic phases of maturity.

Production velocity: from manual hand-off to AIOps engine

The shift from Tactical to strategic Operational and Technical engineering practice is defined by automation. Vertex AI Platform unifies the environment and automates the pipeline. When one-off projects turn into repeatable frameworks for generating output, time to value and ROI accelerate exponentially and trust and reliability scale across organizations:

Automation via Vertex AI Platforms

The MLOps pipelines you used to build our CI/CD workflow in Chapter 7 using Vertex AI become an engine for strategic repeatability. By defining training, testing, and deployment as a single, sharable, and versioned entity, the platform drastically reduces deployment risk and accelerates time to market for validated use cases. Additional time gained by using these tools can be reinvested in human review, oversight, and even user testing.

Accelerating in a unified environment

By combining tools such as Colab Notebooks, BigQuery integration, and foundation model access within Vertex AI Workbench and Vertex AI Studio, the platform eliminates the context switching and setup time that characterizes Tactical phase friction. This unity frees developers to focus valuable time on model building, not tasks like infrastructure management.

Achieving Transformational AIOps

On Vertex AI Platform, the goal is not just automation but self-optimization. Managed model serving allows for one-click deployment that handles, for example, unpredictable traffic. At the Transformational phase, AIOps agents monitor that serving environment, automatically triggering retraining or scaling adjustments based on live performance decay and ensuring continuous value with little human intervention. We walked through the details of AIOps in detail in Chapter 7.

Vertex AI is the catalyst for maturity. It enforces governance by providing lineage and ethical tooling, delivers velocity through pipeline automation, and guarantees integration by connecting models directly to enterprise data. This platform approach transforms the organization from managing fragile pilots into a strategic firm that builds high-quality, repeatable AI assets, setting the stage for transformational self-optimization.

Gemini Enterprise

Unlike Vertex AI Platform, which can be thought of as a factory for creating, training, and deploying AI and agentic systems, Gemini Enterprise is Google's all-in-one agentic platform built for every user, persona, and workflow across the enterprise. Gemini Enterprise is a central hub for AI agents, knowledge discovery, and enterprise search. The platform sits on top of and orchestrates all of the AI assets, including prebuilt agents like Deep Research, Idea Generation, and Data Insights Agent as well as no-code agents (built with natural language) and high-code agents created elsewhere, including those developed within Vertex AI Platform. Importantly, Gemini Enterprise moves beyond a simple chatbot by acting as a single, secure, conversational hub that unifies an enterprise's data, tools, and people to automate complex, multistep workflows. Different editions of Gemini Enterprise allow every business to choose how to explore the evolution of their culture, employees, and strategy to meet the AI era with readiness and intentionality.

Because this book is for both practitioners and executive business leaders, we highlight the value of both Vertex AI Platform and Gemini Enterprise. It seems nearly impossible to talk about one without the other because Vertex extends the work of developers and other builder teams, while Gemini Enterprise fundamentally de-silos access to the assets that these (and other!) teams create. We're seeing a major shift in an organization's need to support not just a handful of enterprise AI products, but hundreds, if not thousands, of models, agents, and other AI assets within a single business unit. Maturity of leadership strategy, talent and culture, and technical capabilities requires centralized access to a full suite of tools for every user and every workflow.

Learning Labs

To reinforce the strategic concepts covered in this chapter and formalize your knowledge, we recommend exploring the certification guides and learning paths available in the Chapter 8 folder of the book's GitHub repository (*https://oreil.ly/fs-iu*). Key resources you will find linked there include:

- **Certifications**
    - Google Cloud Generative AI Leader (*https://oreil.ly/djsPF*): An excellent option for non-technical leaders who want to develop familiarity with how AI is driving fields such as HR, marketing, finance, sales, and more.
    - Cloud Digital Leader (*https://oreil.ly/81Y1E*): We also love this certification for a fundamental understanding of Google Cloud products, concepts, and services.
    - Professional Cloud Architect (*https://oreil.ly/d1ovk*): Ideal for those designing the infrastructure behind the agents. This validates proficiency in enterprise cloud strategy, solution design, and architectural best practices. It emphasizes the Google Cloud Well-Architected Framework (*https://oreil.ly/-sm4j*), ensuring your AI solutions are secure, efficient, and cost-optimized.
    - Professional Machine Learning Engineer (*https://oreil.ly/vFYY0*): The definitive certification for practitioners building and productionizing AI. This exam covers architecting low-code AI solutions, orchestrating ML pipelines (MLOps), and operationalizing generative AI solutions using foundational models.

We encourage you, reader, to dive into the unknown—whether you're in a technical or business role. Get curious, go outside of your comfort zone, and explore something new. Google's professional certifications (*https://oreil.ly/yhvPx*) and training (*https://oreil.ly/gxczu*) cover a broad range of topics from security operations to database engineering to network engineering and DevOps and MLOps engineering.

Conclusion

We hope this book has left you in a different place than where you started, reader. Along the way, we've shared perspectives and insights with as much objectivity as possible, but undoubtedly through the lenses of our own lived experiences and backgrounds. Please accept these chapters as a current view of an ever-changing field, where models, platforms, and products are evolving on an almost day-to-day basis! Yet the foundations of what we've discussed here, and the introduction to the types of choices and decisions you'll be faced with, will apply into the future, regardless of new models, frameworks, and products. We challenge you to apply 10X thinking to your AI and agentic strategy and to keep the principles of responsible AI at heart while doing so. We also encourage you to bring your ideas, concerns, and questions about the AI and agentic future to the greater community. This is a moment where dialogue and conversations in this space are critical; we believe in the advancement of knowledge through open sharing and contributions from every perspective.

Before we conclude, we wanted to take a moment for personal reflection. The advancements discussed in this book—from the evolution of the LLM to the orchestration of complex agentic systems—represent the beginning of a profound transformation. In the following section, each of us want to share our own perspectives about what we're excited about and our vision for the future of this field, including the transformative impacts we hope to help realize through our own contributions.

Thank you all for being a part of this journey with us!

Steph

My background in infectious disease biology directly informs my passion for AI, particularly its potential to solve complex challenges in global health. AI is not just about writing code; it can be a critical tool for understanding and improving human and ecosystem well-being. Today, we're witnessing the evolution from general-purpose AI toward highly specialized agent systems. This is evident in the life sciences, where TxGemma (*https://oreil.ly/YeBwA*) is accelerating therapeutic development by predicting drug properties and optimizing clinical work, and in biology, where Google DeepMind's AlphaFold (*https://oreil.ly/sgQuJ*) system helps to predict the 3D structures of biomolecules—a fundamental breakthrough that has already informed scientific discovery across diverse scientific disciplines. At a global scale, some of the biggest challenges are being met by tools such as Google Earth AI (*https://oreil.ly/1Bgle*). This comprehensive platform uses specialized geospatial models orchestrated by Gemini-powered Geospatial Reasoning (*https://oreil.ly/K_HlN*). This framework allows AI to automatically connect disparate data—such as weather forecasts, satellite imagery, and population maps—to provide crucial, lifesaving lead time for communities threatened by natural disasters such as floods, tornados, wildfires and epidemics.

While many applications of AI are truly novel and transformative at large scales, the possibility for AI to transform basic tasks and reduce manual toil is equally compelling. LLMs are making it possible for scientists and physicians to understand and summarize large, complex documents (*https://oreil.ly/LtM_K*) and get more precise insights at a faster speed than ever before (*https://oreil.ly/gyt1R*). This translates into more time with patients, faster time to discovery, and a more comprehensive view of incredible amounts of data within moments. I am most excited to see how specialized AI tools and general models for understanding the world will come together in the next one to two years. Increasing "connectedness" of AI (e.g., via agents) will truly bring a new era of understanding and possibly emergent properties that could be applied to address some of the most pressing human and environmental challenges in completely new ways.

Ayo

The convergence happening now between AI, robotics, and spatial computing represents a fundamental shift in how we'll interact with technology. We're moving from AI that generates text to AI that navigates and manipulates the physical world—while simultaneously guiding humans through complex physical tasks via augmented reality.

The technical evolution is striking. The same transformer architectures that power our language models now enable robots (*https://oreil.ly/Dknsi*) to learn motor skills across different physical forms. World models like Genie 3 (*https://oreil.ly/xmnY5*) can generate consistent, interactive environments that maintain physical properties for minutes—not just creating pretty pictures, but spaces where agents can actually train. And with XR (*https://oreil.ly/0tqIS*) platforms integrating these capabilities, we're seeing AI assistants that understand both what you're looking at and what you're trying to accomplish.

What makes this moment unique is the practical convergence of these technologies. A surgeon practicing a complex procedure no longer needs a cadaver lab. They can work in generated environments with infinite anatomical variations, with AI providing real-time guidance. Field technicians troubleshooting equipment failures get overlay instructions adapted to exactly what their camera sees. These aren't distant possibilities; they're systems being built today with the same ADK frameworks and Vertex AI pipelines we've covered in this book.

Having worked in computational biology, I've seen firsthand how AI transforms our understanding of complex systems, such as AlphaFold (*https://oreil.ly/amd5T*) revolutionizing protein structure prediction and single-cell analysis revealing previously invisible cellular states. That same pattern of AI making the invisible visible and the complex tractable is currently happening across every field where physical and digital worlds intersect.

The frameworks and practices we've detailed throughout this book—multiagent orchestration, comprehensive evaluation strategies, production-grade MLOps—these aren't just for chatbots and document analysis automation. They're the foundation for systems that will fundamentally change how we learn, work, and solve problems. The question isn't whether this convergence will happen, but how quickly we can build the infrastructure and practices to deploy it responsibly and effectively.

Sarita

My vision for this technology is crystallized at the intersection of operational efficiency and human equity in healthcare. We often talk about AI discovering new drugs, but I am obsessed with how AI will revolutionize the *delivery* of care.

The true bottleneck in healthcare isn't just data; it's the *interface*—the complex, fragmented, and often legacy software that clinicians are forced to navigate. This is where Google's latest work on the Computer Use model becomes transformative. I envision autonomous agents, powered by this model, that can *see* and *operate* these UIs just as a human would.

This is the practical foundation for a true human-computer artificial general intelligence (AGI) in the clinic. Imagine a revenue cycle management (RCM) agent that flawlessly processes claims, not by relying on brittle APIs, but by operating the billing portal itself. Imagine a supply chain agent that anticipates an ICU's needs and then logs into three different vendor systems to orchestrate the order.

This isn't about replacing humans—it's about liberating them from the keyboard. It's about building a collaborative partner that handles the 90% of administrative toil that leads to burnout, allowing clinicians to focus entirely on their patients.

Furthermore, this same technology is the key to my passion for equity. The research that Ayo and I have conducted into a "Multicultural Medical Assistant (*https://oreil.ly/LWVpo*)" is built on this new paradigm. We can build agents that act as powerful equalizers, understanding a patient's accent during intake *and* ensuring that data is entered correctly into the electronic medical record (EMR), regardless of the UI.

The 10X future I'm working toward is one where AI scales not just data processing, but *empathy* and *efficiency* in equal measure, by finally mastering the complex digital environments where care is delivered.

Lavi

My focus is on the fundamental architecture of this new computing paradigm. We are currently in the "artisan" phase of GenAI, hand-crafting bespoke agents and proof-of-concepts. My vision is about what it takes to move to the "industrial" phase.

I believe the next five years will not focus on bigger models, but on the *connective tissue*. The real, hard challenge is in building the durable, scalable engineering primitives for this new era. I'm not just excited about what agents can *do*, I'm obsessed with *how* they will be orchestrated, managed, and trusted at enterprise scale.

The problems we need to solve are systemic. How do we guarantee robust state management for agents designed to run for days, not seconds? How do we build observability into a system that is inherently non-deterministic? What are the secure, high-bandwidth protocols—like the MCP we discuss—that will become the TCP/IP for a new internet of agents?

The work we're doing in LLMOps and agentic frameworks is not just about developer tools. It's about defining the "operating system" for intelligence. My passion is to build this production-grade platform, enabling any enterprise to compose, deploy, and—most importantly—*debug* these autonomous systems with the same confidence they have in traditional, compiled code. The ultimate goal is reliability.

Further Reading for Leaders

The following resources can guide teams from the Tactical to the Strategic maturity phase of Vision and Leadership:

- Google Cloud. 2026. "AI Agent Trends 2026" (report), *https://oreil.ly/dMBgP*
- Harvard Business Impact Perspectives. 2025. "Succeeding in the Digital Age: Why AI-First Leadership Is Essential" (report), *https://oreil.ly/JGny9*
- Iansiti, Marco and Lakhani, Karim R. 2020. *Competing in the Age of AI: Strategy and Leadership When Algorithms and Networks Run the World* (book)
- Bachman, Michael, Boomi Head of Research, Architecture, and AI Strategy. 2023. "AI and the End of Business As Usual: A Framework for the AI Ready Enterprise" (report), *https://oreil.ly/FhSH4*
- Boston Consulting Group. 2024. "The Leader's Guide to Transforming with AI" (report), *https://oreil.ly/1g9N0*
- QuantumBlack, AI by McKinsey. 2025. "Seizing the Agentic AI Advantage: A CEO Playbook to Solve the Gen AI Paradox and Unlock Scalable Impact with AI Agents" (report), *https://oreil.ly/H1NIv*
- Axis Intelligence. 2025. "AI Governance Framework Fortune 500 Implementation Guide: From Risk to Revenue Leadership" (report), *https://oreil.ly/HgeRZ*
- Google Cloud. 2025. "ROI of AI 2025" (report), *https://oreil.ly/1TkJa*
- Generative AI Leader Certification by Google Cloud

The following resources can guide teams from the Tactical to the Strategic maturity phase of the Talent and Culture dimension:

- IBM. 2024. "Upskilling and Reskilling for Talent Transformation in the Era of AI" (report), *https://oreil.ly/BROhS*
- Boston Consulting Group. 2024. "Five Must-Haves for Effective AI Upskilling" (report), *https://oreil.ly/0H-3w*
- Forbes. 2025. "Workforce Reskilling Is the Competitive Edge in the Agentic AI Era" (report), *https://oreil.ly/ao1Kp*
- Google Cloud Skills Boost online platform, which provides a vast catalog of learning materials for individuals and organizations to develop their cloud expertise, gain practical experience, and validate their skills for career advancement in the cloud computing field

Some resources to consider for teams operating at the Transformational phase of AI and agentic maturity include the following:

- Google Cloud. 2025. "14 Ways Googlers Use AI to Work Smarter" (blog post), *https://oreil.ly/oCN6-*
- Google Cloud. 2025. "1,001 Real-World Gen AI Use Cases from the World's Leading Organizations" (blog post), *https://oreil.ly/HmgTK*
- Gartner. 2025. "Emerging Tech Impact Radar: Generative AI" (report), *https://oreil.ly/ou4Gr*
- Microsoft. 2025. "Redesigning How We Work at Microsoft with Generative AI" (report), *https://oreil.ly/_apdy*
- Forrester. 2025. "Ground Your Workforce AI Strategy In Human Experience: Put Employees At The Center Of Your AI Efforts To Drive Business Success" (report), *https://oreil.ly/4DDDh*

Index

About the Authors

Ayo Adedeji is a senior developer relations engineer on Google Cloud's AI Platform team and specializes in bridging advanced AI technologies with practical developer solutions. With a background as an ML engineer in healthcare, Ayo's expertise spans computational biology, big data processing, and foundation models. He holds engineering degrees from Stanford and Johns Hopkins and is passionate about helping developers across industries harness the power of Google Cloud to build innovative, responsible AI solutions.

Lavi Nigam is a machine learning engineer and AI/ML advocate at Google, passionate about democratizing AI and making it accessible to all. He currently leads the charge in bringing Gemini, Google's cutting-edge generative AI model, to developers worldwide through the Google Cloud Vertex AI ecosystem. In addition, he is focused on building scalable LLMOps and Generative AI Agents design patterns to help enterprises efficiently use, manage, and deploy these powerful models. His deep understanding of MLOps and Google Cloud's infrastructure empowers him to guide businesses in building robust, scalable, and production-ready AI systems. He is a recognized thought leader in the field, named one of the "40 Under 40 Data Scientists" by *Analytics India Magazine*.

Sarita A. Joshi is an AI specialist at Google Cloud, helping healthcare organizations architect enterprise generative AI solutions and Agentic systems. With a background spanning consulting, R&D, and product engineering at industry giants like Amazon, Accenture, and Philips Healthcare, Sarita brings a unique blend of technical acumen and strategic vision. A recognized leader in the scientific community, she serves on the Editorial Board of the *IEEE Journal of Translational Engineering in Health and Medicine* (*JTEHM*) and a keynote speaker and peer reviewer for top conferences, leveraging her expertise to help practitioners bridge the gap from prototype to production.

Stephanie Gervasi is a senior customer engineer in AI/ML with Google Cloud. Steph has worked in academia, industry, and in the nonprofit sector to imagine, build, and deploy AI/ML solutions. She has managed and led strategy development for Data Science and Predictive Analytics teams and created the first Responsible AI Playbook and Technical Toolkit for Fair AI at a national health payer organization. Steph has given local and international talks on AI/ML and has over 25 peer-reviewed publications, including collaborative research papers with academic institutions such as MIT and the University of Pennsylvania. Steph received a PhD in Infectious Disease Dynamics from Oregon State University and a master's in Ecological Sciences from the University of Michigan.

Colophon

The animal on the cover of *GenAI on Google Cloud* is a male regent bowerbird (*Sericulus chrysocephalus*). Endemic to Australia, these beautiful birds are found throughout the rainforests of eastern Australia, from central Queensland to New South Wales.

One of the most striking features of the male regent bowerbird is its plumage, which is silky black with golden feathers around its head, nape, and wings. The male's bill and eyes are also yellow. Females, by contrast, have dull plumage and are dark to light brown. On average, regent bowerbirds usually measure 10 to 12 inches long and weigh between 76 and 110 grams. Their diet mainly consists of fruits, berries, and insects.

Male regent bowerbirds are known for building bowers, which are intricate nest-like structures that are solely used to attract mates. These bowers are meticulously built using sticks and twigs and are then decorated with shells, seeds, leaves, and berries. Regent bowerbirds are known to mix a muddy gray-blue "saliva paint" in their mouths, which they also use to decorate their bowers. Females, on the other hand, are responsible for building actual nests, since they are the ones who incubate and care for the chicks (males do not participate in raising their young). The nests females build are usually a shallow saucer of twigs lined with leaves; they are constructed far away from the male's bower.

Being a common species, the regent bowerbird is currently listed as least concern on the IUCN Red List of Threatened Species, although they do face certain threats, such as habitat loss. Many of the animals featured on O'Reilly covers are endangered; all of them are important to the world.

The cover illustration is by José Marzan Jr., based on an antique line engraving from *Cassell's Natural History*. The series design is by Edie Freedman, Ellie Volckhausen, and Karen Montgomery. The cover fonts are Gilroy Semibold and Guardian Sans. The text font is Adobe Minion Pro; the heading font is Adobe Myriad Condensed; and the code font is Dalton Maag's Ubuntu Mono.

O'REILLY®

Learn from experts. Become one yourself.

60,000+ titles | Live events with experts | Role-based courses
Interactive learning | Certification preparation

Try the O'Reilly learning platform free for 10 days.

www.ingramcontent.com/pod-product-compliance
Lightning Source LLC
Chambersburg PA
CBHW080929220326
41598CB00034B/5729